D0086117

# Principles of Banking

## Eighth Edition

**David Buzzell**
**Sally Spasovski**

AMERICAN
**BANKERS**
ASSOCIATION

This publication is designed to provide accurate and authoritative information in regard to the subject matter covered. It is sold with the understanding that the publisher is not engaged in rendering legal, accounting, or other professional service. If legal advice or other expert assistance is required, the services of a competent professional person should be sought.

*From a Declaration of Principles jointly adopted by a Committee of the American Bar Association and a Committee of Publishers and Associations*

The American Bankers Association is committed to providing innovative, high-quality products and services that are responsive to its members' critical needs.

To comment about this product, or to learn more about the American Bankers Association and the many products and services it offers, please call **1-800-BANKERS** or visit us at our website: **www.aba.com**.

This textbook has been approved by the American Institute of Banking for use in courses for which AIB certificates or diplomas are granted. The American Institute of Banking is the105-year-old professional development and training affiliate of the American Bankers Association. Instructional materials endorsed by AIB have been developed by bankers for bankers.

American Institute *of* Banking

AMERICAN **BANKERS** ASSOCIATION ®

© 2004 by the American Bankers Association
Eighth Edition

All rights reserved. No part of this publication may be reproduced, stored in a retrieval system, or transmitted in any form or by any means—electronic, mechanical, photocopying, recording, or otherwise—without prior written permission from the American Bankers Association.

Cover Photo: ©Jon Feingersh/Masterfile

Printed in the United States of America
10 9 8 7 6 5 4 3 2

Catalog Number: 3002279          ISBN: 0-89982-563-X

# Contents

**EXHIBIT LIST**                                             VII

**FOREWORD**                                                  IX

**PREFACE**                                                  XIII

**ACKNOWLEDGMENTS**                                          XVII

**ABOUT THE AUTHORS**                                        XXI

**CHAPTER 1        BANKING AND YOU**

WHAT YOU WILL LEARN                                            1

INTRODUCTION                                                  2

The Role of a Bank Employee                                   2

The Bank as an Organization                                   6

Bank Services                                                 8

A Bank's Role in Its Community                               10

Partnerships and Outsourcing                                 11

Mergers and Acquisitions                                     12

SUMMARY                                                      13

SELF CHECK & REVIEW                                          13

ADDITIONAL RESOURCES                                         14

**CHAPTER 2        THE EVOLUTION OF BANKING**

WHAT YOU WILL LEARN                                          15

INTRODUCTION                                                 16

Banking and the Economy                                      16

U.S. Banking System: 1700s through 1913                      16

Banking in the 20th Century                                  21

Banking in the 21st Century                                  28

Federal Reserve System                                       32

Regulators and Regulations                                   36

SUMMARY                                                      38

SELF CHECK & REVIEW                                          41

ADDITIONAL RESOURCES                                         41

**CHAPTER 3        MANAGING AND REPORTING BANK INVESTMENTS
                   AND PERFORMANCE**

WHAT YOU WILL LEARN                                          43

INTRODUCTION                                                 44

Annual Report | 44
Importance of Financial Information | 49
Management of Bank Funds | 50
Maximizing Asset Return | 53
Fee Income | 57
Performance Measures | 58
Budgeting and Planning | 58
SUMMARY | 59
SELF CHECK & REVIEW | 60
ADDITIONAL RESOURCES | 61

**CHAPTER 4    DEPOSIT ACCOUNTS**

WHAT YOU WILL LEARN | 63
INTRODUCTION | 64
The Deposit Function | 64
Deposit Account Products | 65
Deposit-Related Services | 68
Ownership of Deposit Accounts | 73
Opening a Deposit Account | 76
Deposit Regulations | 78
SUMMARY | 79
SELF CHECK & REVIEW | 80
ADDITIONAL RESOURCES | 81

**CHAPTER 5    PAYMENTS**

WHAT YOU WILL LEARN | 83
INTRODUCTION | 84
Checks as a Payment System | 84
The Check Payment Process | 86
Electronic Payment Systems | 97
Cash as a Payment System | 101
Laws and Regulations | 102
SUMMARY | 103
SELF CHECK & REVIEW | 104
ADDITIONAL RESOURCES | 105

**CHAPTER 6    LENDING**

WHAT YOU WILL LEARN | 107
INTRODUCTION | 108
The Lending Function | 108
Loan Categories | 110
The Lending Process | 114

Loan Policy                                    120
Legal Requirements                             121
SUMMARY                                        123
SELF CHECK & REVIEW                            124
ADDITIONAL RESOURCES                           125

CHAPTER 7        SPECIALIZED PRODUCTS AND SERVICES
WHAT YOU WILL LEARN                            127
INTRODUCTION                                   128
Trust Services                                 128
Investment Services                            132
Cash Management                                136
Capital Markets                                138
Insurance Services                             139
Global Banking                                 141
SUMMARY                                        143
SELF CHECK & REVIEW                            144
ADDITIONAL RESOURCES                           145

CHAPTER 8        BUILDING RELATIONSHIPS:
                 SALES AND CUSTOMER SERVICE
WHAT YOU WILL LEARN                            147
INTRODUCTION                                   148
Selling in Today's Environment                 148
Meeting Customer Expectations                  151
Cross-Selling and Referrals                    155
The Purchasing Process                         156
Product Development                            158
SUMMARY                                        160
SELF CHECK & REVIEW                            161
ADDITIONAL RESOURCES                           162

CHAPTER 9        SAFEGUARDING CUSTOMERS, BANK ASSETS,
                 AND THE NATION
WHAT YOU WILL LEARN                            163
INTRODUCTION                                   164
Safeguarding Customers                         164
Safeguarding Bank Assets                       171
Safeguarding the Nation                        178
SUMMARY                                        180
SELF CHECK & REVIEW                            181
ADDITIONAL RESOURCES                           181

## ANSWERS TO SELF CHECK & REVIEW

| | |
|---|---|
| Chapter 1 | 183 |
| Chapter 2 | 184 |
| Chapter 3 | 186 |
| Chapter 4 | 188 |
| Chapter 5 | 190 |
| Chapter 6 | 191 |
| Chapter 7 | 193 |
| Chapter 8 | 195 |
| Chapter 9 | 196 |

## GLOSSARY 199

## INDEX 219

# Exhibit List

## CHAPTER 1

Exhibit 1.1 Typical Commercial Bank Organization     7
Exhibit 1.2 A Hypothetical Financial Holding Company Organizational Chart     9
Exhibit 1.3 The Flow of Money     9

## CHAPTER 2

Exhibit 2.1 Milestones in the Evolution of the U.S. Banking System     17
Exhibit 2.2 Timeline of Banking Legislation in the 20th Century     21
Exhibit 2.3 Innovations in Banking in the 20th and 21st Centuries     23
Exhibit 2.4 Consumer Protection Laws     24
Exhibit 2.5 Federal Reserve Districts and Branch Cities     33
Exhibit 2.6 Fed Tools and Their Effects     35
Exhibit 2.7 Categories of Federal Reserve Regulations     39

## CHAPTER 3

Exhibit 3.1 Consolidated Statement of Condition     45
Exhibit 3.2 Consolidated Profit-and-Loss Statement     48
Exhibit 3.3 Interest Rate Comparison     55

## CHAPTER 4

Exhibit 4.1 Bank's Relationship with Depositor and Borrower     64
Exhibit 4.2 Characteristics of Deposited Items     71
Exhibit 4.3 Account Ownership     73

## CHAPTER 5

Exhibit 5.1 Parties to a Check     84
Exhibit 5.2 Elements of a Negotiable Check     85
Exhibit 5.3 The Check Payment Process     87
Exhibit 5.4 Visual and Nonvisual Tests for Inspecting a Check     89
Exhibit 5.5 Presenting Checks for Payment and Posting     91
Exhibit 5.6 Check Sorting and Bundling     93
Exhibit 5.7 Recognizing Substitute Checks     96
Exhibit 5.8 Point of Sale Online and Offline Debit Card
        Transaction Processing     98
Exhibit 5.9 Process Flow for Preauthorized Payment     100
Exhibit 5.10 U.S. Cash Distribution System     101

## CHAPTER 6

Exhibit 6.1 The Lending Process     114
Exhibit 6.2 Sample Loan Interview Questions     115
Exhibit 6.3 The Five C's of Credit     116

## Chapter 7

Exhibit 7.1 Controlled Disbursement                                           137

## Chapter 8

Exhibit 8.1 The Purchasing Process                                            156
Exhibit 8.2 New Product Development                                           159

## Chapter 9

Exhibit 9.1 The New $20 Bill                                                  176
Exhibit 9.2 Know your Money—Raised Banknote                                   177

# *Foreword*

## THE INDUSTRY AND YOU

Banking is a dynamic industry constantly responding and adapting to the forces of the marketplace. Competition is increasing. Laws and regulations are changing. New products and services are emerging every day. And customers are becoming more sophisticated.

To keep pace, bank employees of today are expected to deliver top-quality service to bank customers, whatever their financial needs may be. In doing so, employees are asked to exceed their customers' expectations all the time. No question about it: a banking workplace is a high-performance environment.

For that reason, most banks understand that their most valuable asset is neither the cash in the vault nor the loans on the books. Banks' most valuable asset is their people.

To compete effectively, banks need to attract, develop, and retain a highly skilled staff. In today's workplace, employees need to possess specific competencies to be effective. But effective employees also look beyond their current responsibilities and search for ways to further their professional growth and development.

### *Your Learning Resource*

More than likely, if you are reading *Principles of Banking*, then you are either new to banking, considering banking as a career, or interested in knowing more about one of America's most important industries. It is also highly likely that you are enrolled in an AIB course with the same name as this textbook.

Most students of *Principles of Banking*, whether they are members of an AIB class or independent students of banking, have been directed to the class or to the book by a supervisor, mentor, or friend. Ask any experienced banker the question, "I'm new to banking and want to know more about the industry, what would you advise?" Don't be surprised to hear: "Take POB." Or, more specifically, enroll in an AIB *Principles of Banking* (POB) class offered in a classroom or online.

Your decision to experience *Principles of Banking* is a sound one. You will engage in a unique learning experience, one that is sure to benefit you now and in the future. From the career standpoint, well-trained and informed employees, who display a strong grasp of banking and banking operations, are often viewed as superior performers and, therefore, prime candidates for promotion. There are numerous examples of bankers entering our industry as tellers or in other entry-level positions and later becoming senior managers, including many who eventually become the CEOs of their banks.

*Principles of Banking*—the textbook and the course—introduces bankers to banking principles and operations, the financial services industry in general, and the issues and forces that affect banking and financial markets. More than an orientation to banking, *Principles of Banking* will help you round out the training you received in acquiring your current skills while it provides the foundation for your long-term development as a banker.

### *Developing Your Banking Knowledge, Skills, and Abilities*

In banking, as in other industries, the terms training and development often are used interchangeably. But they have different meanings. Training usually is associated with the need to apply new knowledge, skills, or abilities to a new job or a current job as soon as possible, in order to perform new tasks or different tasks, or to perform the same task differently.

Development, on the other hand, is a learning process that requires more time and is often less precise than training. Development is associated with a variety of learning activities that help us reach a readiness stage for assuming additional job responsibilities, learning more sophisticated knowledge or skills, or taking on a different job or a new step in our careers.

*Principles of Banking* provides banking knowledge that is immediately useful on the job while it also offers the foundation for new learning and career opportunities. Of course, what you learn—through either training or development activities—depends on your willingness or desire to learn, among many other factors.

Training tends to be driven either by business goals or the performance expectations of the positions we hold. For example, today, you would be hard pressed to find a bank that does not offer a sales or customer service course as part of its regular training offerings. Why? The answer is obvious: sales and customer service are core requirements of virtually every job in the bank.

To be successful in any job requires mastery of a unique set of competencies – the specific tasks and activities that individuals need to perform in carrying out their duties and responsibilities. Competencies require a mix of knowledge, skills, abilities, and personal qualities. When competencies are mastered at the level of proficiency required for a position, they lead to competence—the ability to perform at a professional level in a position or profession.

Through ongoing research on key jobs in banking, ABA identifies what bankers need to know and be able to do to be competent in their jobs. Through this research, we have determined that a general understanding of banking, banking principles, and banking operations is important to success in virtually any position in the industry.

ABA's research would suggest the content included in *Principles of Banking* has direct applicability to a broad spectrum of positions in banking, from the Customer Service Representative (CSR) and Personal Banker, to the Consumer Lender and Branch Manager. This unique course provides a foundation of banking knowledge that will prepare you to acquire new understanding or skills in your current position or get ready for new career opportunities.

For example, Personal Bankers, sometimes referred to as Financial Services Representatives or Associates, represent a key job in most banks. Personal Bankers provide quality service to customers, conduct basic banking transactions, cross-sell, and resolve customer problems consistent with bank policies and procedures as well as related regulatory requirements. According to ABA research findings, superior Personal Bankers "have a good sense of the financial services industry and their own competitive market, and use that understanding to help build and retain customer relationships." They also "understand the banking system and banking operations in general."

## *Your Career*

Banks offer exceptional career opportunities for those who make the commitment and take the initiative to grow in their careers. Developing a career path that is right for you is not always simple or obvious, but it is manageable. It is a process that will continue throughout your working life. The key is to focus on becoming evermore valuable to your bank by learning.

Most banks offer employees the opportunity to grow and to be challenged. However, banks, like organizations in many other industries, also are asking their employees to assume increasing responsibility not only for their long-term professional development, but also, in some cases, for identifying training opportunities to enhance their current job performance. Often, it is up to the individual to take the initiative to map out a career plan and act on it.

Learning about yourself, your organization, and your industry cannot be overemphasized in managing a career and preparing for future opportunities. Where you learn, whether in a structured classroom, on the job, or on your own, is not important as long as you learn continually, adding to your knowledge and skills.

With *Principles of Banking*, you are on your way to developing the learning foundation on which to build your banking career. It will help you become more successful today and prepare you for tomorrow.

Congratulations!

# Preface

*Principles of Banking* (POB) is an entry-level textbook intended to give those who are new to banking a broad understanding of banking today. POB introduces fundamental banking concepts and principles, the basics of how banks operate as a business, and the responsibilities of bank employees in a customer-focused financial services environment. Specific objectives are to

- explain the context, structure, and operation of banks as profit-making enterprises that rely on employees to provide customer-focused service (Chapter 1)

- describe the evolution of the U.S. banking system that has led to opportunities and responsibilities of banks and bank employees today (Chapter 2)

- explain the business operations of banks, from managing assets and liabilities to maximizing returns on loans and investments, minimizing expenses and risks, monitoring financial performance, and planning for the future (Chapter 3)

- describe the types of deposit products and services, the bank's function in opening a deposit account, and laws and regulations relating to deposits (Chapter 4)

- explain the check as a negotiable instrument and the payment process from the time a check is written by the drawer to when it is received by the paying bank and rendered on the customer's statement (Chapter 5)

- understand electronic payments and cash as a payment system, and laws and regulations relating to payments (chapter 5)

- identify the types of loans banks offer to their customers, the lending process, and laws and regulations pertaining to lending (Chapter 6)

- describe the specialized trust, investment, capital markets, insurance, cash management, and global banking services that banks offer to fulfill the financial needs of their customers (Chapter 7)

- explain the building of customer relationships by meeting customer expectations, understanding the purchasing process, and through effective sales and marketing practices (Chapter 8)

- describe the ways banks protect customer information, safeguard customer and bank assets, deter financial crimes, and help protect the nation's financial system against misuse and corruption (Chapter 9)

This eighth edition of POB incorporates changes that have occurred in banking during the past three years, including

- additional responsibilities of bank employees to act ethically and maintain customer confidence, following the recent corporate governance scandals and the passage of the Sarbanes-Oxley Act (chapter 1)

- strategic approaches, such as partnership and outsourcing arrangements, being adopted by banks to provide services in a more efficient and less costly manner (chapter 1)

- recent legislation and regulations that affect banking, including the financial privacy provisions of the Gramm-Leach-Bliley Act, the USA PATRIOT Act, the Fair and Accurate Credit Transaction Act, and the Sarbanes-Oxley Act (chapter 2)
- approaches, including developing fee-based services, adopted by banks to maximize the use of assets and increase profitability (chapter 3)
- the diversity of deposit account products and services offered by banks to consumers and businesses, including Internet banking services (chapter 4)
- deposit account opening procedures, including those required by the USA PATRIOT Act (chapter 4)
- check negotiability and the check payment process described through the roles of parties to a check (chapter 5)
- innovations in the electronic processing of checks fostered by the Check Clearing for the 21st Century Act (chapter 5)
- using debit cards as a payment device for both online and offline transactions (chapter 5)
- electronic bill payment via the Internet (chapter 5)
- the loan products made available to consumers, businesses, and state and local governments, and the lending process (chapter 6)
- specialized products and services banks offer to meet customers' total financial needs, including new trust, investment and brokerage, cash management, capital markets, insurance, and global banking services (chapter 7)
- importance of customer service, cross-selling, and referrals to building customer relationships (chapter 8)
- threats to the security and confidentiality of customer information, including computer attacks and identity theft (Chapter 9)
- types of bank fraud (Chapter 9)
- ways banks fight crimes that threaten the economic stability and national security of the United States (chapter 9)

In addition to text updates, this edition was restructured. Chapters were reorganized, condensed, and redesigned to make the material easier to teach and comprehend. The text format is different from the past. The text, typeset in a one-column format, features sidebars that highlight relevant information. Graphics, photos, and prominent color visually enhance the reading and learning experience. Instructional design features include:

- learning objectives at the beginning of the chapter that convey what can be expected to be learned from the material presented
- an introduction that introduces topics covered in the chapter
- informational inserts: "Banker Profiles," "Historical Facts," "Did You Knows?" "By the Numbers," "Customer Tips," and "Situations" that contain topical material related to the concepts in the chapter
- graphs and exhibits that supplement chapter content
- definitions in sidebars for key terms bolded in the text
- a summary that reviews the chapter's main points

- self-check review questions for testing comprehension of chapter content
- a list of additional resources, including publications and Web sites, that contain material related to chapter content
- a separate section at the back of the book with answers to chapter self-check review questions
- a glossary that provides definitions for terms used in the text
- an index that can be used to locate content quickly

Chapter 1 introduces the general responsibilities of a bank employee and the bank to customers, the bank's owners (stockholders), and the community in which it operates. Bank employees serve customers in many capacities while being accountable to other employees and upholding the policies and procedures of the bank. To better serve their customers, banks continually seek ways to improve their products and services and take advantage of new opportunities.

Chapter 2 covers the larger picture of the role of banking in the U.S. economy. It looks at the development of the U.S. banking system, events and factors driving banking-related legislation, and the opportunities and responsibilities of banks in the 21st century. This larger picture helps in understanding how providing financial products and services to customers is an important function in the larger business and social system.

In supplying essential products and services to customers, banks generate assets and liabilities, with the ultimate objective of producing a profit for stock-holders. Chapter 3 looks at how banks operate as a business and how their perform-ance is reflected in financial reports that show where and how the bank acquired funds, how the funds were put to work, and the results achieved.

The subject of Chapter 4 is a core bank product: the deposit account. Checking, savings, money market, and time deposit accounts are discussed in this chapter. Also explained are different ways bank customers can deposit funds. The type of deposit account opened by a customer and the way in which the account is titled determines the ownership of the account, which, in turn, has a bearing on account opening procedures.

Whereas bank customers make deposits, they also move money out of their accounts. Chapter 5 looks at payments, specifically the instruments and procedures used to transfer money, make payments, and settle debts among individuals, businesses, governments, and financial institutions. The core of this chapter is the check payment function, from paying for products and services or cashing a check at the teller window, to processing the check through the clearing system where it eventually arrives at the paying bank for debit to the account of the check writer.

Chapter 6 covers a traditional primary function of banks: lending to consumers and businesses. This chapter presents an overview of the lending function, looks at the many consumer and commercial loan products marketed, and reviews each stage of the lending process: from loan application to loan administration and review.

Although banks once focused on offering checking and savings accounts and making loans, they now seek to meet the total financial needs of their customers.

Chapter 7 looks at the specialized financial products and services that banks offer today. This includes trust and agency services; investment products such as stocks, bonds, mutual funds, and annuities; investment advice and financial planning services; cash management services; capital market services; insurance products, and global banking services.

The key to bank profitability and success is building long-term relationships with customers. Chapter 8 looks at how this can be achieved by providing excellent customer service and developing and selling services that meet customer needs and expectations.

The text concludes by considering the stewardship responsibilities of banks. Banks have a special duty to protect customer information, safeguard customer and bank assets, deter financial crimes, and help protect the nation's financial system against misuse and corruption. It is for these reasons that banking has been called a "public trust." Chapter 9 looks at these issues and the role of bank employees in helping safeguard customers, bank assets, and the nation.


David Buzzell
Sally Spasovski

# *Acknowledgments*

The creation of *Principles of Banking*, 8th edition, was the result of pooling creative talent within and outside of the American Bankers Association. A design task force of ABA experts in banking, training, and publishing reviewed the information provided by ABA Local Training Providers, instructors, and students. Special thanks are extended to the following ABA experts who provided valuable service for the design of the new edition.

Douglas Adamson
Executive Vice President
Professional Development Group

Diane Allessi
Director
Training Development
Professional Development Group

Teri Callahan
Director
American Institute of Banking
Professional Development Group

Wendi Calvert
Associate Director
Creative Services
Communications Group

Peter Carlivati
Director
Educational Relations and
Quality Standards
Professional Development Group

Susan Einfalt
Manager
Graphics Design
Communications Group

Maryann Johnson
Associate Director
Programs
Professional Development Group

Theresa Londquist
Instructional Designer
Training Development
Professional Development Group

Janita Ponze
Project Manager
Training Development
Professional Development Group

Developing a textbook and related course materials require the skills of different professionals. The American Bankers Association extends grateful thanks to the members of the development team. David Buzzell, author, quickly condensed, modified, updated, and revised the text of the 7th edition to meet the expectations of the design plan. Sally Spasovski, instructional designer, reviewed drafts to ensure all instructional design elements were addressed according to the design plan and content presentation was appropriate for the student, adding new graphics and details. Sally also authored the Instructor's Manual, a course component, which was reviewed by David Buzzell. Tom Cameron, editor, reviewed and edited the final manuscript to ensure content is presented consistently and with quality, proofed the layout, and developed the index. Wendi Calvert, Associate Director, Creative Services, American Bankers Association, took the final manuscript and carefully incorporated it into the new textbook layout design she created in consultation with the course design task force. Roxanne Shields, Senior Graphic Designer, and Heather Fields, Associate Director, Marketing, American Bankers Association, coordinated the cover design. Janita Ponze, Project Manager, investigated the required changes with local training providers and instructors, obtained decisions from the course design team for the course materials, and worked with the reviewers, development team, and production team to guide the project along. She, along with some members of the design team, also reviewed the manuscript.

A new feature for this edition is the Banker Profile. John Blanchfield, Director for Agricultural and Rural Banking; Kathryn Kelly, Assistant Director, ABA Education Foundation; and Howard Walseman, Group Director, Professional Certifications and Memberships, provided assistance in enlisting the support and contributions of the following bankers who graciously shared their professional biographies:

Charles D. Christy
Executive Vice President and CFO
Citizens Banking Corporation
Flint, Michigan

B.A. Donelson
Chairman
First State Bank
Stratford, Texas

Richard G. Dorner, CFMP, CLBB
President and CEO
Ann Arbor Commerce Bank
Ann Arbor, Michigan

Elizabeth A. Duke
Executive Vice President
Community Bank Development
SouthTrust Bank
Virginia Beach, Virginia

Chris Huffman
Vice President and Marketing Officer
The First National Bank in Trinidad
Trinidad, Colorado

Dianne E. Kolb, CFSSP
Vice President and Director of Security
Fulton Financial Corporation
Lancaster, Pennsylvania

Michael D. Maher, CRCM
Senior Vice President
Enterprise Risk Management
Wells Fargo Home Mortgage
Minneapolis, Minnesota

Steve Martin, CFMP
Vice President, Marketing
Canandaigua National Bank & Trust
Canandaigua, New York

Denise McClelland, CTFA
Senor Vice President
Wells Fargo Private Client Services
Long Beach, California

Sandra J. Pattie
Executive Vice President and
Chief Operating Officer
BankNewport
Newport, Rhode Island

Ernest McD. Skinner
Vice President and
Community Relations Director
Citibank, F.S.B., Mid-Atlantic Region
Washington, D.C.

The American Bankers Association and the authors thank reviewers of the seventh edition textbook or the eighth edition manuscript and provided valuable input for this new edition of *Principles of Banking*. They contributed to both substance and presentation of content. Special appreciation is extended to:

Richard E. Beck, Jr.
Senior Vice-President
Corporate Sales Manager
STAR Financial Bank
Fort Wayne, Indiana

John J. Byrne
Director
Center for Regulatory Compliance
American Bankers Association
Washington, D.C.

Harrison H. Buxton, III CTFA
Senior Investment Advisor and
Vice President
Columbia Management Advisors
Bank of America- Private Bank
Hartford, Connecticut

Paula B. Cravens
Director–KBA Education Alliance
Kentucky Bankers Association
Louisville, Kentucky

Nessa E. Feddis
Senior Federal Counsel
Government Relations
American Bankers Association
Washington, D.C.

Richard Ferguson
Vice President
Commercial Loans
Adirondack Trust Company
Saratoga Springs, New York

G. Jay Francis
Vice President and Director
Security, Contingency Planning and BSA
Univest Corporation of Pennsylvania
Souderton, Pennsylvania

David H. Friedman
Vice President (Retired)
Financial Services
Federal Reserve Bank of New York
New York, New York

Clayton I. Garrett, Jr.
Marketing, Training and Security
Jonestown Bank and Trust Company
Jonestown, Pennsylvania

Carl H. Gregg
Branch Manager
Main Office
The National Bank Of North East
North East, Pennsylvania

William C. Hood, III
Compliance Generalist
Government Relations
American Bankers Association
Washington, D.C.

Jon A. Hooks Ph.D., CFA
Professor of Economics and Finance
Albion College
Albion, Michigan

Doug Johnson
Senior Policy Analyst
Government Relations
American Bankers Association
Washington, D.C.

Maryann Johnson
Associate Director
Program Development Group
American Bankers Association
Washington, D.C.

Tom Judd
Associate Director
Technical Services Division
American Bankers Association
Washington, D.C

Dianne E. Kolb, CFSSP
Vice President and Director of Security
Fulton Financial Corporation
Lancaster, Pennsylvania

Theresa Londquist
Instructional Designer
American Bankers Association
Washington, D.C.

Brenda Marlin, CFMP
Associate Director
ABA Marketing Network
American Bankers Association
Washington, D.C.

James D. McLaughlin
Director
Regulatory and Trust Affairs
American Bankers Association
Washington, D.C.

Sarah "Sally" Miller
Director, Center for Securities,
Trust and Investments
Government Relations Division
American Bankers Association
Washington, D.C.

Janita Ponze
Project Manager
Training Development
American Bankers Association
Washington, D.C.

John C. Rasmus, Esq.
Senior Federal Administrative Counsel
Government Relations
American Bankers Association
Washington, DC

Steve Schutze
Director
eStrategies
American Bankers Association
Washington, D.C.

Paul A. Smith
Senior Counsel, Government Relations
American Bankers Association
Washington, D.C.

Paul A. Stauffer
Assistant Manager,Jonestown Branch
Jonestown Bank and Trust Company
Jonestown, Pennsylvania

Rob Strand
Senior Economist
American Bankers Association
Washington, D.C.

Mathew H. Street
Deputy General Counsel for State
Relations and ABA Secretary
American Bankers Association
Washington, D.C.

Kevin Thiele
Assistant Vice President
Wahoo State Bank
Wahoo, Nebraska

Mark O. Thomas
Compliance Officer
Platte Valley State Bank & Trust Company
Kearney, Nebraska

L.H. Wilson
Associate General Counsel
American Bankers Association
Washington, D.C.

Thomas J. Zukosky
Vice President, Dealer Finance Group
PNC Bank
Scranton, Pennsylvania

# *About the Authors*

David Buzzell is a writer specializing in the financial services industry. He has written extensively about bank compliance, trust, auditing, corporate governance, risk management, commercial and consumer lending, deposit operations, and employee benefits and human resource issues. Over the past 19 years, he has written, designed, and produced newsletters and magazines; written textbooks; developed training programs and seminars; and written and produced a variety of other materials, including articles for newspapers and journals, marketing brochures, and internal management documents.

Sally Spasovski is a training consultant with 20 years experience in instructional design and training delivery. She began her career as a consumer and small business lender, valuable experience in her current role as a training consultant to the financial services industry. In addition to working with major U.S. banks, she has developed self study, classroom, and web-based training courses for the American Bankers Association in topic areas including consumer lending, small business lending, trust services, and sales.

# Banking and You

# What You Will Learn

*After studying this chapter, you should be able to*

- discuss various employee roles in banking
- describe a bank's organizational structure
- explain bank products and services
- describe the role of banks in the communities they serve
- discuss the benefits of banking partner and affiliate relationships
- explain the reasoning for acquiring or merging with another bank
- define the bolded key terms that appear in the text

## Situation

Customers Matthew and Verna, who came to the United States several years ago from the Caribbean, always have wanted a home of their own. Although they have found the house they want, they now need a mortgage to buy it. Another customer, Tamara, has her own successful interior decorating business. She has never worked for a company that offered a pension plan. She would like to set aside a portion of her income for retirement security but is unsure what plans are available for a person in her situation.

# Introduction

Banks do much more than accept deposits or make loans. They provide a variety of banking products and services to meet the diverse requirements of their customers. Although banks offer products and services, the banker is the primary link between the customer and the bank. For their part, customers place their trust in the knowledge and professionalism of bankers. Bankers, however, play the critical role in the relationship. To serve the customer well and to fulfill day-to-day responsibilities, bankers must possess a thorough working knowledge of banking, and bank products and services.

Banks not only address the financial needs of individual customers, they also contribute to the community, to the economy, and to the financial services industry as a whole. As businesses that operate for the benefit of their stockholders, banks seek ways to operate efficiently and profitably. To achieve these goals, banks may form business alliances and merge with or acquire other financial institutions.

In today's era of bank mergers and acquisitions, market forces have changed the traditional delivery of products and services. Many bank services now are delivered electronically through ever changing organizational structures.

## THE ROLE OF A BANK EMPLOYEE

The banker's primary responsibility is to professionally represent the bank's interest in every interaction with bank customers, bank employees, bank vendors, or other community members. Bankers must possess good judgment, be able to address requests promptly, follow procedures, and establish a banking relationship that meets the goals of the customer and the bank.

## BANK EMPLOYEES SERVE CUSTOMERS

Customer-focused banks provide customers with exceptional personal service, maintain complete confidently, and conduct business in a professional manner. "Customers," however, are not only depositors and borrowers. Bank employees, as well, depend on one another to fulfill job responsibilities. A helpful and pleasant attitude combined with job knowledge leaves a positive impression with customers and fellow employees.

## BANK EMPLOYEES ARE RESPONSIBLE

In addition to specific job duties, bank employees are responsible for upholding the bank's policies and procedures. Moreover, employees are responsible to those they report to and for those reporting to them. Most important, they are responsible to the bank's customers and to the bank's stockholders.

## BANK EMPLOYEES MAINTAIN CUSTOMER CONFIDENCE

The strength of the financial services industry is based on customers' confidence in its institutions and employees. Because they handle and safeguard the funds and assets of others, banks must uphold the highest standards of business ethics. By law, banks must report even minor deviations from established bank policies to regulatory authorities. These policies should be explained in the bank's code of ethics.

### *Code of Ethics*

A **code of ethics** is a set of guidelines adopted by the board of directors and implemented by management to direct employee actions that may reflect on the bank. Typically, a code of ethics establishes bank policies about, for example, employees receiving gifts from customers, serving on public boards, taking outside jobs, and reporting suspicious activities.

In light of recent corporate governance scandals and the passage of the **Sarbanes-Oxley Act** in 2002, it is more important than ever for employees to adhere to the ethical values expressed in a bank's code of ethics.

Normally, employees are required to read the code of ethics and periodically certify they are in compliance. Most codes of ethics address the following:

- *Personal conduct.* As safekeepers of other people's money, banks are held to high standards of employee conduct. In fact, banks are prohibited from employing persons who have committed dishonest acts or have been convicted of certain crimes. Dishonest and fraudulent activity of any kind is not tolerated. Employees who have been arrested or charged with a crime of any nature should report the facts and circumstances immediately to their supervisor or to the human resources department.

- *Conflict of interest.* In light of the Sarbanes-Oxley Act, avoiding a conflict of interest is especially important. As a representative of the bank, every employee is obligated to act in the best interest of the bank, its customers, and stockholders. Bank employees should avoid situations where personal or financial interests or relationships might influence or appear to influence professional judgment.

**Historical Fact**

In 1897, the ABA Bureau of Education distributed a pamphlet to educate the public on the role of banks and bankers. *What Is a Bank?* was so popular that over 1 million copies were distributed the first year.

*(American Bankers Association)*

**Code of Ethics**—A formal set of guidelines that represent a company's policies of corporate governance and individual conduct.

**Sarbanes-Oxley Act**— A federal law intended to improve the governance of public corporations by holding boards of directors, management, and auditors to high standards of conduct and accountability.

**Conflict of Interest**—A situation in which an action taken by an individual in an official capacity may benefit that individual personally to the detriment of the employer.

- *Compliance*. Banks are subject to many laws and regulations, and employees have a personal responsibility to carry them out. With equal employment opportunity regulations, for example, an employee must not participate in any form of job bias, and bank employees must report acts suggesting discrimination.

- *Accepting gifts*. Employees may not accept money or gifts of significant value from customers or anyone else when the purpose of the act is to influence or compromise the employee's performance.

- *Outside activities*. Employee conduct, both at work and away from work, reflects on the bank's reputation and its image in the community. Participating in civic, social, educational, and charitable activities is encouraged. If a question, however, arises about the activities of an outside organization that an employee supports, the employee should put the bank's interests first.

- *Confidentiality*. Bankers are obligated to avoid unauthorized use or release of a customer's confidential information. Indeed, bank customers have a right to expect personal information to be kept strictly confidential. State and federal privacy laws, including the **Gramm-Leach-Bliley Act**, limit how banks may share personal financial information with affiliates and third parties. Never should a customer's financial information be the subject of discussion or gossip among family members, friends, and acquaintances.

- *Purchasing defaulted property*. Bank employees should not purchase repossessed or foreclosed property or otherwise enrich themselves at the expense of customers. This prohibition is in keeping with a bank's sense of responsibility toward its customers.

- *Notification of violations*. Bank employees are obligated to report suspected wrongdoing by another employee. Again, an employee's overriding responsibility is to act in the bank's best interests and in the best interests of its customers and stockholders.

## BANK EMPLOYEES ARE PROFESSIONALS

Bank employees work with customers, other employees, and managers on a regular basis. In these working relationships, a banker's professional attitude and appearance set the tone for the entire bank. Skilled bank professionals are

- *Organized*: keep work areas neat, answer messages, answer customer inquiries promptly, get to work on time

- *Positive*: recognize the importance of customer service, maintain a positive attitude, are honorable and sincere

- *Confident*: dress appropriately, maintain eye contact, treat customers with courtesy, respect, and empathy, maintain a business-like posture, know the bank's products, act decisively

- *Attentive*: listen, solve problems, keep promises, pay attention to details

**Gramm-Leach-Bliley Act**—The financial modernization law that permits banking organizations to engage in a broad range of financial activities, including incidental and complementary activities. The law created the financial holding company structure, which owns companies engaged in nonbanking activities. It also includes provisions on financial privacy and security and ATM disclosures.

# Bank Employees Have Career Opportunities

As banking services and applications continue to expand, so do career opportunities in the world of banking. There always will be a need for employees who enjoy working with customers on a daily basis, such as customer service representatives, tellers, and other front-office staff and supervisors.

Many other career opportunities are available, ranging from accounting, auditing, and compliance to lending, sales, trust services, human resources, and corporate support services. Banks also are major employers of technology and operations specialists. As they enter new lines of business under the financial modernization laws, banks are employing more people with skills allied with banking, for example, insurance and securities sales representatives. The following are just some of the areas where bankers enjoy career growth.

## Sales and Business Development

To reach potential customers and keep existing customers informed, banks promote the benefits of financial products and services. Of course, it is every banker's job to sell, but some bank employees are dedicated to this task full time.

Sales and business development are critical in today's highly competitive financial services environment. In larger banks, sales teams specialize according to product. Retail banking, business banking, insurance, investment products, and trust services, for example, are sales avenues open to today's bankers. In smaller banks, a business development manager may promote and sell all of the bank's products and services.

## Operations

Operations departments offer employees the opportunity to work behind the scenes. By servicing deposits and loans and processing transactions, these departments provide support to the customer-contact staff. Operations personnel are among the first to use new technology and software applications to efficiently accomplish increasingly challenging tasks.

## E-Business or E-Commerce

E-business or e-commerce is a major growth area for banks. Opportunities abound in Web design and hosting, business-to-business endeavors, and Internet services.

## Technology

Technology has transformed traditional jobs in banking and created new jobs. Examples of technology careers available in banking include

- servicing and supporting mainframe, personal computer (PC), and local area networks (LAN)
- computer programming
- software training
- support for information security, transaction processing, and electronic commerce

## Banker Profile

**Elizabeth A. Duke**
*Executive Vice President, Community Bank Development, SouthTrust Bank, Virginia Beach, Virginia*

Elizabeth Duke began her career in banking as a part-time teller. She went on to become CFO and later CEO of a community bank. She also served as a Director of the Federal Reserve Bank of Richmond. She is now an executive with SouthTrust Bank, a major regional bank.

Continuing education is important and rewarding to Ms. Duke. "I'm living proof. In six years I finished three AIB certificates, the Virginia Bankers School of Bank Management, two ABA investment schools, ABA's Stonier Graduate School of Bank Management, and an MBA." Then she became an instructor for AIB and the banking schools. "I did it because it was a way to give back to the industry. I was grateful for the chance to interact with bankers and learn from their experiences, and to build lifelong friendships."

Ms. Duke, active with the American Bankers Association for over 20 years, will become ABA's first woman Chairman in 2004.

- internet banking management
- automated teller machine support
- Web site maintenance
- customer support

## BANK EMPLOYEES HAVE TRAINING OPPORTUNITIES

Banks have a long history of training employees for current and new positions within the bank. In addition to in-bank, job-specific training, many banks offer reimbursement for education and training as part of their benefits packages. Employees can receive American Institute of Banking (AIB) credit and diplomas, Institute of Certified Bankers certified status, college degrees, other specialty certifications and designations, and a variety of education and training opportunities for free or at a reduced cost—just for working at a bank.

# THE BANK AS AN ORGANIZATION

Most banks in the United States are commercial banks. Originally, commercial banks concentrated on meeting the deposit and credit needs of businesses. Today, commercial banks serve both the consumer and business markets. Savings banks, savings and loan (S&L) associations, and cooperative banks originally focused on serving the saving and mortgage needs of middle and lower income consumers.

## TYPICAL BANK ORGANIZATION

As a **corporation**, a bank is a legally chartered business enterprise with owners (stockholders), directors, and officers. It is operated for profit. A bank's charter is granted either by the state in which it is organized or by the federal government through the Office of the Comptroller of the Currency.

A bank may be publicly owned or closely held. A publicly owned company sells stock to the public, and the stockholders participate in the bank's governance. A closely held or privately held bank is owned by one or more individuals or a family.

The bank's stockholders elect a **board of directors**, which is the governing body of the corporation. Directors, who ultimately are responsible for the bank's operations, regulatory compliance, and performance, can be held legally liable for their actions. Directors appoint the bank's officers. The board of directors usually functions through various committees, such as an audit and compliance committee, risk committee, credit committee, trust committee, corporate governance committee, and compensation committee.

The chairman of the board, often the bank's chief executive officer, is responsible for the basic policies that guide the bank. The bank's president, typically the chief operating officer, is responsible for implementing policies and supervising operations. Depending on the size and scope of the bank, various departments may be created so that specific individuals are responsible for certain functional areas. Exhibit 1.1 shows the typical organization of a commercial bank.

**Did You Know ...**

In 2002, the banking industry employed about 1.8 million wage and salary workers. More than seven out of ten jobs were in commercial banks, and the remainder were concentrated in savings institutions and credit unions.

*(Bureau of Labor Statistics)*

**Corporation**—A business organization treated as a legal entity and owned by a group of stockholders (shareholders). The stockholders elect the directors, who serve as the active, governing body to manage the corporation's affairs.

**Board of Directors**— The governing body of a corporation ultimately responsible for its financial performance, consisting of individual directors who are elected by the stockholders.

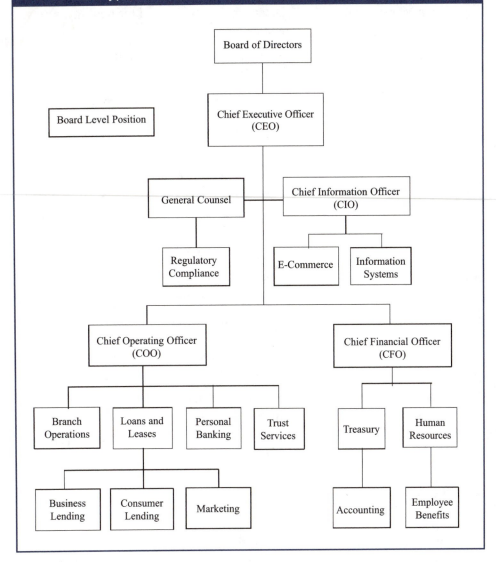

Jane started at the bank as a bank teller. She retires this year as a senior vice president in charge of human resources. In the interim, she received an AIB General Banking diploma and a bachelor's degree from a local college, paid for by the bank's education reimbursement program. She regularly reads ABA's *Human Resources Solutions* on **www.aba.com** and attends conferences sponsored by ABA and her state association, thus staying current professionally.

While specific titles may vary, a typical bank has the following departments and functions.

| Department | Function |
|---|---|
| Accounting and Finance | Organizes, records, and reports all transactions that represent the financial condition of the bank, including how efficiently and profitably the bank is operated |
| Audit and Loan Review | Makes sure the bank is safe from risks such as internal and external fraud and under-performing loans |
| Commercial or Business Banking | Delivers loan, deposit, and payment services to businesses |
| Compliance | Ensures that all bank staff and departments are in compliance with banking laws and regulations |
| Consumer Banking | Delivers loan, deposit, and payment services to individuals |

## Banker Profile

**Ernest McD. Skinner**
*Vice President and
Community Relations
Director, Citibank, F.S.B.,
Mid-Atlantic Region,
Washington, D.C.*

In his work, Ernest Skinner brings education programs to children and adults across the Washington, D.C., area. He participates in the ABA Education Foundation-sponsored Teach Children to Save program.

While it is natural for a community relations banker to be involved, Mr. Skinner is active in community affairs beyond his job. He is president of the Immigrant Empowerment Council, serves on the Advisory Board of Directors for D.C. Small Business Development Center, and is a member of many area civic organizations.

In 2002, Mr. Skinner was named among the "Fifty Influential Minorities in Business" by the Minority Business and Professionals Network, Inc.

A native of Trinidad and Tobago, Mr. Skinner holds degrees from Howard University and Columbia University.

| Department | Function |
|---|---|
| Funds Management | Balances the bank's need for liquidity, safety, and income |
| Human Resources | Recruits, trains, develops, and compensates bank staff |
| Information Systems and Operations | Provides information to the bank and its customers; processes transactions by using mainframe, personal computer, Internet, and other electronic media |
| Insurance | Provides insurance services for consumers and businesses |
| International | Services the bank's international consumer and business needs, such as letters of credit and foreign exchange |
| Internet Banking | Provides banking services delivered over the Internet or other electronic channels |
| Marketing and Sales | Identifies potential customers, learns what they want, and devises strategies for promoting and delivering the bank's products and services to its market area |
| Wealth Management | Provides personalized service to valued, high-net-worth customers |
| Trust | Administers trust activities for individuals and businesses |

## BANK HOLDING COMPANIES AND FINANCIAL HOLDING COMPANIES

Some banks are organized as bank holding companies (BHCs). A BHC is a company that has control over one or more banks or other BHCs. A bank does not have to be large to choose a BHC structure.

Financial holding companies (FHCs) were authorized by the Gramm-Leach-Bliley Act so that banking organizations could engage in a broad array of financially related activities. For example, in addition to offering deposit and loan products, banks operating as an FHC may offer services, such as securities and insurance sales. A BHC that meets certain eligibility requirements may apply for FHC status.

BHCs and FHCs can own banks in more than one state, thus facilitating interstate banking. Exhibit 1.2 shows a typical organizational chart for an FHC.

## BANK SERVICES

Banks provide individuals and businesses with a wide range of financial services, including traditional deposit and credit services, nontraditional services such as insurance sales and securities brokerage, and electronic banking services.

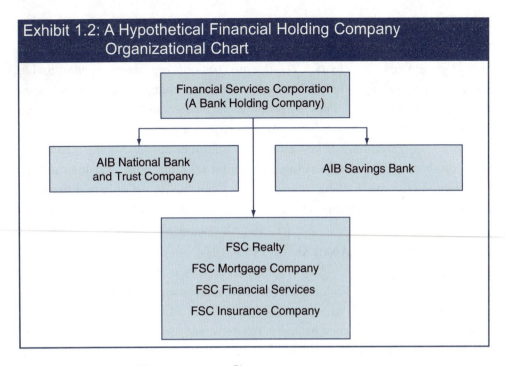

## Exhibit 1.2: A Hypothetical Financial Holding Company Organizational Chart

Financial Services Corporation
(A Bank Holding Company)

AIB National Bank
and Trust Company

AIB Savings Bank

FSC Realty

FSC Mortgage Company

FSC Financial Services

FSC Insurance Company

## TRADITIONAL FINANCIAL SERVICES

In its simplest terms, traditional banking involves accepting money from those who have it (depositors) and loaning it to those who need it (borrowers), as shown in Exhibit 1.3. The difference between the interest banks pay for deposits and the interest banks earn from loans is the income banks use to fund their operations and generate a profit.

Why do depositors choose to save their money in a bank rather than in a coffee can buried in the back yard? Banks provide a secure way for depositors to safeguard their savings. Banks also pay depositors for the use of their money in the form of interest on their savings. In addition, bank customers benefit from deposit accounts by having a safe, easy way to clear checks and pay bills.

How do loan customers benefit? Loans significantly increase customers' buying power and improve their quality of life by funding large purchases. Without loans, for example, many consumers would be unable to buy a house, a car, or afford a college education for their children. Business customers use loans to expand their markets, purchase inventory, buy new equipment, and modernize facilities.

Banks complement basic deposit and loan services with related products and services that benefit individuals and businesses, while allowing banks to grow and be profitable. These include trust, payment, and safekeeping services.

## Exhibit 1.3: The Flow of Money

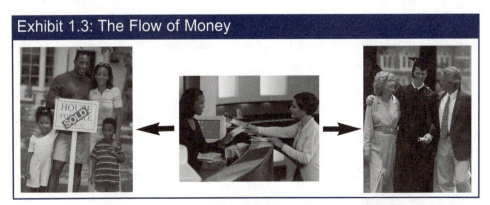

**Did You Know ...**

Between 2002 and 2003, the number of people conducting online banking transactions grew 80 percent, from 12.9 million to 23.2 million.

*(Nielsen//Net Ratings)*

## NONTRADITIONAL FINANCIAL SERVICES

Using the financial holding company structure, banks may own companies that engage in nonbanking activities. As a result, banking organizations can provide securities underwriting, offer a full range of insurance products, engage in merchant banking, and enter other lines of business that were, until late 1999 with the passage of the Gramm-Leach-Bliley Act, prohibited activities.

Banking organizations have become financial services supermarkets, offering one-stop shopping for customers to purchase, for example, both a car loan and car insurance. A customer looking to invest money can choose not only certificates of deposit but also investment products such as mutual funds and annuities.

## ELECTRONIC FINANCIAL SERVICES

For bank customers, convenience is an important reason for maintaining a primary relationship with a bank. With the advent of computer technology, financial services have been revolutionized. As a result, most banks now offer online banking services. Customers can verify account balances, pay bills, and apply for loans online. Now that electronic signatures are recognized as legally valid, banks can offer customers online loan closings and other contractual arrangements.

## MARKETING AND CROSS-SELLING SERVICES

With traditional and nontraditional services, and all the possibilities technology offers, banks now offer a wide range of products and services. One important challenge for bank marketing departments is making customers aware of new products and services that will simplify or enhance the fulfillment of their financial needs. Many customers still go to an insurance company for insurance, a brokerage company for investments, and a bank for a checking account, without appreciating that they may be able to address all these services at one bank.

One strategy for broadening the purchase of bank products and services is **cross-selling**. For example, if a customer wants a mortgage, a banker may cross-sell other products, such as a

**Cross-selling**—A marketing and sales practice whereby additional products and services are offered to a current customer.

- safe deposit box to store mortgage papers
- checking account with automatic payment to ensure a mortgage is paid on time
- home owner's policy through the insurance subsidiary
- personal line of credit to help cover the incidental expenses of new home ownership

Meeting customer needs is a key factor in bank profitability. Bankers who cross-sell services to customers help the customer meet financial needs and the bank meet financial objectives.

# A BANK'S ROLE IN ITS COMMUNITY

Banks provide a safe and convenient place for customers to take care of their financial needs. However, banks are much more than mere service providers to customers, the community, and the economy. When banks do their jobs well, they build strong communities, help families grow, educate children, help develop businesses, and generally improve the quality of life in a society.

## BANKS PROVIDE FINANCIAL SERVICES

Banks provide an expanding menu of traditional, nontraditional, and electronic services to a broad range of customers, including individuals, businesses, and governments. The banking industry's response to the **Community Reinvestment Act (CRA)** underscores the integral role banks play in making financial services available in their communities to help improve the lives of low- to moderate-income consumers and business owners. In keeping with CRA's goals and objectives, banks are meeting neighborhood credit and community development needs and delivering financial services to an increasingly diverse population. For example, many ATMs now display information in as many as six languages.

**Community Reinvestment Act**—A federal law mandating that federal bank regulators regularly evaluate how financial institutions help meet the credit needs of their communities, including low- and moderate-income sections of the local community, and publicly rate the bank's performance.

## BANKS PROVIDE CUSTOMER SERVICE

Bank customers seek the knowledge and understanding of a bank employee who can assess their problems and suggest appropriate solutions. A bank employee, whether a teller, customer service representative, or branch manager, can help respond to a college student's need for an education loan, a small business owner's need for an Individual Retirement Account (IRA), or a retiree's need for trust services. Customers' lives are made easier by the bank professional's knowledge of bank products and understanding of individual financial needs.

**Payment system**—A communication system that permits the exchange of information necessary to carry out transfers of funds. The payment system extends from point of acceptance through to the paying bank.

## BANKS CONTRIBUTE TO THE ECONOMY

Banks contribute to the economic well being of community and nation in many ways. Through the **payment system**, banks facilitate the flow of money throughout the United States and around the world. Without the payment system, national and global economies would collapse. By making loans and providing a safe place to deposit money, banks allow communities to grow and prosper. Small business and agricultural loans are examples of how banks directly contribute to the economic vitality of their communities.

Banks also provide jobs and generate profits for their stockholders, thus contributing to a vibrant local, regional, and national economy.

## BANKS PROVIDE COMMUNITY SUPPORT

Banks support countless charitable organizations with financial contributions and volunteer support. They directly contribute to building or restoring communities through community development foundations. In addition to providing the capital that helps businesses and communities grow, many bank employees become active in all aspects of community life.

# PARTNERSHIPS AND OUTSOURCING

To meet business needs, banks traditionally relied on their own employees and resources. This strategic approach is changing as the banking industry becomes more competitive and operational technology advances. To provide services in a

**Outsourcing**—The practice of turning over part or all of a bank's operations to a third-party provider.

more efficient and less costly manner, it is now common for banks to partner with one or more banks or **outsource** services to third-party vendors.

Currently, banks form many of these alliances by offering joint lending programs and sharing management, administration, and financing responsibilities. Banks employ outside companies to service, repair, maintain, and upgrade their computer hardware and software, thus ensuring access to the latest technology. To take advantage of opportunities in insurance sales, many smaller banks join cooperative ventures with other banks. Banks of all sizes hire training consultants to provide in-house job training.

While banks may have given up some of the independence and ability to customize they enjoyed in the past, these alliances provide significant cost savings, greater choice for consumers, and a high level of customer service. Partnering and outsourcing free up bank capital and allow banks to make other profitable investments that will improve financial performance and create benefits for employees.

# MERGERS AND ACQUISITIONS

For more than two decades, the number of banks in the United States has steadily declined. This decline is not the result of bank failures; the banking industry historically has been very strong, and in recent years banks have enjoyed record profitability. Nor is the decline primarily caused by customer migration to other financial service providers. Rather, the number of banks is declining because of mergers and acquisitions.

Many banks combine forces (merge) or purchase other institutions (acquire) to form larger banking companies. Through mergers and acquisitions, some banks eliminate duplicate efforts and thereby become more profitable. They are taking advantage of economies of scale by

- reducing or eliminating departments that perform the same tasks
- closing branches that are in close proximity and combining their services in one location
- using data processing centers that support the larger volume of combined banks, thus eliminating distinct systems

Banks also combine forces as a way of entering new geographic areas and expanding market share. Through mergers and acquisitions, banks extend their reach across state boundaries throughout the United States and into global markets.

Although the trend is toward larger banks, small community banks continue to play a significant role in the economy. They are well suited to providing relationship-based personal services and financial products that require extensive knowledge of the customer, such as small business and farm lending.

**Did You Know ...**

In 1982, there were 14,451 commercial banks. Because of mergers and acquisitions, 20 years later there were 7,887. However, during that time, the number of branches increased from 39,783 to 66,185, making it more convenient than ever to visit a bank.

*(Federal Deposit Insurance Corporation)*

# SUMMARY

- Bank employees are responsible for more than their specific job duties. They serve bank customers in many capacities while being accountable to other employees and upholding the policies and procedures of the bank. They maintain customer confidence by conducting themselves ethically and avoiding conflicts of interest. Bank employees are professional in attitude, appearance, and work habits. Individuals with these attributes will find that banking offers a wide variety of career opportunities with potential for advancement.

- Most banks are corporations owned by stockholders. A bank may be closely held by one or more individuals or a family, or publicly held by investors. Stockholders appoint the board of directors, and the board's committees oversee management on behalf of the stockholders. The chairman of the board, who often serves as the bank's chief executive officer, is the lead member of management. Typically, a bank is organized into numerous departments, each responsible for a specific area of operations—for example, consumer banking, human resources, or marketing.

- To better serve customers, banks continually seek ways to expand their product and service offerings. Banks offer traditional banking services, such as deposit accounts and loans, and nontraditional services, such as insurance and securities products. Banks also take full advantage of new opportunities made possible through the electronic delivery of financial services. As with any business, a bank's profitability depends on its ability to meet customer needs. Employees who know their bank's products as well as their customers' needs match the two.

- Banks benefit their communities in many ways, from providing the public with financial services to financing community development activities and supporting charitable activities.

- To remain profitable in the future, banks must continue to operate efficiently and effectively. Mergers and acquisitions and strategic alliances with peers and vendors allow banks to compete in markets of all sizes.

# SELF CHECK & REVIEW

1. If all bankers are expected to sell products and services as part of their job, why is sales and business development a separate career path for bankers?

2. During a period of several years, a bank has experienced losses whereas other banks have been profitable. Who ultimately is accountable for the bank's poor financial performance?

3. What are nontraditional bank services, and why do banks want to provide them?

4. How do banks contribute to their communities?

5. What are the benefits of banking partner and affiliate relationships?

6. Why might a bank consider acquiring or merging with another bank?

**Learning Check**

# ADDITIONAL RESOURCES

*ABA Banking Journal*, **www.ababj.com**

American Bankers Association, **www.aba.com**

*Banking and Finance Terminology*. Washington, D.C.: American Bankers Association, 1999.

*Banking Basics*. Federal Reserve Bank of Boston, **www.bos.frb.org**

*Careers in Banking*. Washington, D.C. : ABA Education Foundation

Job Resume Bank, American Bankers Association, **www.aba.com**

Nielsen//NetRatings, 2003, **www.nielsen-netratings.com**

Occupational Outlook Handbook, 2004–2005 Edition, Bureau of Labor Statistics, U.S. Department of Labor, **www.bls.gov/oco/cg/cgs027.htm**

# The Evolution of Banking

**2**

# What You Will Learn

*After studying this chapter, you should be able to*

- describe the role of banking in the nation's economy
- explain the development of the U.S. banking system
- discuss banking events and legislation in the 20<sup>th</sup> and early 21<sup>st</sup> centuries
- describe the structure and functions of the Federal Reserve System
- identify bank regulators and major bank regulations
- define the bolded key terms that appear in the text

# Introduction

*Understanding the role of banking in the economy and the forces behind change in the U.S. banking industry are important factors to understanding how interactions between bankers and customers influence the nation's business and social system. By driving banking-related legislation and laying the foundation for the opportunities and responsibilities of the 21st century, the events of the past have shaped the banking system of today.*

## BANKING AND THE ECONOMY

Banks serve an important role in the national economy. They manage money. Banks safeguard the money of individuals, businesses, and the government. As financial intermediaries, banks transfer money from one party to another. They also create money through the commercial lending process, whereby funding from loans is added to business demand deposit balances. After paying reserve requirements at the Federal Reserve Bank, these monies are available for more bank loans.

One important function banks play in the economy is to serve as a conduit for economic and social policy. Through banks, the Federal Reserve System can take measures to control the money supply. As depositories for government accounts, such as the treasury, tax, and loan accounts, banks are a resource for government economic policy. Banks also serve the government's national economic and social goals by complying with laws and regulations that implement them.

Thus, banks have an influential, some would say powerful, position in the nation's economy and society. They fund loans, offer financial services to consumers and businesses, provide access to the payment system, create money, help expand and contract the money supply, and are a force for economic and social change. It was not always this way, however. The U.S. banking system as we know it developed over the past three centuries, and it is still evolving.

## U.S. BANKING SYSTEM: 1700s–1913

Banking in the 1700s and 1800s bears little resemblance to banking today. The financial system then was unreliable. Depositors had no assurance that money left in a bank would be there when they wanted to withdraw it or that it would have the same value. Two merchants from different areas of the country, for example, had difficulty consummating transactions because neither merchant had faith in the other's bank.

In today's banking system, depositors know their money is safe and insured by the federal government. Money changes hands almost instantaneously through checks, credit cards, debit cards, wire transfers, and computer. When today's depositors take money to a bank, they can choose to open a checking or savings account or invest in a certificate of deposit, money market fund, or any number of other products to meet their financial needs.

The U.S. banking system passed through historic developmental milestones, emerging from the chaotic, unstructured, and unregulated days of the 1700s to the creation of the Federal Reserve System—setting the stage for banking as we know it today (exhibit 2.1).

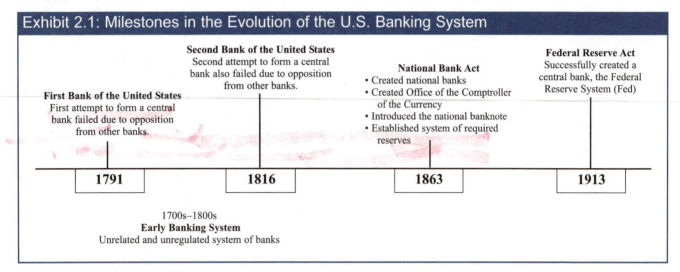

**Exhibit 2.1: Milestones in the Evolution of the U.S. Banking System**

**First Bank of the United States**
First attempt to form a central bank failed due to opposition from other banks.

**Second Bank of the United States**
Second attempt to form a central bank also failed due to opposition from other banks.

**National Bank Act**
• Created national banks
• Created Office of the Comptroller of the Currency
• Introduced the national banknote
• Established system of required reserves

**Federal Reserve Act**
Successfully created a central bank, the Federal Reserve System (Fed)

1791     1816     1863     1913

1700s–1800s
**Early Banking System**
Unrelated and unregulated system of banks

## THE EARLY BANKING SYSTEM

During the 1700s and 1800s, the "banking system" consisted of a large number of unrelated and unregulated banks with no common currency and no system to clear notes. This fragmented system created problems for currency. Anyone could own a bank: there were no restrictions on bank ownership and the requirements for capital were very low. Every bank issued its own **banknotes** for currency.

The problem with the early banknotes was that they might not be redeemed for gold or silver as required by state law when presented to the bank. The bank may have been unable to redeem the note because it lacked sufficient gold or silver, or the bank might no longer exist. No standards existed for issuing notes; any bank could issue them in any form.

The unrestricted issuance of banknotes led to counterfeiting and printing notes for nonexistent banks. That the money supply could vary drastically was another concern. With every bank issuing its own notes, the money supply could grow rapidly without control and fuel **inflation**. In fact, inflation became a problem during the early period of banking in this country.

**Banknote**—A note issued by a bank promising to pay the amount of money designated on the face of the note when presented to the bank. Currency issued by an individual bank.

**Inflation**—A continuing increase in the level of prices in an economy, caused by too many dollars and too few goods to be purchased.

**Banknote Issued by the Bank of Morgan, Georgia, 1857**

Although colorful and artistic, early banknotes were easy to counterfeit and their issuance could not be controlled centrally.

*(Source: The Smithsonian Institution, National Numismatic Collection)*

**Did You Know ...**

During the Civil War, the Bureau of Engraving and Printing printed paper notes in denominations of 1 cent, 5 cents, 25 cents, and 50 cents. The reason for this was that people hoarded coins because of their intrinsic value, which created a drastic shortage of circulating coins.

*(Bureau of Engraving and Printing)*

**Chartered**—Authorized by a federal or state regulatory body to conduct banking business.

**Dual banking system**—The banking system in the United States today whereby a bank may be chartered under state or federal government.

## FAILED ATTEMPTS TO FORM A CENTRAL BANK

With confidence in the banking system eroding, Congress approved a new central bank that had direct involvement and backing from the federal government. Opened in Philadelphia in 1791, the First Bank of the United States restored the public's faith and confidence in the banking system. However, existing banks whose notes were redeemed for coin and currency by the new bank strongly opposed it. Opposition from banks was so strong that Congress refused to renew the charter, and the bank closed in 1811.

Without a central bank, many of the previous banking problems recurred, including poorly operated, undercapitalized local banks, limited access to credit, and lack of faith in the currency system. In 1816, Congress responded by creating the Second Bank of the United States. It functioned similarly to the First Bank, with the added responsibility to act as a depository for the federal government. The Second Bank met the same fate as the First Bank, and for basically the same reasons. When the second bank's 20-year charter expired, Congress once again bowed to political pressure and refused to renew the charter. Andrew Jackson, who was elected president in 1828, strongly opposed all forms of centralized government, including centralization of the banking system.

The period from 1836 to 1863 has been described as the darkest in U.S. banking history. The need for a sound and trustworthy banking system had never been greater, yet government was unresponsive. Geographic expansion, population growth, and economic prosperity in the years preceding the Civil War created an ideal climate for commercial banking. However, many banks that opened during this time were undercapitalized, lacked prudent management, and ultimately failed.

### National Bank Act of 1863

In 1862, the U.S. banking system and the economy were in serious trouble. The country was engaged in civil war, government expenditures exceeded revenues, and the inflation rate was high. Government intervention was needed to overhaul and reform the banking system. In 1863, Congress passed the National Currency Act, later renamed the National Bank Act. The National Bank Act founded the banking system. It contained four major provisions that

- created national banks
- created the Office of the Comptroller of the Currency (OCC)
- introduced the national banknote
- established a system of required reserves

### National Banks

National banks were created to instill public confidence in the banking system. Like state banks, national banks are owned in the private sector but are **chartered** by an agency of the federal government. Charter requirements for a national bank are very strict and require the bank to be adequately capitalized and competently managed. The establishment of national banks created a **dual banking system** of national and state-chartered banks that exists to this day. As an incentive for owners to establish national banks, these banks were given the authority to issue a currency, called national banknotes. To encourage state banks to convert their charters, Congress passed legislation imposing a 10 percent tax on notes issued by state banks. To distinguish national banks from state banks, national banks are required to either include the word "national" in their name—for example, Union National Bank and Trust Company—or add the words "National Association" (abbreviated as "N.A.") to the end of their name—for example, Citibank, N.A.

### Office of the Comptroller of the Currency (OCC)

The OCC was created by the National Bank Act to charter, examine, and issue regulations governing national banks.

### National Banknotes

Congress authorized the national banknote to address problems associated with every bank being able to issue its own notes. Only national banks were given the authority to issue national banknotes. With the exception of the issuing bank's name, the notes were a standard design, which helped reduce rampant counterfeiting. National banks issuing notes were required to buy and pledge Treasury bonds as security against the notes. This requirement served three purposes: It raised money for the federal government, it gave the public confidence in the notes, and it kept the amount of each bank's notes proportionate to its capital.

### Required Reserves

Depositors were reluctant to put money in banks because there was no assurance that banks would be able to meet their demands for withdrawals. The National Bank Act addressed this problem by establishing a system of reserve requirements whereby every national bank was required to keep reserves against its deposits and notes as additional protection for depositors. The concept behind the **reserve requirement** was that the bank would have available in a money center bank either cash or demand deposit balances to meet depositor withdrawal demands.

**Reserve requirement**— A monetary policy control rule, issued by the Federal Reserve, that requires a bank to set aside a portion of its cash assets against its outstanding checkable deposits.

**Float**—The dollar amount of deposited cash items that have been given immediate, provisional credit but are in the process of collection from drawee banks. Also called uncollected funds.

**National Banknote, 1902**

National banknotes brought uniformity in size and format to America's currency, but were not readily obtainable when the government began redeeming the securities that collateralized the notes.

*(Source: The Smithsonian Institution, National Numismatic Collection)*

## ESTABLISHING THE FEDERAL RESERVE SYSTEM

Although the National Bank Act went a long way toward restoring confidence in the banking system, it still fell short of solving all the problems. Three remaining weaknesses were an inadequate check collection system, resulting in float and check fraud, an inflexible currency, and the pyramiding of reserves.

**Federal Reserve Act, 1913**
National check clearing
system
  • 12 Federal Reserve
    districts
  • reduced float
  • faster check collection
Decentralized reserves
  • bank reserves within the
    Federal Reserve district
  • local control over bank
    reserve requirements
Federal Reserve Notes
  • notes not backed by
    government securities
  • basic form of U.S.
    currency today

To address these weaknesses, Congress passed the Federal Reserve Act of 1913. The Federal Reserve Act included three key provisions: a national check clearing system, decentralized reserves, and the issuance of Federal Reserve notes. The following describes the problems of the National Bank Act and the solutions provided by the Federal Reserve Act.

## *National Bank Act of 1863 Problems*

## *Federal Reserve Act of 1913 Solutions*

### Inadequate Check Collection System

The check collection system was slow, complicated, and obstructed by poor communications. Checks could take weeks to travel coast-to-coast for posting and payment. Collection and transportation costs were deducted from the face amount. Checks were returned unpaid because accounts closed or for insufficient funds. When larger banks served as clearing centers, checks traveled through a number of banks before reaching their destination.

### National Check Clearing System

Federal Reserve Banks receive and clear checks from member banks. The Federal Reserve Bank (or processing center) presents checks to paying banks either directly or indirectly through another Federal Reserve Bank (or processing center). Federal Reserve Banks offer check-clearing, collection, and return items services to banks.

### Inflexible Currency

The money supply, tied to the level and value of government bonds, was unable to expand as needed by the economy. A national bank only could issue notes when it purchased bonds to pledge as security. Whereas the economy expanded, the amount of notes did not.

### Federal Reserve Notes

The Federal Reserve issued Federal Reserve notes. Because the notes do not have to be backed by government securities, the limitations of national banknotes are eliminated. Federal Reserve notes are the basic form of U.S. currency today.

### Pyramiding of Reserves

Requiring banks to hold their own reserves lead to instability and bank panics. Smaller banks used larger city banks as depositories for reserves. City banks, in turn, placed their reserves with larger money center banks. The result was a concentration of pyramided reserves in the New York City money center banks. To pay interest on these reserve accounts, New York banks used deposited funds to make short-term loans, usually to brokerage firms. When smaller depositing banks needed to withdraw reserves to meet obligations, the New York banks were compelled to raise funds quickly by calling in loans. Delays led to bank panics.

### Decentralized Reserves

The 12 Federal Reserve Districts solved the problem of pyramiding reserves. The Federal Reserve Board has the authority to set and change reserves as needed, within limits. Member banks keep their reserves in the Federal Reserve Bank or branch located in their district. The reserves are spread across the country rather than centralized in one location.

# BANKING IN THE 20TH CENTURY

During the 20th century, Congress passed legislation in response to events that threatened the U.S. banking system. Two pivotal events were the Great Depression and the savings and loan (S&L) crisis. Other legislation supported the public's demands for consumer protections in banking transactions, the changing financial market conditions, and the need to offer new products and services to meet consumer needs (exhibit 2.2).

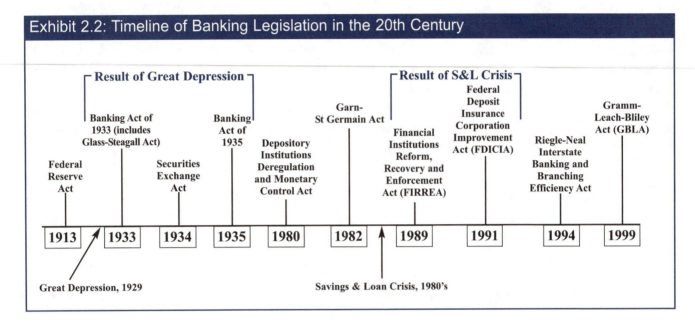

**Exhibit 2.2: Timeline of Banking Legislation in the 20th Century**

## THE GREAT DEPRESSION AND NEW BANKING PROTECTIONS

The creation of the Federal Reserve restored customers' confidence in the banking system and provided a powerful boost to the economy. The 1920s was a period of national prosperity and optimism, and the stock market soared. Investors were convinced that the stock market would continue to rise. No one wanted to be left out, and if people did not have funds to invest in the stock market, they simply borrowed from banks, paying for a percentage with their own money and financing the rest—a practice called **buying on margin**. Stock was used as collateral for the loans.

On October 28, 1929, the stock market crashed and the lives of most investors changed dramatically. The day of the market crash, paper values decreased by $14 billion. The crash triggered the most severe economic depression this country has ever experienced. Referred to as the Great Depression, it lasted more than ten years, during which the unemployment rate reached 25 percent. Unable to collect on loans, banks suffered losses, bankruptcy, and closed their doors. By 1933, over 8,300 commercial banks (about half the nation's banks) had failed. As a result, customers lost about $7 billion in deposits.

Once again, the public lost faith in the banking system. Many people lost their life savings. What had gone wrong? History can be a good teacher, and after the Great Depression, five factors were identified as the main contributors.

- *Paying interest on demand deposits.* Banks were allowed to pay interest on demand deposits. To attract deposits and fund loans, banks continually

**Buying on Margin**—Using borrowed funds, plus some equity, to purchase assets such as stock.

## Banker Profile

**Mike Maher**
*Senior Vice President,
Enterprise Risk Management,
Wells Fargo Home Mortgage,
Minneapolis, Minnesota*

"In the compliance profession, we have the privilege of giving voice to the conscience of our organizations. We not only comply with the letter of the law, we also strive to understand what laws and regulations are trying to achieve and what is fair for our customers."

Affiliated with the compliance field since he graduated from college, Mr. Maher continued his professional development. He became a Certified Regulatory Compliance Manager (CRCM) and a Certified Risk Professional (CRP). "Never stop learning. Change is constant in the financial industry. We must keep our knowledge and skills on the cutting edge."

Mr. Maher serves the banking industry by supporting ABA professional programs such as the Institute of Certified Bankers and ABA's National Compliance School, as well as authoring articles and books.

increased the interest they paid. This growing interest expense lowered bank earnings; as a result, banks eased credit policies so more loans could be made to offset interest expenses.

- *Securities (stock) underwriting*. Banks were allowed to underwrite securities issues. They could buy entire issues of new stock and place them on the market. A bank would guarantee the sale and collect a handling fee. Banks also would lend money to borrowers to purchase stock underwritten by the bank. In theory, the bank could make money on both the loan interest and the securities sale.

- *Lack of margin requirements*. Some banks exercised caution and required margins as high as 50 percent, but more controls were needed. If stock purchasers had been required to put up more cash, the number of stocks purchased would have been reduced, and banks would not have been exposed to so much risk.

- *Lack of depositor protection*. When banks failed, depositors lost their deposits and had no recourse against the banks.

- *Insufficient liquidity provided to banks*. The Federal Reserve's stringent lending rules prevented them from lending sufficient reserves to troubled banks to keep them open.

### Resulting Legislation

During the 1930s, Congress enacted several pieces of legislation to reform the banking system and address the factors believed to have contributed to the stock market crash. Three acts in particular—the Banking Act of 1933 (containing sections referred to as the Glass-Steagall Act), the Securities Exchange Act of 1934, and the Banking Act of 1935—had a pervasive influence on the banking business that continues to this day.

| | |
|---|---|
| **Banking Act of 1933** (contains sections referred to as the Glass-Steagall Act) | • Prohibited banks from paying interest on demand deposits<br>• Raised minimum capital requirements of national banks<br>• Prohibited member banks of the Federal Reserve System from underwriting securities issues and from affiliating with organizations dealing in securities<br>• Allowed the Federal Reserve Board to forbid any member bank to use Reserve credit for speculative purposes<br>• Created the Federal Deposit Insurance Corporation (FDIC) to protect depositor accounts at FDIC-insured banks |
| **Securities Exchange Act of 1934** | Gave the Federal Reserve authority to set margin requirements. All loans made by banks that were collateralized by securities were subject to the margin requirements. |

| **Banking Act of 1935** | Referred to as the Federal Deposit Insurance Act of 1935, this act amended the Banking Act of 1933 and authorized the FDIC to |

- Set standards for operations at FDIC member banks
- Examine those banks to ensure compliance with the standards
- Take action to reduce the potential of troubled banks failing
- Pay depositors if an insured bank failed

## SOCIAL CHANGE AND CONSUMER PROTECTION

The Great Depression ended with the advent of World War II when manufacturing geared up and people returned to work to meet the demand for military equipment and supplies. Banking reforms enacted by Congress helped keep the financial system sound and functioning.

The decades following the Great Depression were marked by restrictive regulations that limited banks' competitiveness. Nevertheless, there were several innovations in credit and investment products to meet marketplace demands (see exhibit 2.3). In the 1950s, the credit card was introduced. Early in the 1960s, the certificate of deposit (CD) was offered, and by the end of that decade, automated teller machines (ATMs) appeared, which began a revolution in the delivery of bank services.

### Exhibit 2.3: Innovations in Banking in the 20th and 21st Centuries

|  |  |
|------|------------|
| 1946 | First drive-in banking service offered by Exchange National Bank of Chicago |
| 1947 | First lockbox developed by First Chicago Bank |
| 1952 | First bank credit card issued by Franklin National Bank, New York |
| 1960 | Magnetic Ink Character Recognition (MICR) technology helps automate check handling |
| 1961 | First negotiable certificate of deposit is offered by First National City Bank (now Citibank) to selected corporate customers |
| 1966 | First truly paperless point-of-sale (POS) system instituted by Hempstead Bank in Syosset, New York, in 32 retail establishments |
| 1969 | Automated teller machines introduced by several banks |
| 1972 | Automated Clearing House (ACH) payment mechanism established as an electronic alternative to the traditional paper-based check collection system |
| 1974 | Telephone bill payment services initiated by the savings and loan industry |
| 1980 | Home banking infrastructure was first developed, laying the groundwork for Internet banking |
| 1994 | Banks began to create a presence on the World Wide Web |
| 2000 | Electronic signatures gained legal validity for consumer transactions, breaking down a barrier to e-commerce |
| 2001 | Electronic bill payment and presentment systems go online |
| 2003 | A new negotiable instrument, the "substitute check," was created by law to support digital imaging of checks and electronic check payment processing |

Along with these innovations came social change. Before 1968, little, if any, federal law protected consumers in their dealings with banks and other financial institutions. Consumer protection was primarily a state responsibility. Most states prohibited usurious interest rates and set ceiling rates on loans to consumers.

The 1968 Consumer Credit Protection Act, of which Title I is the Truth in Lending Act, was a turning point. The act required all lenders to make meaningful disclosure of their credit and leasing terms to enable consumers to compare the various terms available. Lenders were required to provide consumer borrowers with specific written information on the cost of credit, especially the two most important measures of the cost: the finance charge—the amount of money paid to obtain credit—and the annual percentage rate (APR)—the finance charge expressed as an annual percentage of the funds borrowed. The APR allows a comparison of credit costs regardless of the dollar amount of the costs or the length of time over which payments are made. After 1968, Congress significantly expanded the Truth in Lending Act and enacted other statutes to require disclosure of still more information to depositors and borrowers, and to curb various unfair and deceptive lending practices (see exhibit 2.4).

## Exhibit 2.4: Consumer Protection Laws

Since the late 1960s, Congress has enacted a broad range of laws to protect consumers in their financial transactions with banks. These laws include the

- Truth in Lending Act
- Fair Housing Act
- Fair Credit Reporting Act
- Flood Disaster Protection Act
- Equal Credit Opportunity Act
- Fair Credit Billing Act
- Real Estate Settlement Procedures Act
- Home Mortgage Disclosure Act
- Consumer Leasing Act
- Community Reinvestment Act
- Fair Debt Collection Practices Act
- Electronic Fund Transfer Act
- Right to Financial Privacy Act
- Federal Trade Commission Improvement Act
- Expedited Fund Availability Act
- Fair Credit and Charge Card Disclosure Act
- Home Equity Loan Consumer Protection Act
- Women's Business Ownership Act
- Truth in Savings Act
- Bank Sales of Insurance Act
- Financial Privacy Act
- Fair and Accurate Credit Transactions Act

## NEW COMPETITORS AND LEVELING THE PLAYING FIELD

Before the 1980s, banks were constrained in the types of products and services they could offer. The constraint hampered their ability to compete on an equal basis with other financial service providers.

For example, banks had legal limits imposed on the amount of interest they could pay on savings and time deposits. In 1961, in an attempt to offer a product for which banks could offer competitive interest rates, New York banks introduced a $100,000 or greater CD. Because of the size and terms, large-denomination CDs were exempt from interest rate restrictions. However, few customers could afford to invest $100,000 for a CD.

Meanwhile, **brokerage firms** introduced the money market mutual fund designed for customers with less than $100,000 to invest. For these customers, banks could offer traditional savings accounts only, which paid considerably less than money market funds.

As interest rates increased in the mid- to late-1970s, the gap between what banks and their competitors were offering for deposits grew. Many customers withdrew their money from insured savings accounts in banks and invested in higher-earning products with other financial service providers, a process known as **disintermediation**. One of the problems with disintermediation, however, is that it decreases the supply of loanable funds available to banks.

Competition was a new experience for banks, and they struggled to adjust. State-chartered banks that voluntarily belonged to the Federal Reserve began to question whether their membership was worthwhile. Although, as members, they used Fed services, they did not earn interest on the reserves held by the Fed. Some national banks, whose membership in the Fed was required, considered changing to state charters to free up their Fed reserves.

## New Competitors

Banking legislation enacted between 1933 and 1980 needed to be revisited to respond to the changing marketplace. For years, banks competed among themselves with little other competition for traditional banking services. Most bank deposits were demand deposits on which the bank paid no interest. This all changed when nonbank institutions, not subject to the same regulatory controls, entered the market. Banks faced significant competition from other providers of financial services.

- *Credit unions*. Credit unions offer financial services to members who, by law, must share a common bond, such as being teachers or federal employees. Because credit unions are exempt from federal taxes, offer a range of services, and often occupy employer-provided facilities, they have minimal expenses and can offer products and services at a reduced cost to their members.

- *Savings and loan associations (S&Ls)*. Originally chartered to provide mortgage credit to their customers, to encourage the flow of deposits into S&Ls, the Federal Reserve allowed S&Ls to pay a higher interest rate on deposits than stipulated for banks. S&Ls are either mutual in structure, so they are owned by depositors, or are stock companies. For years, commercial banks preferred not to make long-term mortgage loans, a decision that allowed the S&L industry to grow without competition.

- *Savings banks*. Many savings banks are former savings and loan associations. They operate and are member-owned or are stock companies in much the same way. Savings Banks are insured by the FDIC. Many S&Ls have changed their charters and names to federal savings bank (FSB) primarily to have the word "bank" in their title. Others have dropped the word "savings" altogether to distance themselves from S&Ls and to be recognized as offering more financial services.

- *Brokerage firms*. Brokerage firms help customers buy stocks, bonds, and mutual funds. Their investment products are not FDIC-insured, but the

**Brokerage Firm—**
A business that arranges contracts for the purchase and sale of stocks and bonds.

**Disintermediation—**
The withdrawal of money from a financial institution and deposit of the funds in another type of investment product in order to earn higher rates of interest.

Securities Investor Protection Corporation (SIPC) offers some protection for brokerage customers.

## Leveling the "Playing Field"

Beginning in 1980, the tight rein on banking powers was relaxed when Congress enacted a series of laws that dismantled prior regulation and gave banks more freedom to compete. These new laws included the following:

| | |
|---|---|
| **Depository Institutions Deregulation and Monetary Control Act of 1980** | This act redefined banking powers and allowed banks and S&Ls to offer new products. S&Ls and credit unions could make commercial loans and offer trust services. Banks could offer **NOW** accounts (negotiable order of withdrawal accounts), an interest-bearing checking account, often called "interest checking." Over time, limitations on interest rates paid on deposits were phased out. FDIC coverage was increased from $40,000 to $100,000. Reserves were required for checking account deposits. |
| **Garn-St Germain Depository Institutions Act of 1982** | With this act, banks and other depository institutions could offer the **money market deposit account (MMDA)**, often called "high interest savings accounts" and the super NOW account. |
| **Riegle-Neal Interstate Banking and Branching Efficiency Act of 1994** | Full interstate banking across the country, regardless of prior federal law or state law, was allowed. Affiliate banks within bank holding companies may function as branches for each other. National banks could operate branches across state lines by acquiring banks in other states. However, state law continued to control intrastate branching, the practice of opening branches within a particular state, and to authorize banks within their borders to open new branches across state lines. |

Many bankers, however, felt that Congress did not go far enough in the deregulation effort to allow banks to compete against brokerage firms and other providers. The provisions of the Banking Act of 1933 (Glass-Steagall Act), including those prohibiting banks from underwriting securities and paying interest on demand deposits, remained intact.

## THE SAVINGS AND LOAN CRISIS

Not every law passed in the 1980s was intended to break down regulatory barriers. Banking legislation is often passed in reaction to a crisis. In the 1980s, commercial banks suffered huge losses from deteriorating loan portfolios, and many banks failed. Banks that granted loans to less developed countries had to add billions of dollars to loan loss reserves because full repayment on these loans became

---

**NOW Account—An** interest-earning transaction account on which check-like instruments (negotiable orders of withdrawal) may be used. This transaction account is not a demand deposit account. The bank must reserve the right to require the depositor to give seven days' advance notice before withdrawing funds, a requirement that is rarely imposed.

**Money Market Deposit Account (MMDA)—A** type of savings account created in 1982 that pays a market interest rate and allows account holders limited check-writing privileges.

unlikely. Banks with large loan concentrations in real estate development and the oil and gas industries also experienced losses because these industries faltered. Real estate sales plummeted in many parts of the country, and overbuilding, financed largely by banks, resulted in unoccupied office space.

The S&L industry was less regulated than the banking industry, and the consequences were severe. From the late 1980s to mid-1992, many thrift institutions failed, and the number of S&Ls and savings banks declined by over one-half. The industry fallout became known as the S&L crisis because the Federal Savings and Loan Insurance Corporation (FSLIC) did not have enough funds to pay depositors of failed associations, and the housing market (mortgages) was seriously affected by S&L failures.

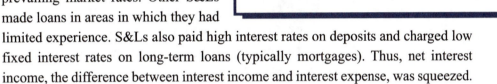

**Net Interest Spread**

The interest income on a bank's portfolio of loans is $3.5 million. The interest paid on deposits to fund those loans is $1.5 million. What is the bank's net interest spread?

**By The Numbers**

**$3.5 million - $1.5 million = $2 million**

Narrowing interest rate spreads and inexperience with new deposit and loan products contributed to the S&L crisis. To keep or attract deposits, some S&Ls paid interest rates above prevailing market rates. Other S&Ls made loans in areas in which they had limited experience. S&Ls also paid high interest rates on deposits and charged low fixed interest rates on long-term loans (typically mortgages). Thus, net interest income, the difference between interest income and interest expense, was squeezed. Losses were inevitable.

## Resulting Legislation

Congress enacted two laws in response to the 1980s S&L crisis:

**Financial Institutions Reform, Recovery and Enforcement Act of 1989 (FIRREA)**

- Reformed and consolidated the federal deposit insurance system. Disbanded the Federal Savings and Loan Insurance Corporation. FDIC now administrates Bank Insurance Fund (BIF) and Savings Association Insurance Fund (SAIF).

- Established the Office of Thrift Supervision (OTS) to supervise savings associations.

- Funded closing insolvent S&Ls, sold their assets, and paid depositors where necessary.

- FDIC allowed to borrow from the Treasury to recapitalize BIF.

**Federal Deposit Insurance Corporation Improvement Act of 1991 (FDICA)**

- Required on-site examinations, annual audit requirements, and revised bank accounting standards for domestic and foreign-owned banks.

- Required new safety and soundness standards for operations and management, officers and directors, and compensation.

- Mandated bank assessments of credit exposure to correspondent banks.
- Prohibited state-chartered banks engaging in activities not permitted for national banks.

# BANKING IN THE 21ST CENTURY

Legal and regulatory barriers erected after the Great Depression once prevented banks from offering many types of financial products and services. But the barriers gradually were lowered by legislation such as the Garn-St Germain Act, as well as by forward-looking regulatory actions and judicial decisions. For the 21st century, the banking industry sees opportunity, responsibility, and accountability.

## OPPORTUNITY: GRAMM-LEACH-BLILEY ACT

Enacted in late December 1999, the Gramm-Leach-Bliley Act (GLBA), hailed as the most significant overhaul of financial services industry laws since the Great Depression, is one of the most influential acts of the 21st century. GLBA (also known as the Financial Services Modernization Act of 1999) repealed key provisions of the Banking Act/Glass-Steagall Act of 1933 and provided the financial services industry with the tools needed to compete in today's economy. Banks, securities firms, and insurance companies can enter each other's businesses and affiliate with each other. As a result, banks now may offer a full complement of financial services—from loans and deposits to life insurance and mutual funds.

GLBA is far-reaching legislation, and its provisions do more than open the door for banks to enter new markets. Other provisions protect customer financial privacy, for example. GLBA authorized activities are

- lending, exchanging, transferring, and investing for others
- safeguarding money or securities for others
- insurance underwriting and sales activities
- investment or economic advisory services
- securitization
- securities underwriting and dealing activities
- "closely related to banking" activities previously approved for bank holding companies by the Federal Reserve Board
- certain products offered overseas, such as travel agency services
- **merchant banking** and equity investment activities

**Merchant banking**—The buying and selling by banks of shares in the unregistered securities in companies.

Banks may offer these products and services in holding company affiliates or financial subsidiaries. In addition, the law authorizes the Federal Reserve Board and the Department of Treasury to use their regulatory powers to approve bank petitions to engage in other financial activities not listed under the law.

To facilitate engagement in new activities, the law created financial holding companies (FHCs) and financial subsidiaries. Bank holding companies and other financial services companies may elect status as FHCs. GLBA specifies the new powers that may be exercised in each type of banking organization. For example, annuity sales may be conducted in the bank, in a bank subsidiary, or in a holding company affiliate.

GLBA benefits community banks as well as large banks and holding companies. It provides new structural options and business opportunities. The law removes restrictions, so all banks may compete in the rapidly changing marketplace.

## RESPONSIBILITY: FINANCIAL PRIVACY AND PROTECTING THE NATION

Because of its important role in the economy, the banking industry remains one of the most highly regulated industries. Within the last few years, banks have taken on a number of new responsibilities in the areas of privacy, corporate governance, and anti-money laundering.

### Financial Privacy

Although GLBA provides new business opportunities for banks, it also imposes new requirements, particularly the obligation to protect the privacy of customer financial information. Information is one of a bank's most important assets. The increase in the types of products and services banks may now offer brings with it the increase in the exchange of consumer financial information. GLBA includes provisions to protect financial privacy and assures customers that their personal information will not be shared with third parties without their permission. The law accomplishes this by

- requiring banks to establish a privacy policy and disclose the policy to customers at account opening and annually thereafter
- requiring banks to protect the security and confidentiality of customer information by implementing physical, technical, and administrative safeguards, which among other things, would bar unauthorized access
- preventing banks from conveying certain account information to unaffiliated third-party marketers
- giving customers the right to instruct their bank not to provide information about them to nonaffiliated third parties.

Before a bank may disclose any nonpublic personal information to a nonaffiliated third party, the customer must have the opportunity to "opt out" of the disclosure.

Protecting the privacy of customer financial information is a critically important component of bank compliance and customer relations. If customer information is disclosed to unauthorized third parties, the bank's relationship with customers is damaged, its reputation in the community is tarnished, and earnings and profitability can be put at risk.

Another repercussion of the failure to protect customer information is **identity theft**. This crime exacts a financial and emotional toll on its victims. An identity thief can use ill-gotten personal information of another to obtain credit, merchandise, and services. One of the best weapons for combating identity theft is a strong

**Identity theft**—A crime involving the possession of identifying information not lawfully issued for that person's use or the attempt to access the financial resources of that person through the use of illegally obtained identifying information.

Justin opened checking and savings accounts when he graduated from college. Recently, he inherited money from his grandmother. Because he is satisfied with his bank's service, he deposits the money into his account. His banker suggests that he talk to a financial counselor, who offers him a mutual fund. Justin inquires about the stock market and is surprised when the financial counselor can help with that, too. He is surprised even more when he asks to withdraw money to pay his car insurance bill and is referred to the bank's insurance agency for a quote. Justin leaves thinking how convenient it is to get all of his financial needs taken care of in one place—and with people he knows and trusts!

customer information privacy program. Communicating with customers about how to protect their identifying information is another recommended policy.

### USA PATRIOT Act

In the aftermath of the terrorist attacks of September 11, 2001, Congress decided to broaden the intelligence-gathering powers of law enforcement agencies in an effort to prevent future attacks. In October 2001, the Uniting and Strengthening America by Providing Appropriate Tools Required to Intercept and Obstruct Terrorism Act—better known as the USA PATRIOT Act—was enacted.

Financial institutions, including banks, are on the first line of defense in the war against terrorism. Terrorist organizations, as is true of all other criminal enterprises, need financing. They engage in money laundering and other illegal practices through legitimate financial institutions to hide their transactions.

The USA PATRIOT Act places responsibilities on financial institutions to track and prevent the illegal transfer of funds, including

- adopting and enforcing anti-money laundering programs
- implementing customer identification programs
- reporting certain currency and other transactions to the government
- reporting suspicious activities, including possible terrorist financing schemes, to the government

Some of these requirements are not new to the banking industry. Since 1987, banks have had to maintain anti-money laundering programs. Since 1996, banks have been required to report suspicious activity under the Bank Secrecy Act (BSA). BSA requires banks to report cash transactions that exceed $10,000 in any single day and to maintain other records.

The USA PATRIOT Act also requires banks to adopt written customer identification programs. Banks must require new customers opening bank accounts to produce identifying information, and banks must maintain records of the information used to verify the person's identity. Banks must determine whether the person appears on any lists of known or suspected terrorists or terrorist organizations provided to the financial institution by any government agency. Federal law enforcement agencies also can demand financial information from banks about individuals or entities that are suspected of terrorism or money laundering.

### The FACT Act

The Fair and Accurate Credit Transaction Act of 2003 (FACT Act) was signed into law by President Bush on December 4, 2003. The FACT Act contains provisions intended to prevent identity theft, improve consumer access to consumer reports, enhance the accuracy of consumer reports, and limit sharing certain consumer information. The act adds a new section to the Fair Credit Reporting Act, by restricting the circumstances under which consumer reporting agencies may furnish reports containing medical information about consumers. It also prohibits creditors from obtaining or using a consumer's medical information when determining eligibility, or continued eligibility, for credit. The FACT Act will affect how banks use consumer reports, furnish credit information, and share consumer information with affiliates.

## ACCOUNTABILITY: THE SARBANES-OXLEY ACT

A little over ten years after the S&L crisis, another crisis produced legislation with implications for the banking industry. This time, however, financial institutions largely escaped direct culpability. The crisis involved commercial companies such as Enron, an energy services company, and WorldCom, a giant in the telecommunications industry. Both companies came to symbolize mismanagement and weak **corporate governance**.

During the late 1990s, stock prices increased dramatically. However, the rise in stock prices for some companies was not due to solid financial performance. Rather, prices were inflated artificially through accounting practices that exaggerated the value of contracts and holdings, or disguised losses by structuring deals based on inflated revenue and profit projections. Meanwhile, some executives and directors used their insider knowledge and sold their stock shortly before accounting irregularities were disclosed and stock prices plummeted. Employees who owned company stock through their retirement savings plan had no forewarning and subsequently lost their life-long savings.

**Corporate governance—** The manner in which directors, management, and auditors handle their responsibilities toward shareholders.

| Chronology of Major Banking Legislation and Events | |
|---|---|
| 1791-1811 | First Bank of the United States |
| 1811-1816 | Bank failures increase |
| 1816-1836 | Second Bank of the United States |
| 1836-1863 | Chaos in the banking system |
| 1863-1864 | National Bank Act (Office of the Comptroller of the Currency established) |
| 1913 | Federal Reserve Act (Federal Reserve System created) |
| 1929-1939 | Great Depression |
| 1933 | Banking Act, including Glass-Steagall Act, (FDIC Created) |
| 1934 | Securities Exchange Act |
| 1935 | Banking Act (Federal Deposit Insurance Act) |
| 1968 | Truth in Lending Act |
| 1970-1980 | "Disintermediation" in the banking system |
| 1980 | Depository Institutions Deregulation and Monetary Control Act |
| 1982 | Garn-St Germain Depository Institutions Act |
| 1988-1992 | Savings and loan crisis |
| 1989 | Financial Institutions Reform, Recovery, and Enforcement Act (FIRREA) |
| 1991 | Federal Deposit Insurance Corporation Improvement Act (FDICIA) |
| 1994 | Riegle-Neal Interstate Banking and Branching Efficiency Act |
| 1999 | Gramm-Leach-Bliley Act (Financial Modernization Act) |
| 2001-2003 | Corporate accountability scandals |
| 2001 | USA PATRIOT Act |
| 2001 | Sarbanes-Oxley Act (SOX) |
| 2003 | FACT Act |

With the collapse of several large companies, investors lost confidence in the earnings and profit figures announced by public corporations. As investor confidence plunged, so did the stock market.

To restore investor confidence in publicly held corporations, Congress passed the Sarbanes-Oxley Act of 2001 (SOX). The law imposes new responsibilities on company executives, boards of directors, audit committees, and accounting firms. A company's chief executive officer and chief financial officer must attest personally that the information contained in company reports is complete and accurate. Companies also are required to have an audit committee responsible for overseeing the company's accounting and financial reporting processes and audits of its financial statements.

SOX stipulates that an accounting firm may no longer provide audits for a company if the firm also provides the company with non-audit services such as bookkeeping, appraisal or valuation services, or investment advisory services unrelated to the audit. External auditors also must attest to the fairness and accuracy of the company's financial statements.

SOX applies only to public companies—that is, companies that issue stock to the public. However, the federal banking agencies issued guidelines and regulations that apply SOX-like requirements to all banks, publicly owned or closely held.

# FEDERAL RESERVE SYSTEM

As the United State's central bank, the Federal Reserve System plays an important role in the banking system and the economy. Duties of the Federal Reserve System fall into four general areas:

**Duties of the Federal Reserve System**

- Conduct monetary and credit policy
- Supervise and regulate banking institutions
- Maintain stability of the financial system
- Provide certain financial services

- conduct the nation's monetary policy by influencing money and credit conditions in the economy in pursuit of full employment and stable prices

- supervise and regulate banking institutions to ensure the safety and soundness of the nation's banking and financial system and to protect credit rights of consumers

- maintain the financial system's stability and contain systematic risk in financial markets

- provide certain financial services to the U.S. government, the public, financial institutions, and foreign official institutions, including playing a major role in operating the nation's payment system

The Fed has the authority to issue rules, regulations, and guidelines that apply to both national banks and state member banks. The regulations provide the Fed with the means to carry out congressional policies and to control the flow of money and credit. Regulating banks and regulations will be discussed later. This section reviews the structure of the Federal Reserve System and provides an overview of two Fed duties: controlling monetary policy and providing certain financial services.

## STRUCTURE OF THE FEDERAL RESERVE SYSTEM

The Federal Reserve System consists of 12 Federal Reserve Districts. Exhibit 2.5 shows the 12 districts and the cities where each Federal Reserve Bank and each Federal Reserve branch is located.

Each Federal Reserve District contains a Federal Reserve Bank with a board of directors. Each Federal Reserve Bank is owned by member banks in the district. The member banks hold stock in the Reserve Bank. Although the Federal Reserve Banks are privately owned, the stockholders (member banks) do not control the system as stockholders normally control a company. Instead, member banks exercise control through election of six of the nine directors of the local Federal Reserve Banks, three of which cannot be bankers. The remaining three directors are appointed by the Board of Governors of the Federal Reserve System, and these also cannot be bankers. The activities of the Federal Reserve Banks and the overall activities of the Fed are directed by the Board of Governors of the Federal Reserve System.

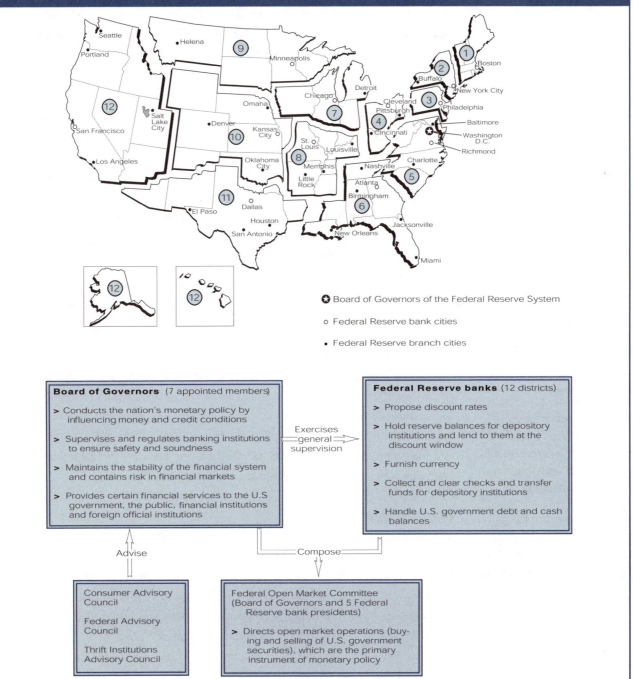

Exhibit 2.5: Federal Reserve Districts and Branch Cities

✪ Board of Governors of the Federal Reserve System

o Federal Reserve bank cities

• Federal Reserve branch cities

**Board of Governors** (7 appointed members)

> Conducts the nation's monetary policy by influencing money and credit conditions

> Supervises and regulates banking institutions to ensure safety and soundness

> Maintains the stability of the financial system and contains risk in financial markets

> Provides certain financial services to the U.S government, the public, financial institutions and foreign official institutions

Exercises general supervision →

**Federal Reserve banks** (12 districts)

> Propose discount rates

> Hold reserve balances for depository institutions and lend to them at the discount window

> Furnish currency

> Collect and clear checks and transfer funds for depository institutions

> Handle U.S. government debt and cash balances

Advise

Compose

Consumer Advisory Council

Federal Advisory Council

Thrift Institutions Advisory Council

Federal Open Market Committee (Board of Governors and 5 Federal Reserve bank presidents)

> Directs open market operations (buying and selling of U.S. government securities), which are the primary instrument of monetary policy

### Board of Governors of the Federal Reserve System

The Board of Governors consists of seven members appointed by the president of the United States and confirmed by the Senate. The governors are appointed for terms of 14 years. One term expires every two years, thus insulating the governors from political pressure. No two members of the board may come from the same Federal Reserve District. The President of the United States appoints one of the governors as chairman and another as vice chairman for four-year terms. These terms do not coincide with that of the President, thus providing further insulation from political pressure.

### Federal Reserve Banks

Each Federal Reserve District has a Federal Reserve Bank, and most Reserve Banks have branches. The structure of the 12 district banks allows them to serve the needs of the local members and to ensure local representation at the national level. The local Federal Reserve Banks also provide information on the regional economy in the form of surveys, statistical reports, and tables of financial data.

## FEDERAL RESERVE'S MONETARY AND CREDIT POLICY

Control of the nation's money supply is a primary duty of the Fed. The Federal Reserve has the responsibility to ensure that the money supply does not outpace the needs of the economy. The Fed can shape the economic environment by taking specific actions to influence the flow of money and credit. It has three tools it can use: reserve requirements, discount operations, and open-market operations.

### Reserve Requirements

The Federal Reserve requires banks to set aside a portion of their cash assets in a noninterest-bearing reserve account at the Federal Reserve as a means of safeguarding customer deposits. The Fed can change the reserve requirement to decrease or increase the amount of money a bank has available to lend, and thus influence the money supply in the economy.

Banks whose reserves at the Fed are more than required may lend excess reserves, called **Fed funds**, to another bank whose reserves are temporarily short. These transactions, which take place by adjusting the reserves of the two institutions on the Fed's account books, typically occur overnight. The rate charged, called the Fed funds rate, is set by the banks, not the Fed. The Fed does establish the rate's range and influences it by increasing or decreasing the reserves available.

### Discount Operations

The Federal Reserve can influence loan demand and credit availability through the **discount rate**. Unlike the Fed funds rate, the discount rate is set by each of the 12 Federal Reserve Banks, subject to veto by the Board of Governors.

The Fed can use the discount rate to encourage or discourage bank borrowing and subsequent bank lending to customers, depending on the effect it is trying to make on the money supply. To increase the money supply, the Fed lowers the discount rate, thereby lowering the cost of funds to banks and encouraging borrowing and business growth and activity. To decrease the money supply, the Fed

---

**Fed funds**—Excess reserves held by member banks in accounts at the Federal Reserve that are loaned with interest on a daily basis to other member banks.

**Discount rate**—The rate of interest charged by the Federal Reserve Banks on loans it makes to financial institutions.

raises the discount rate, thereby increasing the cost of funds to banks and thus discouraging borrowing and decreasing growth of the money supply.

## Open-Market Operations

The most powerful and frequently used tool available to the Fed is the open-market operations conducted by the Federal Reserve Bank of New York for the **Federal Open-Market Committee** (FOMC). The FOMC consists of the seven members of the Board of Governors plus the president of the New York Federal Reserve Bank and four other Reserve bank presidents. The FOMC is responsible for system-wide administration of monetary policy. At FOMC meetings short- and long-term monetary needs are determined. Then a directive is issued to the Federal Reserve Bank of New York, the designated agent, to buy or sell government obligations for Federal Reserve District Banks using selected government securities dealer firms.

**Federal Open-Market Committee (FOMC)**—The Federal Reserve committee that sets monetary policy and issues guidelines for open-market operations. It purchases and redeems U.S. government obligations through the Federal Reserve Bank of New York to implement monetary policy.

The purchase or sale of government securities by the Fed immediately increases or decreases the money supply and affects the availability of short-term credit.

The open-market operations of the New York Fed can have an immediate effect on the money supply and the availability of credit, whereas changes in reserve requirements and the discount rate usually have a delayed effect. Exhibit 2.6 summarizes the effect of the basic Federal Reserve monetary and credit tools on the economy.

### Exhibit 2.6: Fed Tools and Their Effects

| | | |
|---|---|---|
| Reserve Requirements | Increase | Rarely used because its effects can be too disruptive. It decreases the money supply. |
| | Decrease | It stimulates the economy by increasing the supply of loanable funds. |
| Discount Operations | Increase Discount Rate | Can have moderately fast effect on banks and economy, but banks are typically reluctant to borrow. It discourages borrowing and the money supply shrinks when inflation is becoming a problem. |
| | Decrease Rate | Has opposite effect during economic recovery when the Fed wants to expand business activity. |
| Open Market Operations | Purchase Securities | Immediate, powerful effect on banks and economy. Increases money supply in paying for purchases by crediting the reserve accounts of banks. |
| | Sales | Tightens credit by reducing money supply in times of rising inflation. |

*(Source: Amaury Betancourt, Loan Review Examiner)*

## FEDERAL RESERVE SERVICES

One of the original purposes of the Federal Reserve System was to provide basic banking services to member banks, and it did so free of charge until 1980. Then, Congress mandated the Fed to provide services to nonmember banks, and to charge both members and nonmembers for the services. Fed services that carry a fee are special packaging and transportation of coin and currency, check processing, fedwire, automated clearing house, settlement, and securities safekeeping.

| | |
|---|---|
| **Coin and Currency** | The Fed supplies banks with coin and currency to meet customers' withdrawal demands. It accepts shipments of coin and currency from banks and ensures that damaged currency is removed from circulation. |
| **Check Processing** | The Fed offers check clearing, collection, and return items services to banks. |
| **Fedwire** | This payment service is an electronic transfer of funds and government securities between financial institutions that have accounts at Federal Reserve banks. |
| **Automated Clearing House (ACH)** | The Fed is the primary provider of ACH services, which are paperless electronic debit and credit transactions. As with checks, the Fed sorts ACH transactions and presents them to the paying or receiving bank. |
| **Settlement** | When banks send checks to local clearing houses or use Fedwire, payment is made by netting amounts presented and due to participating members. Final postings are sent to the Fed, which provides a settlement service, or payment, through Federal Reserve accounts. |
| **U.S. Government Services** | The Fed serves as the U.S. government's bank. For example, income tax refund checks are drawn on the Fed. The inflow of all funds to the federal government goes ultimately through the Fed. As the fiscal agent for the U.S. Treasury, the Fed is responsible for issuing and redeeming all federal government obligations. |

# REGULATORS AND REGULATIONS

The U.S. banking industry is highly regulated, subject to regulation by one or more banking agencies that supervise banking activities, enforce regulations, and issue guidelines.

## BANK REGULATORS

The Federal Reserve System is one of the five regulatory groups with the authority to supervise bank activities. The other agencies are the Office of the Comptroller of the Currency (OCC), the Federal Deposit Insurance Corporation (FDIC), the Office of Thrift Supervision (OTS), and state banking departments.

## Office of the Comptroller of the Currency (OCC)

The OCC, part of the Treasury Department has jurisdiction over national banks. The OCC is responsible for chartering, examining, and supervising national banks. All applications for national bank charters, all requests by any national bank for opening new domestic or foreign branches or for offering new services, and all mergers or acquisitions involving national banks must have OCC approval. The OCC also issues rules and regulations governing bank investments, lending, and other activities.

## Federal Reserve (Fed)

The Fed is responsible for supervising and examining

- all bank holding companies, their nonbank subsidiaries, and their foreign subsidiaries
- state-chartered banks that are members of the Federal Reserve System and their foreign branches and subsidiaries
- Edge Act and agreement corporations through which U.S. banks conduct operations abroad

In addition to issuing regulations for member banks, the Fed rules on merger and branching applications of state-chartered member banks and activities for bank holding companies.

## Federal Deposit Insurance Corporation (FDIC)

The FDIC is responsible for supervising and examining state-chartered commercial banks that are not Federal Reserve System members (nonmember banks) and state-chartered savings associations. The FDIC also has the authority to examine other FDIC-insured institutions for deposit insurance purposes.

National banks, and state-chartered banks that elect to be members of the Federal Reserve, are required to belong to the FDIC. Other commercial banks may join the FDIC if they wish. Savings banks, which had been given the right to become members of the Federal Reserve System, are permitted to join the FDIC. The FDIC arranges a resolution for each failing institution and promotes the safety and soundness of insured depositories by identifying, monitoring, and addressing risks to the insurance fund.

## Office of Thrift Supervision (OTS)

All federally chartered and many state-chartered thrift institutions, which include savings banks and savings and loan associations, are regulated and examined by OTS. In 1989, OTS was established as a bureau of the U.S. Department of the Treasury.

## State Banking Departments

The United States has a dual banking system of national and state-chartered banks. Banks that opt for a state charter also can decide whether to become members of the

Federal Reserve and the FDIC. Each state has its own banking department responsible for chartering, supervising, and examining state-chartered banks within the boundaries of the state. Banks' applications for state charters are submitted to the banking departments of the individual states and banks must pass qualifying tests. If the proposed new bank desires membership in the Federal Reserve System and the FDIC, its application must be reviewed and approved by those agencies as well. State banking departments also examine the branches and agencies of foreign banks operating in their state.

## BANK REGULATIONS

When Congress passes banking-related legislation, it directs the Fed and other federal regulators to formulate regulatory requirements that implement the law. That the banking industry is one of the most highly regulated industries reflects its important role in the U.S. economy. Bank legislation and regulations have served to

- protect the U.S. banking system
- support changing financial market conditions
- protect consumers

The Federal Reserve has implemented 30 regulations. Each regulation is assigned a letter of the alphabet. Having used letters A to Z (except for R), the regulations started over at AA and now extend through EE. See exhibit 2.7 for a short list of the regulations by categories.

## SUMMARY

- The banking system in the United States has been evolving for more than 200 years. Major changes in the way banks are regulated often have resulted from reactions to crises. The industry has gone from a completely decentralized and unregulated system in the 19th century to one of the most highly regulated sectors of the economy in the 21st century.

- The early U.S. banking system was unstructured and unregulated, and it could not support the needs of a growing industrial nation. Two attempts were made to establish a central banking system, and both failed. Then in 1863, Congress passed the National Bank Act, which created national banks, the OCC, national bank notes, and a system of reserves. The National Bank Act did solve many of the problems plaguing the banking system, but others remained. The national banknote was an inflexible form of currency. There was no check collection system, and reserves were concentrated in money center banks. Bank panics resulted.

- The Federal Reserve Act of 1913 was passed to address the weaknesses that remained after the National Bank Act. The Federal Reserve Act established the Federal Reserve System and, by creating 12 Federal Reserve Districts, solved the problem of the pyramiding of reserves and the lack of a check collection system. The Federal Reserve note, which constitutes our basic currency today, solved the inflexible currency problem.

- The economy's rapid expansion after World War I led to some ill-advised investment and banking practices. The stock market crash of 1929 followed, which in turn contributed to many bank failures and the Great Depression. In 1933, Congress passed the Banking Act, which contains the Glass-Steagall Act, and which placed

## Regulation

### Monetary Policy

A    Loans to depositories
D    Reserve requirements
T, U, X    Credit by banks, by brokers and dealers, and by others; rules for margin borrowers

### Bank Safety and Soundness

F    Limitations on interbank liabilities
L    Restrictions on interlocking directorates in banking
O    Loans to officers, directors, and stockholders
Q    Interest on demand deposits prohibition
W    Transactions between banks and their affiliates

### International Banking and Bank Holding Companies

K    Activities of U.S. banks overseas and U.S. operations of foreign banks
Y    Activities of bank holding companies

### Federal Reserve Membership and Reserve Banks' Procedures

EE    Payments under netting agreements among banks
H    Membership requirements for state-chartered banks
I    Stock ownership requirements for banks joining the Federal Reserve System
J    Check-processing and Electronic Fund Transfer (EFT) procedures
N    Reserve banks' relations with foreign banks and governments
S    Reimbursement for providing customers' banking records to government

### Consumer Protection

AA    Consumer complaint procedures concerning unfair or deceptive practices
B    Equal credit opportunity
BB    Community reinvestment
C    Home mortgage disclosure
CC    Availability of deposited check funds
DD    Truth in Savings
E    Electronic fund transfer
G    Disclosure and reporting of Community Reinvestment Act related agreements
M    Consumer leasing
P    Privacy of Consumer Financial Information
V    Fair Credit Reporting
Z    Truth in Lending

For more information on regulations see Federal Reserve Board of Governors Web site **www.federalreserve.gov**.

significant controls on banks. The act prohibited payment of interest on demand deposits, prohibited banks from underwriting stocks or affiliating with organizations dealing in securities, raised capital requirements, authorized the Fed to forbid use of reserve credit for speculative purposes, and created the FDIC.

- Before 1968, little, if any, federal law protected consumers in their dealings with banks and other financial institutions. The 1968 Consumer Credit Protection Act, of which Title I is the Truth in Lending Act, was a turning point. The act requires, among other things, that lenders provide consumers with finance charge and APR information.

- In 1980, an era of deregulation began. Congress passed the Depository Institutions Deregulation and Monetary Control Act. The law allowed banks to compete more effectively with nonbank competitors by lifting some restrictions on banking activities, such as allowing NOW accounts, an interest-bearing checking account. The Garn-St Germain Act, which followed, allowed banks to compete with mutual funds and other investment products, by offering money market deposit accounts. Later the Riegle-Neal Interstate Banking and Branch Efficiency Act of 1994, allowed, for example, national banks to operate branches across state lines.

- During the late 1980s, such factors as narrowing interest rate spreads and inexperience with the new deposit and loan products caused unprecedented losses to S&Ls. Commercial banks also experienced high loan losses. By passing FIRREA in 1989, Congress stepped in to avert significant individual losses. FIRREA provided the FDIC with greater administrative control over both the bank and savings association insurance funds. In 1991, FDICIA was passed requiring banks to meet new safety and soundness standards.

- The 21st century brings new opportunities and responsibilities. The Gramm-Leach–Bliley Act provides opportunities for banks to offer other financial services, such as investment and insurance products. At the same time, public concern over identity theft and the privacy of financial information imposes new legal obligations on banks. The terrorist attacks of September 11, 2001, for example, led to the enactment of the USA PATRIOT Act, which now requires banks to implement customer identification programs and report suspicious activities to federal government agencies.

- The Federal Reserve has the authority to issue rules, regulations, and guidelines that apply to both national banks and state member banks. The Fed controls the flow of money and credit by using reserve requirements, discount operations, and open-market operations. The Fed also provides many basic banking services to member and nonmember banks.

- In addition to the Federal Reserve, banks may be supervised by the Office of the Comptroller of the Currency, the Federal Deposit Insurance Corporation, the Office of Thrift Supervision, and state banking departments.

- The Federal Reserve, one regulatory agency that issues regulations, has implemented 30 regulations for its member banks. Regulations implement banking legislation. Each regulation is assigned a letter of the alphabet. The Truth in Lending Act is Federal Reserve Regulation Z.

# SELF CHECK & REVIEW

**Learning Check**

1. What is the role of banks in the U.S. economy?

2. What is inflation?

3. Why is the National Bank Act of 1863 important?

4. What is meant by dual banking system? Does the dual banking system exist today?

5. What was the singular achievement of the Federal Reserve Act?

6. What Federal Agency was created by the Banking Act of 1933 and why?

7. What are the four basic duties of the Federal Reserve?

8 What events contributed to the bank failures in the late 1980s and early 1990s?

9. What legislation guarantees that a bank customer's financial records will be kept private? What are the basic privacy provisions?

10. What are five regulatory groups with the authority to supervise bank activities?

# ADDITIONAL RESOURCES

**Resources**

*ABA Bank Compliance Magazine*, Washington D.C.: American Bankers Association.

*ABA Bankers News,* Washington D.C.: American Bankers Association.

*ABA Banking Journal*, American Bankers Association. **www.ababj.com**

American Bankers Association, **www.aba.com**

Board of Governors, Federal Reserve, **www.federalreserve.gov**

Federal Deposit Insurance Corporation, **www.fdic.gov**

Federal Reserve Bank of New York, **www.ny.frb.org**

Office of the Comptroller of the Currency, **www.occ.treas.gov**

Office of Thrift Supervision, **www.ots.gov**

*Reference Guide to Regulatory Compliance*, Washington D.C.: American Bankers Association, 2004.

# Managing and Reporting Bank Investments and Performance

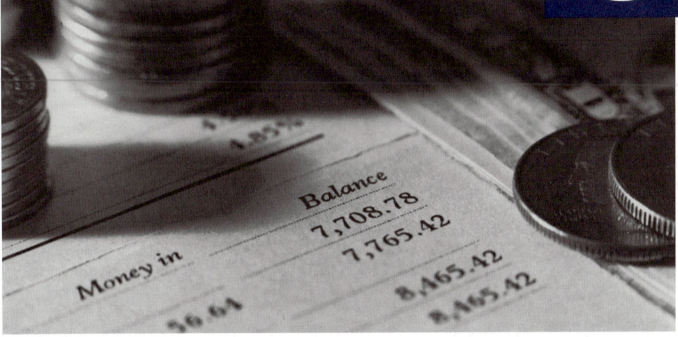

# What You Will Learn

*After studying this chapter, you should be able to*

- describe the annual report and its two key financial statements: profit and loss statement and statement of condition
- explain why financial statements are important to various bank constituent groups
- discuss the role of the Asset and Liability Management Committee and funds management goals and objectives
- explain how banks maximize loan and investment returns
- identify the key performance measures in banking
- describe the role of budgeting in achieving bank objectives
- define the bolded key terms that appear in the text

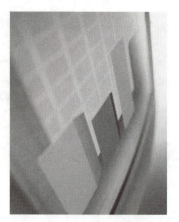

# Introduction

*Banks, like any other business, supply products and services, generate assets and liabilities, and produce a profit for stockholders. As businesses, banks report their performance through financial statements and ultimately in the annual report to owners. These reports demonstrate the performance results of a bank and its employees. They show where and how a bank acquired funds, how the funds were put to work, and the results achieved.*

## Situation

The Jayson Investment Group manages the pension fund for ACME Corp., a large manufacturing business with more than 3,000 employees. Mr. Jayson is considering investing in several bank stocks. He has read annual reports and other financial data from your bank and has set up a meeting with senior management and auditors to discuss future projections. If Mr. Jayson is satisfied with the bank's prospects, he will invest a large sum of money for the ACME Corp. pension fund.

## ANNUAL REPORT

Once a year, a bank issues an annual report that presents a picture of a bank's operations and financial condition. The annual report is management's summation of a bank's achievements over the course of the year. It describes management's perspective of the past year, including significant achievements, and looks at future objectives. It includes information about a bank's financial position and business performance. Four main components make up an annual report: promotional information, analysis, financial statements, and an audit report. Many banks publish annual reports on the Internet. (See Additional Resources for a sample.)

| | |
|---|---|
| **Promotional information** | Promotes the company to investors, including photographs of the bank at work, and nonfinancial statistics such as contributions to the community. |
| **Analysis** | Analysis of management's business strategies and developments. |
| **Financial statements** | Will include the statement of condition and income statement, and may include statement of cash flows, usually with comparisons to prior years. |
| **Audit report** | A written statement by contracted accountants attesting to the financial reports provided. |

The two key financial statements for a bank are the statement of condition (balance sheet) and the profit and loss statement (income statement). Abbreviated statements are in the annual report. These reports are important to understand a bank as a business and are important to various bank constituencies.

### STATEMENT OF CONDITION

The statement of condition, or balance sheet, is prepared as of a specific date. For example, it reports total assets, liabilities, and capital accounts of a bank as of December 31 of a given year.

A statement of condition lists all of a bank's assets and liabilities and stockholder equity (net worth). An asset is anything of value owned by or owed to a bank, whereas a liability is anything owed by a bank. For example, loans (owed to the bank by borrowers) are assets of the bank. Deposits (owed by the bank to depositors) are liabilities of the bank.

A statement of condition is a snapshot of the assets, liabilities, and capital of a bank or a company on any given day or a monthly, quarterly, or annual average of the balance in those particular asset, liability, or capital accounts. Exhibit 3.1 shows a typical statement of condition of a financial institution.

**Equity**—The stockholders' investment interest in a corporation, equaling the excess of assets over liabilities and including common and preferred stock, retained earnings, surplus and reserves.

## Exhibit 3.1: Consolidated Statement of Condition

### Assets

| (In thousands of dollars) | December 31 20XX | 20XX | Change |
|---|---|---|---|
| Cash and due from banks | $ 1,649,334 | $ 1,332,586 | $ 316,748 |
| Overseas deposits | 458,313 | 460,396 | (2,083) |
| Investment securities: | | | |
| U.S. Treasury securities | 881,081 | 982,654 | (101,573) |
| Securities of other U.S. government agencies and corporations | 199,318 | 243,420 | (44,102) |
| Obligations of states and political subdivisions | 738,813 | 396,948 | 341,865 |
| Other securities | 88,278 | 92,032 | (3,754) |
| Total investment securities | 1,907,490 | 1,715,054 | 192,436 |
| Trading account securities | 14,846 | 66,140 | (51,294) |
| Funds sold | 168,600 | 108,450 | 60,150 |
| Loans (net of reserve for loan losses and unearned discount) | 9,715,728 | 8,074,132 | 1,641,596 |
| Direct lease financing | 147,860 | 134,472 | 13,388 |
| Premises and equipment, net | 133,506 | 132,320 | 1,186 |
| Customers' acceptance liability | 372,835 | 248,271 | 124,564 |
| Accrued interest receivable | 133,840 | 123,719 | 10,121 |
| Other real estate owned | 34,332 | 13,668 | 20,664 |
| Other assets | 103,939 | 131,711 | (27,772) |
| Total assets | $ 14,840,623 | $ 12,540,919 | $ 2,299,704 |

### Liabilities and Stockholders' Equity

| (In thousands of dollars) | December 31 20XX | 20XX | Change |
|---|---|---|---|
| Demand deposits | $ 3,543,141 | $ 2,937,065 | $ 606,076 |
| Savings deposits | 3,585,808 | 3,485,886 | 99,922 |
| Savings certificates | 1,635,215 | 1,391,107 | 244,108 |
| Certificates of deposit | 1,827,420 | 1,601,707 | 225,713 |
| Other time deposits | 424,592 | 313,811 | 110,781 |
| Deposits in overseas offices | 1,468,003 | 722,950 | 745,053 |
| Total deposits | 12,484,179 | 10,452,526 | 2,031,653 |
| Funds borrowed | 897,189 | 924,501 | (27,312) |
| Long-term debt | 44,556 | 43,766 | 790 |
| Acceptances outstanding | 373,022 | 249,088 | 123,934 |
| Accrued taxes and other expenses | 142,756 | 122,064 | 20,692 |
| Other liabilities | 171,904 | 122,890 | 49,014 |
| Total liabilities (excluding subordinated notes) | 14,113,606 | 11,914,835 | 2,198,771 |
| Subordinated notes: | | | |
| 8.25% capital note to Wells Fargo & Company, due 20XX | 25,000 | 25,000 | —— |
| 4.5% capital notes due 20XX | 50,000 | 50,000 | —— |
| Total subordinated notes | 75,000 | 75,000 | —— |
| Stockholders' equity: | | | |
| Capital stock | 94,461 | 94,461 | —— |
| Surplus | 300,036 | 251,512 | 48,524 |
| Surplus representing convertible capital note obligation assumed by parent corporation | 10,065 | 14,589 | (4,524) |
| Undivided profits | 247,455 | 190,522 | 56,933 |
| Total stockholders' equity | 652,017 | 551,084 | 100,933 |
| Total liabilities and stockholders' equity | $ 14,840,623 | $ 12,540,919 | $ 2,299,704 |

Major categories of assets listed on a bank's statement of condition are as follows:

| Asset category | Description |
|---|---|
| Cash on hand and due from banks | Coin and currency held in a bank's vault, checks in the process of collection, and balances with **correspondent banks** and the Federal Reserve. |
| Investments | Obligations of the federal government and its agencies, obligations of state and local units of government, and stock in the Federal Reserve if the bank is a member. |
| Loans | All indebtedness to the bank, usually subdivided by category. |
| Fixed Assets | Real estate owned by the bank; furniture, fixtures, and equipment. |
| Other short-term assets | For example, fed funds sold and securities purchased under the agreement to resell. |

The following types of liabilities appear on a bank's statement of condition.

| Liability category | Description |
|---|---|
| Deposits | Subdivided into demand deposit, savings deposit, time deposit, domestic deposit, and global deposit accounts. |
| Taxes payable | All federal, state, and local taxes that must be paid. |
| Dividends payable | The directors' approved payment of a **dividend** to the stockholders, before actual disbursement has been made. |
| Other short-term liabilities | For example, fed funds purchased and securities sold under the agreement to repurchase. |

Depending on the size and scope of a bank's operations, various assets and liabilities are listed. They are listed in the order of liquidity so that the first item in each category is the most current and most easily converted into cash. Therefore, "cash and due from banks" is the first asset shown and "deposits" is the first liability listed. Besides showing the balances in the asset and liability accounts, the statement of condition also provides information used to calculate certain performance measurements, such as return on assets (ROA) or return on equity (ROE).

For banks, one of the most important considerations is reporting loans on the balance sheet. Despite a bank's best efforts to collect on loans, it is a fact of banking that not all outstanding loans will be repaid as scheduled. Therefore, each bank calculates a **loan loss reserve** on the basis of past experience with losses, the quality of its current loan portfolio, and the economic and political climate.

Each bank is permitted to reduce its total loan amount by this reserve. The loan loss reserve is not an advance admission by a bank that the full amount of the reserve will be used for charge-offs. Rather, the reserve is a "best guess" about the

**Correspondent bank—** A bank that maintains an account relationship or engages in an exchange of services with another bank.

**Dividend—**A periodic payment, usually made each quarter, by a corporation to its stockholders as a return on their investment. All dividend payouts must be approved by the corporation's board of directors.

**Loan loss reserve—**An amount that is reserved (or set aside) to cover possible loan losses. The loan loss reserve is built up through deductions from net income. As loan losses occur, they are charged to the reserve.

possibility a bank will need loan loss protection against events that may take place in the future.

Unless a bank is insolvent, its total assets are greater than its total liabilities. The excess of assets over liabilities, which is shown in its capital accounts, is the net worth of a bank. Net worth also is called stockholder equity. A fundamental equation in accounting states that total assets must equal total liabilities plus net worth. Thus, if all a bank's liabilities were paid by using assets, the bank's net worth would remain. The standard equation is:

$$\text{Assets} = \text{Liabilities} + \text{Net Worth (Stockholders' Equity)}$$

A statement of condition in an annual report might include other assets and liabilities not included in the totals. These are contingencies for financial events that could occur in the future, so they are not considered part of the current financial picture.

## PROFIT-AND-LOSS STATEMENT

The profit-and-loss statement, also called the income statement, covers a bank's operations over an extended period, such as the quarter or the year ending December 31 of a given year. It shows all revenues and expenses and the resulting profit or loss.

The profit-and-loss statement lists all categories of income by source and all expense categories. Expenses, which are shown subtracted from income, reflect either the profit or the loss experienced by a bank for a specified period. Exhibit 3.2 (on the following page) shows a profit-and-loss statement.

| Statement of Condition (Balance Sheet) | vs. | Profit-and-loss Statement (Income Statement) |
|---|---|---|
| A detailed list of a company's assets, liabilities, and capital (equity) on a specific date. | | Summary of revenue, expenses, and net income earned by a company during a period, such as a quarter or year. |

The following major sources of bank income are listed typically in order of size and importance:

- interest and fees earned on loans
- interest and dividends earned on investments
- fees, commissions, and service charges

The major items of expense, also listed in order of size and importance, are

- interest paid on deposits
- salaries, wages, and benefits
- taxes (federal, state, and local)

A bank's profit-and-loss statement produces a net, or bottom line, figure representing revenues less expenses. This net figure usually is translated into earnings per share. The earnings per share figure tells stockholders how much each share of outstanding stock earned during the designated period. If a bank's total expenses for the period exceed its income, the net figure is negative, indicating a loss.

A bank can use the profit-and-loss statement to analyze its profits and determine its major sources of income and expense. It also can compare its categories of income and expense with those of peer banks. If its expenses are higher than its peers, a bank can adjust its operations to bring them in line with other institutions. Many reference materials, such as data from the FDIC, are available to help banks make peer comparisons.

## Exhibit 3.2: Consolidated Profit-and-Loss Statement

| Interest Income | December 31 | |
| --- | --- | --- |
| (In thousands of dollars) | 20XX | 20XX |
| Interest and fees on loans | $ 823,415 | $ 693,463 |
| Interest on Fed funds sold | 6,429 | 3,496 |
| Interest and dividends on investment securities: | | |
| U.S. Treasury securities | 69,938 | 59,883 |
| Securities of other U.S. government agencies and corporations | 16,520 | 25,228 |
| Obligations of states and political subdivisions | 22,504 | 15,846 |
| Other securities | 7,067 | 7,268 |
| Interest on overseas deposits | 24,394 | 37,658 |
| Interest on trading accounts securities | 4,419 | 3,478 |
| Direct lease financing income | 33,371 | 32,560 |
| Total interest income | 1,008,057 | 878,880 |

| Interest Expense | December 31 | |
| --- | --- | --- |
| (In thousands of dollars) | 20XX | 20XX |
| Interest on deposits | 463,733 | 414,832 |
| Interest on federal funds borrowed and repurchase agreements | 35,193 | 33,019 |
| Interest on other borrowed funds | 17,751 | 12,882 |
| Interest on long-term debt | 21,232 | 19,079 |
| Total interest expense | 537,909 | 479,812 |
| Net interest income | 470,148 | 399,068 |
| Provision for loan losses | 41,028 | 46,379 |
| Net interest income after provision for loan losses | 429,120 | 352,689 |

| Other Operating Income | December 31 | |
| --- | --- | --- |
| (In thousands of dollars) | 20XX | 20XX |
| Trust income | 21,635 | 19,649 |
| Service charges on deposit accounts | 25,511 | 24,254 |
| Trading account profits and commissions | (268) | 1,690 |
| Other income | 43,797 | 23,324 |
| Total other operating income | 90,675 | 68,917 |

| Other Operating Expense | December 31 | |
| --- | --- | --- |
| (In thousands of dollars) | 20XX | 20XX |
| Salaries | 168,085 | 145,746 |
| Employee benefits | 41,028 | 32,126 |
| Net occupancy expense | 34,919 | 31,636 |
| Equipment expense | 20,648 | 19,234 |
| Other expense | 94,331 | 68,317 |
| Total other operating expense | 359,011 | 297,059 |
| Income before income taxes and securities transactions | 160,784 | 124,547 |
| Less applicable income taxes | 73,484 | 61,076 |
| Income before securities transactions | 87,300 | 63,471 |
| Securities gains (losses), net of income tax effect of $(1,233) in 20XX and $48 in 20XX | (1,020) | 40 |
| Net income | $ 86,280 | $ 63,511 |
| Income per share (based on average number of common shares outstanding): | | |
| Income before securities transactions | $4.03 | $3.16 |
| Securities transactions, net of income tax effect | (.05) | |
| Net income | $3.98 | $3.16 |

# IMPORTANCE OF FINANCIAL INFORMATION

The information in a bank's financial statements and reports is important not only to management and the board of directors, but also to stockholders and investors, regulators, other financial institutions, customers, and employees.

## STOCKHOLDERS AND INVESTORS

Stockholders and investors are interested in a bank's financial data because the information may have an immediate effect on stock value. For example, a report of higher-than-expected earnings usually increases the value of bank stock. If the financial data indicate that a bank is performing poorly, the stock value typically will decline.

## REGULATORS

Bank regulators are interested in bank financial reports because they help determine a bank's true financial condition. Regulators are interested particularly in a bank's capital (stockholder's equity).

## OTHER FINANCIAL INSTITUTIONS

Financial institutions judge their own performance relative to their peers, as well as against their own goals. Using **ratio analysis**, they analyze ratios of comparable banks as a way of judging their own performance in the marketplace.

Banks seeking to expand through merger or acquisition are interested in the financial results of other banks. Potential acquirers are looking for bargains. If a bank's performance ratios indicate operational inefficiencies, the bank could be a prime candidate for acquisition. The potential acquirer may be able to reduce expenses or take advantage of economies of scale to turn a lackluster bank into a top performer.

## CUSTOMERS

After federal deposit insurance was established, consumers were less concerned about the strength of financial institutions for many years. However, because bank failures occasionally happen and deposits are insured up to $100,000 only, many people now are concerned about the financial strength of banks. Customers are interested in the financial stability of a bank so their money is put to productive uses and they do not lose their savings. Customers not only shop for interest rates, they also shop for financial stability.

## EMPLOYEES

The financial information produced by a bank affects bank employees. Many employees take pride in the financial results of their organization and are interested in how their bank compares with competitors. Their salaries, bonuses, benefits, and compensation may be tied directly to bank performance. In addition, many banks maintain compensation plans for executive management that are based on bank performance, including performance in relation to peer institutions.

**Did You Know ...**

The banking industry's ROA for 2003 was 1.38% — high by historical standards.

*(Federal Deposit Insurance Corporation)*

**Ratio analysis**—A technique for analyzing a financial statement that examines the relationships among certain key values reported in the statement.

Pat and Larry are moving to the Southwest from the Northeast when they retire in a few months. Careful planning and saving over the years have resulted in a substantial retirement investment portfolio that they want to transfer to a bank near their new home. In the 1980s, they had their life savings in a financial institution that failed. Although they did not lose any money, they did not have access to their funds for some time and were scared about the potential loss. Since then, they have become very knowl-edgeable about finan-cial matters. When they move, they want to make sure the bank they select to handle their accounts is well managed and solid.

A primary goal of management and employees is to increase stockholder value by ensuring bank financial results are positive. Attaining financial goals helps motivate employees, especially if they are allowed to share in the profits. Many banks have profit-sharing plans that give employees a stake in the bank's financial results. Some banks are entirely employee-owned.

# MANAGEMENT OF BANK FUNDS

Managing assets (loans and investments) and liabilities (deposits) is a fundamental challenge of banking. It is far more complex than simply making sure the rate charged for a loan is higher than the rate paid for deposits.

A common misconception is that banks possess huge pools of money belonging only to themselves and that they can lend and invest these funds as they see fit. If this were true, a bank would risk only its own funds when it makes loans. In fact, the opposite is true. Every bank loan represents an effort to put deposits to work safely, prudently, and profitably, while meeting the legitimate credit needs of borrowers.

## ASSET AND LIABILITY MANAGEMENT

When developing a strategy to manage bank funds, every bank takes many variables into account. Most banks use a funds management strategy that simultaneously manages assets and liabilities. Because asset and liability management is so important, banks have an Asset and Liability Management Committee (ALCO) responsible for this function.

ALCO monitors costs of deposits and income from loans. Its goal is to manage the bank's assets and liabilities so that the bank's stockholders receive the maximum long-term gain achievable. To accomplish the feat requires planning for liquidity and controlling risk.

For years, bank management primarily focused on traditional assets such as loans and other investments. Managers were not as concerned about the source of the funds—primarily customers' deposits—that were used to purchase assets. Today, however, customers have a wide variety of options for depositing their money. As a result, managing the liability side of banking is equally important.

Banks work hard to attract new depositors and to retain deposits. Periodically, every bank must decide how much it needs in working funds, where to acquire additional funds, and how much it is willing to pay for these funds in a competitive marketplace.

One of the largest expenses for banks is the interest paid to depositors. A challenge for bankers is to ensure that the interest paid to depositors is less than the interest received on loans. The spread between the two is known as net interest spread. Each bank's net interest spread is important to its efforts to meet payments, generate profits, and grow.

Applying the principles of matched funding, short-term loans are funded with short-term deposits, and long-term loans are funded with long-term deposits. A 30-year loan to purchase a home is funded by longer-term deposits, such as certificates of deposits. A short-term loan or adjustable-rate loan that is repriced or adjusted as market rates change is funded with demand deposits.

**Matched funding** is not applied to individual loans but to entire loan portfolios. Thus, banks are careful to maintain a balance in the types of deposits they attract and the types of loans they make.

## FUNDS MANAGEMENT OBJECTIVES

Because customers entrust their money with banks, a high priority for every bank is a sound funds management program. Responsible to ALCO, the president or CEO at smaller banks and funds management departments at larger banks often manage these programs. A funds management program strives to balance three objectives: liquidity, safety, and income.

### *Liquidity*

**Liquidity** is very important for banks. If it does not have money available when depositors want to make a withdrawal, a bank will fail. When a bank is suspected of being illiquid, depositors will rush to withdraw funds. In the past, depositors' fear that money would not be available for withdrawal has triggered bank panics and failures.

The need for liquidity is tied to both the deposit function and to the lending function. Liquidity enables a bank to meet the loan demands of its customers and helps a bank support the credit needs of its communities, as mandated by the Community Reinvestment Act.

Every bank operates with the expectation that fund inflows will approximate fund outflows over time. Under normal circumstances, new deposits will arrive at a bank each day while checks and orders for withdrawals are being honored.

However, liquidity problems build up over time when fund inflows and outflows do not match. If loan demand is high (because of low interest rates or other market factors) and deposits are low (because funds are being diverted to stock investments or people stop saving), a "credit crunch" could occur. In a credit crunch, banks find it difficult to meet the legitimate borrowing needs of their customers.

Liquidity needs are met through reserves, classified usually as primary and secondary reserves.

| | |
|---|---|
| **Primary Reserves** | Cash on hand, demand deposit balances held at correspondent banks, and reserves kept at the Federal Reserve. Funds that support daily operations. No interest is paid on these deposits. They are available immediately and thus highly liquid. |
| **Secondary Reserves** | Highest quality investments permitted by law such as Treasury bills. They earn interest and can be converted to cash quickly. Back-up source of liquidity because they must be sold and converted to cash. |

Although a bank must maintain adequate liquidity, it cannot overemphasize liquidity by keeping large amounts of currency in its vaults. Excess reserves reduce

**Matched funding**—An asset/liability management technique, whereby the maturity of loans is matched with the maturity of deposits.

**Liquidity**—The ability of a bank or business to meet its current obligations.

**Historical Fact**

In 1907, currency hoarding by the public led to a liquidity crisis in the banking system. Funds available for lending were scarce. The crisis was abated through the intervention of J.P. Morgan and an infusion of government aid.

*(American Bankers Association)*

Joan has a $5,000 certificate of deposit that will mature soon. She has decided to reinvest the money in another certificate of deposit and wants the highest rate of return possible. She is not certain if her bank's rates are competitive with the current market. Joan plans to shop around for the best rate and will move her money to another bank if necessary.

the percentage of a bank's deposits available for lending and lower a bank's income from loans. Therefore, while recognizing the primary importance of liquidity, a bank also focuses on two other obligations in its program of funds management: safety and income.

### Safety

Depositors must be confident that their money is safe. Although deposits are insured to $100,000 by the Federal Deposit Insurance Corporation (FDIC), banks can protect the deposits entrusted to them by avoiding unnecessary risk. Prudent lending practices, adequate loan loss reserves, and strong corporate governance that minimize fraud and mismanagement help protect depositors against loss of funds.

Balancing liquidity, safety, and income is essential for banks. If a bank tried to provide maximum safety by avoiding all risk, it would make few loans and invest only in low-yielding instruments. In being overcautious, such a bank would inevitably neglect the legitimate credit needs of its customers and community and would lose loan interest income.

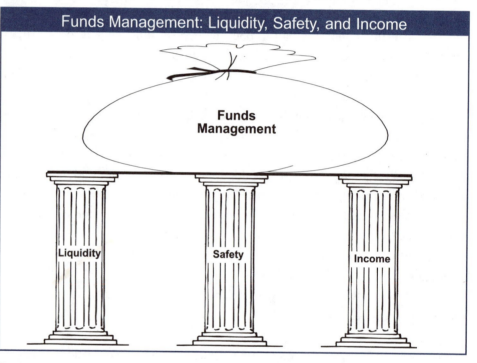

**Funds Management: Liquidity, Safety, and Income**

### Income

The third objective of funds management is income. If liquidity and safety were the only factors a bank had to consider, it could build the largest and strongest vault imaginable, keep as much cash as possible on hand under maximum security, make only those loans and investments that carry an absolute minimum of risk, and fail to meet the income objective.

United States banks are not owned or directly subsidized by the federal government. Banks are owned by their stockholders, and earning a profit for those stockholders is of primary importance. A bank that repeatedly operates at a loss soon loses the confidence of its depositors, its stockholders, and the public.

Throughout U.S. financial history, banks that chose to maximize short-term income at the expense of liquidity and safety were forced out of business because of unsafe practices. Although there may be a short-term gain in profits, unduly lowering credit standards will prove fatal to a bank in the long run when weak loans are uncollected and charged off for a loss. Income, like liquidity and safety, never can be considered alone.

# MAXIMIZING ASSET RETURN

Recall that the primary bank assets are loans and investments. Maximizing the profit earned by these assets is a fundamental objective.

## LOANS VERSUS INVESTMENTS

Two basic differences exist between loans and bank investments. First, banks must give priority to the credit needs of customers and their communities, lending money to individuals, businesses, government, and other banks. Investments, on the other hand, are made chiefly for income purposes. The fact that banks do contribute to the general well-being of a community by buying that community's notes or bonds is secondary to the income objective. Investments are made after the demand for loans has been met. When a bank encounters an increased demand for loans, it may choose to sell some of its investment holdings to obtain additional funds to lend.

Second, banks negotiate directly on loans and indirectly on investments. In making loans, banks negotiate directly with borrowers about the amount, purpose, maturity, interest rate, and other factors, and investigate borrower **creditworthiness**.

In contrast, when banks make investments, they do so indirectly through bond dealers or underwriters, and issuers may not know the purchasers. Banks rely on investment rating services to determine the quality of the investment and the risk involved. Where local issues of securities are not rated, banks may have their own investment portfolio officers rate the issues before investing.

## CREDIT RISK VERSUS MARKET RISK

Whether making a loan or investing funds, a bank faces risks. How well a bank addresses its risks significantly affects its profitability. Two of the major risks a bank must address are **credit risk** and **market risk**.

The chief concern with loans is credit risk. The investments that banks are allowed to make have a lower degree of credit risk than loans. With U.S. government obligations (Treasury bills and notes), there is no credit risk, because the federal government guarantees repayment. There is little credit risk when a state, county, or city guarantees debt securities because they can raise taxes to repay the obligation. The difference between the credit risk of bank loans and investments is reflected in the rate of return or yield on investments. In general, investments produce less revenue for a bank than loans.

With investments, the chief concern is market risk. When a holder wishes to sell a security, market conditions and the overall desirability of the security determine market value—the seller cannot control it. The risk is that the market value at the time of sale may be less than the price the holder initially paid for the security. U.S. government obligations carry no credit risk, but like other investments, they do entail market risk.

**Creditworthiness**—The ability and willingness to repay a loan, largely demonstrated by a credit history.

**Credit risk**—The risk that the borrower cannot or will not repay a loan with interest as scheduled.

**Market risk**—The risk that the market value of a security will decrease because of interest rates and other market conditions.

## Banker Profile

**Charles D. Christy**
*Executive Vice President and Chief Financial Officer, Citizens Banking Corporation, Flint, Michigan*

Charles Christy has been with Citizens Banking Corporation since September 2002. His responsibilities include accounting, finance, treasury, legal, and investor relations. Prior to joining Citizens, he held a number of leadership positions with Bank One, where he specialized in "turnaround" situations.

At Citizens, Mr. Christy helped transform the bank into a line of business organization with 177 branches, trust banking services, and subsidiaries in Wisconsin, Illinois, and Iowa. "We have a management team committed to long-term growth and shareholder value."

Mr. Christy is a graduate of Ohio University. He also graduated with honors from the ABA Stonier Graduate School. He wrote his thesis on "*Leadership: How to Win in a World Where Change is Constant.*"

## LOAN INTEREST

Because interest income is a primary source of bank revenue, choosing the interest rate for each loan is important. The interest rates banks charge on loans reflect the supply-and-demand value of money.

The interest rate charged on a specific loan usually represents a combination of the following factors.

**Cost of funds**

The basic source of loanable funds is customer deposits. Deposits carry a significant cost to the bank in the form of interest paid to depositors and the costs of providing services to depositors such as teller and check clearing services. Banks monitor the cost of funds compared to the interest rate charged on loans.

**Availability of funds**

The Federal Reserve plays a major role in controlling the nation's supply of money and credit by raising or lowering reserve requirements as needed. In addition, the purchases and sales of government obligations, as directed by the Federal Open Market Committee, directly affect the availability of loanable funds.

**Risk factors**

The interest rate charged on loans is affected by the bank's perception of the risk of sustaining losses on loans. Banks also evaluate risk on the type of loan. Unsecured loans, such as credit card loans, are higher risks than secured loans such as mortgages or home equity loans. If a borrower defaults on a secured loan, the collateral backing the loan can provide an alternative source of loan repayment for the bank.

**Term**

The term or amount of time a loan will be outstanding affects the interest rate charged. The longer the loan term, the greater the risk that the borrower's credit standing will deteriorate and jeopardize repayment. The cost of deposits also becomes less certain over time. Therefore, to offset these risks, banks usually charge higher rates for long-term loans than for short-term loans.

## MARKET INTEREST RATES USED IN LENDING

Banks consider another, very important factor in setting the interest rates charged for a loan—the prevailing interest rate in the financial markets.

**Discount rate**

The discount rate is the interest rate the Federal Reserve charges banks for the use of its funds. The discount rate applies to short-term credit extended by the Fed.

**Prime rate**

The prime rate is a base rate that a bank establishes and reflects its determination of such factors as the cost of funds, overhead, loan portfolio risk, and profit objectives. Prime rate, or below prime rate, loans are reserved usually for the bank's best, most creditworthy customers. Otherwise, interest rates are set at a certain percentage above prime rate (such as prime plus 1.25 percent). As a variable interest rate, it is adjusted as the cost and availability of funds change.

**Fed Funds rate**

The fed funds rate is the rate one bank charges another for the overnight use of reserve funds to correct shortfalls on reserve requirements. Exhibit 3.3 shows the relationship among the discount, prime, and fed funds rates.

**LIBOR rate**

LIBOR stands for the London Interbank Offered Rate. It is an international money market interest rate that represents the average rate offered by banks for the interbank placement of Eurodollars. Using LIBOR, banks often add percentages above LIBOR to determine the interest rate.

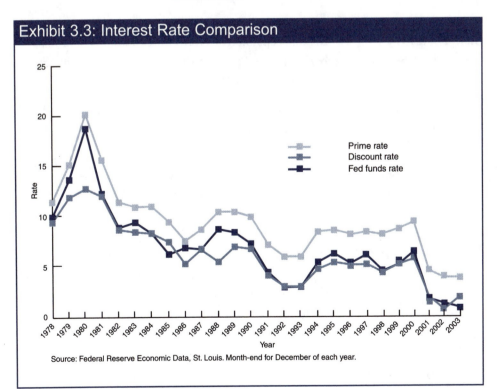

Exhibit 3.3: Interest Rate Comparison

Source: Federal Reserve Economic Data, St. Louis. Month-end for December of each year.

## INVESTMENT DIVERSIFICATION

Another important source of revenue is the profit earned on bank investments. To achieve the appropriate combination of liquidity, safety, and income, banks invest in a variety of instruments with different maturities. This investment practice is called **diversification**.

## INVESTMENT REQUIREMENTS

Banks have legal requirements for investments. First, banks are prohibited from investing directly in any common stock. However, as a result of the Gramm-Leach-Bliley Act, nonbank affiliates of financial holding companies are permitted to make controlling investments in any kind of company, including a nonfinancial firm. This new authority is called merchant banking or equity investment activities.

Second, banks are limited in the percentage of their capital and surplus they can invest in the securities of any one issuer, except investments in U.S. government obligations.

Third, many states require banks to pledge U.S. government obligations to ensure protection for deposits in public funds accounts over and above the coverage provided by the FDIC. Similarly, many states require bank trust departments to set aside federal and state debt issues to protect the pension, trust, and profit-sharing funds they manage.

## TYPES OF BANK INVESTMENTS

A typical bank's investment portfolio consists almost exclusively of four types of holdings: U.S. Treasury (U.S. government) obligations, U.S. government agency obligations, municipal issues, and miscellaneous investments that meet the highest credit standards.

| | |
|---|---|
| **U.S. Treasury Obligations** | Most acceptable **collateral** for Federal Reserve loans to banks. Backed by the full faith and credit of the federal government. |
| *U.S. Treasury Bills* | Maturities of less than one year. Immediately marketable and with limited risk. |
| *U.S. Treasury Notes* | Maturities greater than one year but less than five years. Marketable but with greater market risk than Treasury bills. |
| **U.S. Government Agency Obligations** | Obligations issued by federal government agencies such as the Export-Import Bank, and by federally sponsored agencies such as the Fannie Mae. Guaranteed or protected by the federal government to some extent. Yield higher interest than U.S. government obligations of the same maturity. |
| **Municipal Issues** | Bonds issued by any government or government agency, other than the federal government; for example, state, |

**Diversification**—A method of decreasing the total risk of investments by investing funds in assets of different kinds.

**Collateral**—Specific property pledged by a borrower to secure a loan. If the borrower defaults, the lender has the right to sell the collateral to liquidate the loan.

city, county, town, or school district. Backed by the taxing power of the issuer, they have credit risk and market risk. Income is exempt from federal income taxes and sometimes state and local taxes. They represent bank commitments to the community.

**Types of Bank Investments**
- U.S. Treasury or U.S. government obligations
- U.S. government agency obligations
- municipal issues
- miscellaneous investments of the highest credit possible

*Miscellaneous Investments*

**Banker's Acceptances**

Drafts or bills of exchange banks accept as liabilities by pledging their credit on behalf of customers' credit.

**Negotiable Certificates of Deposit**

Certificates of deposit that can be sold prior to maturity and of $100,000 minimum denomination. Rates may be negotiated with depositor and need to be higher than Treasury bills and commercial paper with the same maturities to be an attractive investment.

**Commercial Paper**

Short-term unsecured obligations of large, financially sound corporations used to raise funds. There is no collateral, only firms' good reputation. Used for short-term funds instead of a bank loan.

**Corporate Bonds**

Long-term debts owed to investors. May be unsecured or secured by collateral. Not used often as bank investment, because after-tax return on other investments usually greater.

# FEE INCOME

The financial services marketplace is competitive. Although banks used to be the only source of deposits and loans, today customers can choose from a variety of financial service providers. As a result, banks seek other income sources. Income from fees is an important component of **noninterest income**. Opportunities for fee-based income are transforming many traditional commercial banks into diversified financial asset service providers. Banks improve fee income in three ways.

**Noninterest income**—Income a bank derives from sources other than interest; for example, fees and service charges, trading income, investment securities gains, and other income.

| *Fee Income Method* | *Examples* |
|---|---|
| Increase existing fees to true cost of service | Increase fees for processing costs and reflect risk of paying checks returned for nonsufficient funds (NSF) |
| Charge for previously free services | Charging for a statement copy |
| Enter into fee-based lines of business | Credit card services, securities processing, global payments, private banking, investment management, and fiduciary services |

# PERFORMANCE MEASURES

How well a bank manages its funds through its lending and investments is a major determinant of its profitability. Net income alone is not a true measure of bank performance. A bank with $1 billion in assets is expected to generate more net income than a bank with $100 million in assets. For this reason, management, investment analysts, state and federal regulatory authorities, and stockholders use other measures to evaluate and compare bank financial performance over time. Return on assets, return on equity, capital ratio, net interest spread, and earnings per share are the measures most widely used.

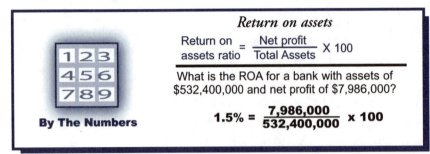

**Return on assets**

Return on assets ratio $= \dfrac{\text{Net profit}}{\text{Total Assets}} \times 100$

What is the ROA for a bank with assets of $532,400,000 and net profit of $7,986,000?

$$1.5\% = \dfrac{7,986,000}{532,400,000} \times 100$$

**By The Numbers**

| Performance Measure | Definition |
|---|---|
| Return on Assets<br>ROA = Net Profit ÷ Total Assets **x** 100 | Measures how well a bank uses assets to produce income. An ROA of 1% is considered good performance. |
| Return on Equity<br>ROE = Net Profit ÷ Total Equity **x** 100 | Measures the rate of return achieved relative to funds invested (equity). The ratio is higher than ROA. ROE of 15% is a benchmark for good bank performance. |
| Capital Ratio<br>Capital Ratio = Capital ÷ Assets **x** 100 | Measures bank's stability and strength. Bank's capital account absorbs losses not covered by current earnings and loan loss reserves. Banks are highly **leveraged** because their capital ratios, higher than other industries, are 6 to 8 percent, normally. |
| Net Interest Spread<br>Interest Earned – interest paid = interest spread | Difference between interest earned on loans and interest paid on deposits. Net Higher the spread, greater the profit, if other expenses remain constant. |
| Earnings Per Share<br>Net Income ÷ average number of shares of stock outstanding = Earnings per share | Establishes income goals, such as $4 per share. Compared with stock's market price to determine value in marketplace. |

**Leverage**—The use of debt securities or borrowed money to increase the return possible on equity capital.

# BUDGETING AND PLANNING

Good financial performance is not achieved automatically. Bank management must plan carefully, set earnings objectives, and structure the balance sheet to achieve its goals.

## THE BUDGETING PROCESS

The budget is the financial plan for attaining the goals set by management.

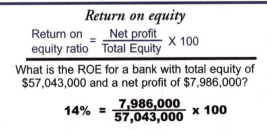

**Return on equity**

Return on equity ratio $= \dfrac{\text{Net profit}}{\text{Total Equity}} \times 100$

What is the ROE for a bank with total equity of $57,043,000 and a net profit of $7,986,000?

$$14\% = \dfrac{7,986,000}{57,043,000} \times 100$$

**By The Numbers**

Although budgeting varies from one bank to another, the basic concept is the same: budgeting means establishing a financial plan for the coming year and perhaps another plan for the next three to five years.

### Capital ratio

Capital Ratio = $\frac{\text{Capital}}{\text{Assets}}$ X 100

What is the capital ratio for a bank with total assets of $2.54 billion and capital of $153 million?

$6.02\% = \frac{153,000,000}{2,540,000,000} \times 100$

**By The Numbers**

In preparing a budget, a bank projects income and expenses. With regard to expenses, most banks base their budgets on amounts spent the previous year. For example, a bank may establish a goal that noninterest expense will not exceed previous-year expenditures by more than 2 percent.

It is difficult to budget for interest income and expense, because a bank must project not only loan and deposit volumes, but also interest rates and the affect rates will have on interest income and expense.

Budgeting is not an exact science, but a properly prepared budget plan offers a blueprint for the future.

## BUDGET VARIANCES

Unforeseen circumstances cause variances from the budget. An expenditure may be incurred earlier than anticipated or business volume may be higher than anticipated. Banks usually do not adjust the budget once it is in place. Instead, they offset negative variances in one part of the budget with cost reductions in another part of the budget.

Variances that cannot be offset that way, such as large loan charge-offs, are identified as permanent variances documented for the negative impact on profitability.

## PERFORMANCE MEASUREMENT AND STANDARDS

In addition to the budget, many banks establish performance measurements for specific units or specific employees to measure productivity and quality. For example, the proof department's productivity measures may find that proof operators' item encoding rate of 1,300 per hour this month, compared to 1,250 last month and 1,150 during the same month last year, shows a notable increase. The rate will be compared with peer banks as well. In general, technology and related process improvements continue to increase productivity.

Another factor is the quality of work. For example, the average proof operator error rate of one per 1,000 items encoded is compared with previous error rates to identify department trends and with peer banks for comparisons.

After obtaining measurements, management then sets standards for the next budget year.

**Did You Know ...**

From 1994 to 2001, U.S. labor productivity in the business sector (measured by output per hour) averaged 2.1. In 2002 and 2003, output more than doubled, averaging 4.7 for the two years.

*(U.S. Department of Labor)*

## SUMMARY

- A bank's annual report typically contains two key financial statements, the statement of condition (or balance sheet) and the profit-and-loss (or income) statement. These statements convey the essential information about a bank's current financial condition and the financial results it has achieved.

- Financial information is used by stockholders, investors, regulators, other banks, customers, and employees in pursuit of their specific goals and objectives. For example, financial information reports provide management with insight on how to improve bank performance.

- A bank's primary assets are its loans and investments. Its principal liability is its deposits. Managing assets and liabilities is a fundamental challenge of banking and is a major determinant of whether a bank operates profitably. ALCO monitors the costs of deposits and the income from loans. Its goal is to manage a bank's assets and liabilities so that a bank's stockholders receive the maximum long-term gain achievable. A funds management program strives to balance three objectives: liquidity, safety, and income.

- To maximize its return on loans and investments, a bank must manage both credit risk and market risk. Because interest income is a primary source of bank revenue, choosing the right interest rate to charge for loans is important. Factors influencing loan interest rate include funds cost, funds availability, risk factors, and loan term. As a starting point for setting loan interest rates, banks look at the market interest rate.

- Banks also seek investment diversification. The investment portfolio of a typical bank consists of U.S. Treasury and government agency obligations, municipal bonds, and miscellaneous investments of the highest credit standards, such as negotiable CDs, commercial paper or corporate bonds issued by financially sound companies.

- A bank's financial performance can be measured on the basis of its return on assets, return on equity, capital ratio, net interest spread, and earnings per share. Each of these measures reflects a different aspect of a bank's strength over a given period.

- Good financial performance is not achieved automatically. Bank management must plan carefully, set realistic earnings objectives, and structure the balance sheet. The budget is the financial plan for attaining the goals set by management. A bank also achieves its goals by continually evaluating employee productivity and work quality.

**Learning Check**

# SELF CHECK & REVIEW

1. What is a bank's largest asset? Its largest liability? Its largest income and expense items?

2. Why is accurate financial data so important to bank stockholders and investors? To federal and state regulators? To customers?

3. What would be the consequences if a bank chose to overemphasize liquidity while neglecting other factors in funds management? What would be the consequences of overemphasizing safety at the expense of liquidity and income?

4. Distinguish between the discount rate and the prime rate.

5. List at least three measures of bank performance, other than net income.

6.  What is the net worth of a bank with the following assets and liabilities?

| | (in thousands of dollars) |
|---|---|
| Cash on hand | $45,400 |
| Investments | 76,600 |
| Loans (net of reserve for loan losses) | 224,300 |
| Fed funds sold | 35,800 |
| Fixed assets | 18,900 |
| Other assets | 12,200 |
| Deposits | 312,700 |
| Fed Fund funds purchased | 68,600 |
| Other liabilities | 4,300 |

7.  What is the net profit (or loss) of a bank reporting the following revenues and expenses?

| | (in thousands of dollars) |
|---|---|
| Interest and fees on loans | $253,700 |
| Interest and dividends on investments | 22,100 |
| Interest paid on deposits | 158,800 |
| Salaries, wages, and benefits | 70,300 |
| Taxes | 11,000 |

8.  What is the earnings per share for a bank with an average of 5,360,000 shares outstanding and net income of $12,450,000?

9.  In what three ways are banks improving fee income?

10. Why is it important for a bank to establish a financial plan (a budget)?

# ADDITIONAL RESOURCES

Resources

American Bankers Association, **www.aba.com**

*Analyzing Financial Statements*, Sixth Edition. Washington, D.C.:
   American Bankers Association, 2003.

*Bank of America Annual Report*, **www.bankofamerica.com/investor/**

*Capital Bank Annual Report,* **www.capitalbank-nc.com/recent_news/annrep.html**

*Citigroup Annual Report,* **www.citigroup.com/citigroup/fin/ar.htm**

*Flagstar Bank Annual Report*, **www.flagstar.com/inside/annual_report.isp**

*Mellon 1st Business Bank Annual Report*, **www.mellon.com/mfbb/annual-report.html**

*Reports of Condition and Income and Thrift Financial Report*, Federal
   Deposit Insurance Corporation, **www2.fdic.gov/Call_TFR_Rpts/search.asp**

*Retail Banking Survey Report*, Washington, D.C., American Bankers
   Association, 2003.

*Statistics at a Glance*, Federal Deposit Insurance Corporation,
   **www.fdic.gov/bank/statistical/stts/index.html**

*The Drive for Quality and CRM, the Evolution of Financial Services Call Center*, Vol. V., Washington D.C., American Bankers Association, 2002.

U.S. Department of Labor, Bureau of Labor Statistics; **www.bls.gov/home.htm**

*Wachovia Bank Annual Report,* **www.wachovia.com/inside/page/1,133_202_257,00.html**

# Deposit Accounts

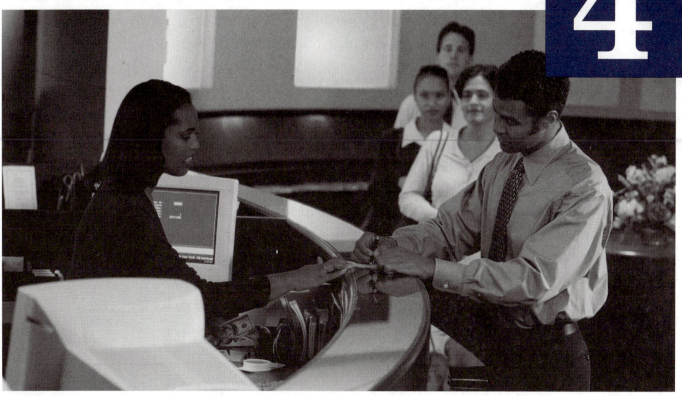

# What You Will Learn

*After studying this chapter, you should be able to*

- describe common deposit accounts offered by banks
- identify deposit-related services provided to deposit customers, including electronic banking services
- describe the types of account ownership
- explain deposit account opening requirements
- describe key banking regulations that apply to deposit products and services
- define the bolded key terms that appear in the text

# Introduction

*Checking, savings, money market, and time deposit accounts are traditional "core" deposit products banks offer customers. Banks use funds generated by deposits to maintain liquidity and to make loans and investments. In turn, loans and investments generate income that enables banks to pay interest on various types of deposits. Along with deposit products, most banks also feature services, such as banking on the Internet, to provide customers convenience in managing their financial affairs.*

*Whether the owners of a deposit account are consumers, businesses, or government entities, legal titling and identification is important. Bank regulations, policies, and procedures address legal concerns. Because the deposit function is important to customers, businesses, and the economy, bank regulations address reserve requirements, electronic fund transfers, funds availability, and account disclosures—all of which govern a bank's deposit relationship with its customers.*

## THE DEPOSIT FUNCTION

The deposit function is the basic banking activity of accepting customers' checks, currency, or other financial instruments for credit to their accounts. Without these deposits, banks would not have enough funds to lend, or invest, and thus pay interest to depositors (see exhibit 4.1).

Millions of dollars are deposited in and withdrawn from banks each day. Consumers and businesses still accept checks for making payments, especially if the payment is large, or if the consumer must mail the payment. The total dollar amount of deposited checks is greater than the amount of coin and currency deposited. As technology improves, electronic payments methods grow as well.

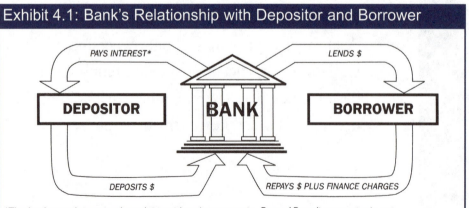

Exhibit 4.1: Bank's Relationship with Depositor and Borrower

*The bank pays interest only on interest-bearing accounts. Demand Deposit accounts do not earn interest.

Electronic payment methods include transfers through direct deposits or direct withdrawal (also known as automated clearing house or ACH transfers), wire transfers, debit cards, Internet transfers, and **point-of-sale** (POS) transactions.

## SAFETY, PRUDENCE, AND CUSTOMER CONVENIENCE

A bank is responsible for safeguarding customer deposits at all times and ensuring that funds are available for withdrawal. If an error or crime occurs that results in a loss of funds, the depositor is protected up to FDIC limits, depending on how the account is titled. Banks are conscious of their responsibility to use deposited funds prudently when making loans and investments. They legally are required to operate in a safe and sound manner. Bank investment and lending policies are set up to honor legitimate requests for withdrawals by their depositors.

In their deposit relationship with a bank, customers value convenience. By maintaining branch offices, banks make it easy for customers to deposit money. For example, banks set up branch facilities in grocery stores and other sites, offer longer banking hours, and make drive-up windows and automated teller machines (ATMs) available. In fact, ATMs represent one of the great advancements in customer convenience in modern banking history. Through linked ATM networks worldwide, bank cardholders can access their accounts for cash withdrawals. ATM machines not only meet customer needs and provide greater convenience, they also reduce transaction costs and allow banks to offer around-the-clock banking services.

Banks also deliver deposit account services electronically. The majority of banks now offer online banking, which provides customers with the ability to check account balances, make automatic bill payments, and conduct other banking transactions over the Internet.

# DEPOSIT ACCOUNT PRODUCTS

Banks offer a wide variety of products and services to meet depositor needs. Before discussing deposit account products and services, it is important to understand the difference between transaction accounts and savings and time deposit accounts.

## TRANSACTION ACCOUNTS VERSUS SAVINGS AND TIME DEPOSITS

Customers may deposit money in a checking, savings, or time deposit account. In each case, the depositor's intention is different. Customers make checking account deposits because they intend to withdraw funds in the near future to pay bills and meet expenses; that is, make transactions. Checking, or transaction accounts, may be demand deposit or interest checking accounts, also known as negotiable order of withdrawal or NOW accounts. Customers generally use savings and time deposit accounts to place funds they do not need immediately, and these accounts pay interest.

### Demand Deposit Transaction Accounts

Demand deposits are so named because the total amount on deposit, or any part of it, is payable "on demand" and can be converted into coin and currency after the deposited funds are collected and available. Customers with balances of $100 in a

**Point-of-sale**—A terminal used to transfer funds from a bank account to pay for purchases.

**Did You Know ...**

By the end of 2003, U.S. commercial banks held a combined $4.3 trillion dollars in deposits and had funded $4.4 trillion in loans.

*(Federal Deposit Insurance Corporation)*

checking account, can write a check for that amount and present it to a teller for immediate payment of $100 in cash.

### *Interest Earning Transaction Accounts*

Traditionally, checking accounts existed only at commercial banks as demand deposits. In the late 20th century, however, thrift institutions, credit unions, and brokerage firms competed aggressively for these checking accounts by introducing interest checking. For their part, credit unions offered **share drafts**, which are similar to checks.

Commercial banks as well adopted negotiable order of withdrawal (NOW) accounts. Withdrawals are made using check-like withdrawal forms. Because NOW accounts, like savings accounts, earn interest, a bank has a legal right to require a seven-day notice before withdrawal. This requirement, however, is rarely imposed.

**Share drafts**—A bill payment device offered by some credit unions. Members of a credit union can write these check-like instruments against their savings share accounts.

### *Savings and Time Deposit Accounts*

Savings accounts differ from demand deposit transaction accounts because technically they cannot be withdrawn on demand. Like interest checking transaction accounts, banks can require a seven-day notice of withdrawal. In practice, few banks actually require a withdrawal notice. Unlike interest checking accounts, transfers are limited to six per month. Savings accounts, like checking accounts, have no maturity date. Deposits and withdrawals can be made at any time over a period of days, weeks, or years.

Time deposit accounts, however, have specific maturity dates, starting at least seven days from the date of deposit. Whenever a time deposit is withdrawn before maturity, an interest penalty usually is imposed for early withdrawal. Banks pay interest on both savings and time deposit accounts.

### *Ratio of Transaction Accounts to Savings and Time Deposits*

The ratio of transaction account deposits to savings and time deposits is important to banks for two reasons. First, a bank pays reserve requirements on transaction accounts. Second, the turnover rate for transaction account deposits is higher than for savings or time deposit accounts.

It is important to remember that every deposit accepted from a customer is a liability—not an asset—for the bank that accepts it. The deposit is an obligation that must be repaid at some future date. Deposits represent the largest percentage of liabilities on almost all bank balance sheets. At the same time, as the bank's raw material, these deposits are the primary source of funds to be put to profitable use as loans and investments. Because time deposits with stated maturities remain with the bank for longer periods than demand deposits, these funds generally are used for longer-term bank loans and investments. High-turnover demand deposit funds are put to short-term use.

## COMMON DEPOSIT ACCOUNT PRODUCTS OFFERED BY BANKS

Most banks offer a diverse selection of deposit account products and services designed to meet the needs of an equally diverse clientele. Some of the more common products offered to consumers are covered here.

| | |
|---|---|
| **Checking accounts** | Transaction accounts that offer check writing privileges. Designed with a variety of terms and features. Bank may impose a monthly service fee or require a minimum balance to avoid a monthly fee, and allow unlimited check-writing privileges. Some checking accounts are marketed to select groups such as seniors. Some offer a **PIN-only debit card** (ATM) or a **signature-based debit card**. If a demand deposit account, it pays no interest. If a NOW account, it pays interest and legally may impose a withdrawal notice requirement. |
| **Statement savings accounts** | Accounts that pay interest on deposits periodically such as monthly or quarterly. Account transfers are limited to six per month. A bank legally may impose a notice of withdrawal. Statements are rendered monthly when there is activity on the account. Withdrawals and deposits are transacted at the teller window, by mail, telephone banking, or through the Internet. |
| **Savings clubs** | Special purpose savings accounts, usually for end-of-year holiday purchases, to pay off high credit card bills due in January or to save for events such as a vacation. |
| **Money Market Deposit Accounts** | Offering higher yields than savings accounts, these accounts also limit monthly transfers to six, three by check and three by preauthorization. Legally, a bank may require a seven-day notice of withdrawal. |
| **Certificates of Deposit (CDs)** | Time deposits with fixed maturities, usually 91 days to five years, and fixed interest rates tied to the maturity and the purchase amount. Withdrawals before maturity incur a penalty charge. |
| **Retirement savings accounts** | Individual Retirement Accounts (IRAs), Roth IRAs, and Simplified Employer Plan IRAs (SEP-IRAs) are among the types of savings accounts that help individuals and self-employed workers save for retirement. Savers can make tax-deductible contributions to accounts that earn tax-deferred interest. |
| **Coverdell Savings Accounts (Education IRAs)** | These accounts allow families to save for educational expenses by making tax-deductible contributions to accounts that earn tax-deferred interest. Often referred to as 529 plans. |

**PIN-only debit card—** A plastic card enabling the cardholder to purchase goods or services or withdraw cash online after entering a personal identification number. The cost of the transaction is debited from the cardholder's bank account (also known as an ATM card).

**Signature-based debit card—**A plastic card enabling the cardholder to purchase goods or services or withdraw cash offline upon signing a receipt. The cost of the transaction is debited from the cardholder's bank account. The card, which may be used for online transactions as well, may carry a VISA or MasterCard logo.

**Historical Fact**

In 1909, the Carlisle Trust Company, Carlisle, Pennsylvania, started the first Christmas savings club. Merkel Landis, the bank's treasurer, originated the idea.

*(American Bankers Association)*

**Health savings accounts** — Tax-deferred health savings accounts. Contributions are tax deductible annually up to 100% of an individual's high-deductible insurance plan's required deductible. Distributions are made according to the plan guidelines, normally involving a withdrawal request form or debit card, and are excluded from an individual's gross income as long as funds are used for defined medical care.

Some of the more common products offered to businesses are as follows.

**Business checking accounts** — Business transaction accounts through which other services are accessed, such as night deposit, merchant services, and various cash management services. Offer detailed statements to help customers organize transaction activity. May be subject to a monthly service charge, a per check deposit, and per check paid charge unless a specified average daily balance is maintained. Usually a demand deposit account.

**Business savings accounts** — Interest-earning accounts used by businesses to accumulate funds for anticipated bills, such as quarterly tax payments.

**Concentration accounts** — A central account for all deposits not invested; typically set up to fund disbursement accounts.

**Certificates of Deposit (CDs)** — Offer higher interest rates than demand deposit or savings accounts. Terms range from 91 days up to 10 years, with the interest rate tied to term and purchase amount. A penalty usually applies for withdrawal prior to maturity.

Negotiable CDs generally require a minimum of $100,000 deposit and can be short term, such as 7 days.

**Money market deposit accounts** — Like consumer money market deposit accounts, they pay higher interest rates than business savings accounts, allow six transfers per month, and legally may require a seven-day notice of withdrawal. Business-related banking services may be attached to the account.

# DEPOSIT-RELATED SERVICES

Banks provide many services to support deposit account products, such as services to facilitate depositing funds into an account, processing deposits once they are made, and providing customers with access to their money and account information.

| | |
|---|---|
| **Pay yourself first** | Determine in advance how much money you plan to keep on deposit each month. If you receive a raise, increase the amount. |
| **Use bank technology** | Consider automatic payroll deductions or automatic transfer from checking to savings. Arrange to have a specific amount transferred to your savings account every pay period. |
| **Pay bills on time and pay more than the minimum amount** | Schedule a time every month to pay bills, and put them in the mail in time to get to the creditor. |
| **Determine needs versus wants** | Do you need to eat out every day for lunch? Do you need that gourmet cup of coffee in the morning? By bringing your lunch to work a couple days a week, you can save hundreds of dollars a year. |
| **Shop around** | Be selective, and get the best prices, services, convenient locations, and lowest fees for credit cards, bank accounts, mortgages, and CDs. |
| **Consider investments** | For long-term goals, such as saving for a home or retirement, look into bonds, mutual funds, real estate, and stocks. |
| **Consult your local bank** | Your banker is the best source of information about accounts and interest rates available at your bank. |

*(Source: ABA Education Foundation)*

## OPTIONS FOR DEPOSITING FUNDS

Customers may make deposits in a number of different ways, including:

| | |
|---|---|
| **Teller window** | Some customers prefer to know when the bank received the deposit and obtain a receipt to prove it. |
| **Night depository** | A locked, secured safe into which the customer may place deposits. The customer is given a key to the night depository to make deposits after the bank is closed. Deposits are processed at the beginning of the next business day. For the most part, small businesses use this service. |
| **Direct deposit** | An electronic banking service that allows depositors to have periodic payments—such as paychecks, Social Security checks, regular dividend payments, and annuity or pension checks—automatically credited to a specified deposit account. Direct deposits are processed through the ACH payment system. |

## Banker Profile

**Chris Huffman**
*Vice President and Marketing Officer, The First National Bank in Trinidad, Trinidad, Colorado*

Chris Huffman has been in banking for 13 years. As Vice President of Marketing, she manages the marketing and advertising needs for the bank, its in-store branch, and out-of-state loan production office.

With a strong commitment to community service, Ms. Huffman supports her bank's involvement in building character and competence in youth through the America's Promise program. Connecting with area schools, Ms. Huffman and colleagues offer free curriculum, class-room visits, instruction on money management, bank tours, and software for home use.

" We believe it is important that children learn the concept of money, respect it, and understand the importance of saving. Providing these educational programs is our way to encourage a lifetime of good spending habits."

Ms. Huffman also believes in professional continuing education. She has participated in ABA training programs, including the American Institute of Banking Course *Principles of Banking*.

| Automatic Transfer Service (ATS) | A preauthorized service that allows for automatic transfer of funds to a customer's checking account to cover checks that have been written and would otherwise cause the account to be overdrawn. Customers may write checks that exceed existing balances and the bank, by prior arrangement (preauthorization), will automatically move funds from the customer's savings account to the checking account to pay the checks. |
| --- | --- |
| Electronic Fund Transfer (EFT) | EFT allows funds to be transferred to and from deposit accounts electronically rather than physically. EFTs can be conducted by telephone or over the Internet using a computer or personal digital assistant. |
| Automated Teller Machine (ATM) | ATMs, which provide a convenient way to make deposits, provide a number of services, such as cash dispensing, balance inquiries, and transfers between accounts. |
| Wire transfer | Funds wired to or from the customer's bank and another bank. Depending on bank policy, wire transfer authorization can be done by telephone, the Internet, or in person. |
| Deposit by mail | Customers make deposits by mail while they are away or to avoid a trip to the bank. The customer simply completes the deposit slip, endorses the checks, and mails the items to the bank. |
| Courier and armored car services | Courier and armored car services provide business customers with convenient and secure deposit pickups when large amounts of cash or valuable securities are involved. |

## TYPES OF DEPOSITED ITEMS

Except for coin and currency, the bank is responsible for collecting funds on other items deposited to accounts and converting them into an available account balance for the customer's use. Depending on the type of item deposited, a bank acts as the customer's agent and collects the funds through a number of different methods.

| Coin and currency | Coin and currency do not require collecting. Customers deposit the money into their accounts, and the bank typically makes some of the funds available that day or on the business day following the deposit. However, there are expenses relating to deposits of coin and currency: teller salaries for handling and processing, cost of shipping excess cash to the Federal Reserve, |
| --- | --- |

**Cash items**

A cash item is not coin and currency. A cash item, for example, a check, flows through the collection process without special handling. Banks make funds available from check deposits according to their funds availability schedule and federal law. Many banks make funds available, up to a certain amount, on the business day after deposit.

*Substitute Check.* Beginning in late 2004, a new type of cash item called the substitute check came into use. It enables banks to truncate paper checks during the interbank collection process and convert them into an electronic image file for processing and payment. The electronic image can be reconverted to paper and included in the customer's account statement.

**Noncash items**

Noncash items require special handling; they cannot be processed in bulk. A draft that cannot be paid unless an auto title is attached is a noncash item. A foreign check that must be converted to U.S. dollars is a noncash item. Upon receipt of noncash items, a teller either enters the items for collection or sends them to a special department for processing. Exhibit 4.2 summarizes the differences between cash and noncash items.

fraud prevention, and security costs. Although individuals or small businesses may not be charged, commercial customers, such as grocery stores, may be charged a fee for handling coin and currency deposits.

**Historical Fact**

On November 1, 1971, Hempstead Bank in Syosset, New York, placed the first truly paperless POS system in 32 retail establishments. By 2000, two-thirds of U.S. households had a debit card.

*(American Bankers Association, National Consumers League)*

---

## Exhibit 4.2: Characteristics of Deposited Items

**Cash Items**

- Give customer immediate, provisional account credit
- Create float (time lag between account crediting and collection)
- May be payable on demand
- Must not have documents attached
- Must not carry special instructions or require special handling
- Inexpensive; processed in bulk
- Payable in U.S. funds

**Example**

- Checks

**Non-cash Items**

- Give customer delayed (deferred) credit
- Do not create float (account not credited until collection is completed)
- May or may not be payable on demand
- May have documents attached
- Require special individualized handling; may carry specific instructions
- More expensive to handle
- May or may not be payable in U.S. funds

**Examples**

- Promissory notes
- Drafts with attached documents
- Coupons
- Checks drawn on banks outside of the United States

## Situation

On her way home from work on Monday, Liz withdraws $100 in cash from the ATM outside her bank. On Tuesday, she goes into the bank and deposits her $700 paycheck at the teller window. On Thursday, she stops at the kiosk in the bank lobby and authorizes a $406 payment on her car loan. Later that evening, Liz sits down at her computer and accesses her bank account through the Internet. She checks her balance and prints out a statement of the activity on her account. All of the transactions she made in the week appear on the screen.

# ACCESSING FUNDS AND ACCOUNT INFORMATION

Customers have a variety of options for accessing funds and account information. Internet banking and debit cards have become popular alternatives to writing checks and in-branch banking.

## Internet Banking

In recent years, internet banking has grown rapidly as more customers use their home or office personal computers (PCs) to access personal and business account information, including balances, transaction history, and tax information. Both consumer and business customers log on to the Internet to purchase CDs and other deposit products.

**Balance inquiry** — Customers can view up-to-the-minute account balance information online.

**Deposit history** — Customers can review interim statements that reveal current account activity or can access and review previous statements. Some banks offer an electronic statement that may be downloaded by the customer; others allow customers to view electronic images of paid checks, front and back.

**Account reconcilement** — Customers can download a file containing the account activity, including deposits made, checks paid, and transfers posted. Items that cannot be matched to the customer's own information, because they have not yet cleared, may be entered manually for reconcilement. When reconciled, a summary of debits and credits is posted, and the customer is given a final balance.

**Account transfers** — Customers access and make transfers among accounts and instruct the bank to make recurring transactions automatically. Generally, a bank provides a confirmation number when a transfer is completed.

## Debit Cards

Debit cards (plastic bank cards) allow customers to obtain cash or purchase goods and services through direct access to balances in checking or savings accounts. A customer swipes a debit card through a point-of-sale (POS) card reader, enters a personal identification number (PIN) if required, and completes the transaction.

Debit card transactions are either online or offline. An online debit card transaction requires a PIN, and the funds are immediately debited from the cardholder's checking account at a bank. An offline transaction requires a customer signature rather than a PIN. Offline debit transactions normally take from 24 to 48 hours to be debited from a checking account. The processing of an offline, signature-based debit card transaction is very similar to a credit card transaction.

# OWNERSHIP OF DEPOSIT ACCOUNTS

Ownership of the account determines the identification and documentation required of the customer to open an account. It also may determine the type of account that may be opened and the account's title. The type of account and the account title determines the rights, obligations, and liabilities of the parties to the account. Exhibit 4.3 shows the two general types of deposit account ownership: consumer and business.

| Exhibit 4.3: Account Ownership | |
| --- | --- |
| **Consumer** | **Business** |
| • Individual | • Sole Proprietorship |
| • Joint | • Partnership |
| • Fiduciary | • Corporate |
| | • Public Funds |
| | • Unincorporated Organization |

## CONSUMER ACCOUNT OWNERSHIP

Types of consumer account ownership are individual, joint, and fiduciary.

### *Individual Account*

An individual account is opened for and owned by an individual. The individual is the sole owner of the account, and no other person has any rights concerning it. When the account owner dies, the account normally becomes part of the owner's estate.

Sometimes a customer may want to give someone else the authority to sign checks or make other decisions for the account. This can be accomplished through a **power of attorney**.

Powers of attorney vary depending on the wishes of the account owner (the **principal**). A general power of attorney gives the attorney-in-fact unlimited authority over the account. A special power of attorney limits the authority to a specific duty or function and to a limited period. A customer may place a power of attorney on a checking account so that bills can be paid, but not on a savings account or CD. A power of attorney ceases at the death of the person who grants it.

### *Joint Accounts*

A joint account is opened in the names of, and owned by, two or more depositors. Joint accounts can be held either in joint tenancy with full right of survivorship or as tenants-in-common.

**Power of Attorney—** A legal document that authorizes a person named as an agent (attorney-in-fact) to act on behalf of another person (the principal).

**Principal—**A party who appoints another to act on his or her behalf, for example, as an agent or attorney-in-fact.

**Right of survivorship—** The right of the surviving tenant(s) to take full possession of specific assets, such as account funds, upon the death of the other tenant(s), without establishing an estate and subject to state laws.

| *Joint Tenancy* | *Tenants-in-Common* |
| --- | --- |
| Bill Wiltshire **or** Peggy Wiltshire | Bill Wiltshire **and** Peggy Wiltshire |
| • Word "or" separates the names of the account holders. | • Word "and" separates the names of account holders. |
| • Either account holder may make deposits, write checks, make withdrawals, transfer funds, access account electronically, stop payment on checks, close the account, or otherwise treat the account as his or her own. | • Account holders must act together. Both signatures are required for deposit to or withdrawal from the account. |
| • Only one signature is required. | • Requires more monitoring. Bank verifies that all account holders sign checks or withdrawal slips. If checks paid with only one signature, bank could be liable to the account holders who did not sign. |
| • Full **right of survivorship**. | |

Establishing identification is just as important in opening joint accounts as it is in opening individual accounts. Joint account holders must be present to sign the signature card. In most circumstances, the account agreement holds each account holder responsible for the transactions on a joint account, including overdrafts.

### Fiduciary Accounts

A **fiduciary** account is opened by a representative for the benefit of another person. Examples include trust accounts, estate accounts, and guardianships.

**Fiduciary**—An individual, bank, or other party to whom specific property is turned over under the terms of a contractual agreement and who acts for the benefit of another party on a basis of trust and confidence.

| | |
|---|---|
| **Trust accounts** | A simple trust, for example, is opened by a mother and father "in trust for" a minor child. This account usually has a basic document and may not involve large balances. When opening the account, the bank obtains identification from the representatives (the parents), just as if opening an account for an individual. |
| **Estate accounts** | An account established for an estate that requires specific documentation, often a document issued by the Probate Court appointing an individual as the administrator or executor of the estate. |
| **Guardianship accounts** | A court-appointed guardian sets up an account to manage funds intended for a ward, a minor, or an incapacitated person. Guardianship accounts can be complicated; they require substantial documentation. Laws governing guardianships vary among states, but in general a guardianship account may be opened only with court documentation. In many cases, withdrawals may be made only by a court order. Policing these accounts usually requires special handling by experienced bank officers. |

In all cases, the fiduciary account has a representative (such as a guardian) and a beneficiary (such as a minor child) or person for whose benefit the account is held. The accounts take many different forms and require different types of documentation, depending on the type of fiduciary relationship and account.

## BUSINESS ACCOUNT OWNERSHIP

The types of business account ownership are sole proprietorship, partnership, corporate, public funds, and unincorporated organization.

### Sole Proprietorship

A sole proprietorship account may be opened in the name of the proprietor (the person owning and operating the business) or in a trade name. "Trading as" (t/a) or the phrase "doing business as" (dba) may be used. For example, if Tabatha Thompson owned a business called The Gift Shop, the account would read "Tabatha Thompson d/b/a The Gift Shop."

When a proprietorship is operated under the individual's own name, a bank requires identification, references, and signature cards to open the account, much as it does in the case of an individual. Often, there is no way to distinguish a sole proprietorship from the individual who is the owner. However, when any name other than the individual's is used, the connection between the owner and the fictitious trade name also should be established legally. The proprietor provides the bank with the legal registration form required by the state. This may be a business certificate, a fictitious name registration, or a certificate of registration of trade name.

A sole proprietor has the right to open an account, make deposits, stop payments, and manage the account. Checks payable either to the proprietor or to the proprietorship may be deposited to the sole proprietorship account. The proprietor can authorize another individual as a signer on the account, but this person would not have the same rights to the account as the owner.

## Partnership

A partnership account may be opened under the names of the individual partners or it may use a trade name. Partnerships are businesses operated by two or more individuals in non-corporate form.

Depending on the terms of the **partnership agreement**, any one member of the partnership may be empowered to act for the others, so that his or her actions are legally binding on the other partners. In opening an account for a partnership, a bank obtains signatures from all partners authorized to issue checks, apply for loans, and otherwise deal with the bank on behalf of the partnership. This form is called a partnership resolution. The bank also obtains a copy of the partnership agreement, and if the partnership operates under a trade name, a copy of the business certificate on file.

## Corporation

A corporate account is opened in the name of the corporation, the owner of the account. The bank legally interacts with the corporation, not the stockholders, directors, or officers. A corporation is identified by its legal name, which may include "Inc.," "Corporation," "Incorporated," or "Limited."

A corporation, like an individual and partnership, is a legal entity, but the similarity ends there. The corporation cannot act independently; it must act through representatives. Stockholders, who own the corporation, elect the board of directors. The board of directors, which is the governing body of the corporation, is responsible for conducting the corporation's business. It establishes who can open and operate a bank account on behalf of the corporation.

To verify the authority to open an account, the bank reviews and obtains a certified corporate resolution, which is filed with the bank. The corporate resolution authorizes certain officers to sign checks or otherwise issue instructions to the bank concerning the account. It also may authorize the corporation to borrow money from the bank.

The bank keeps on file the names, titles, and signatures of the persons who are authorized to transact business on the corporation's behalf. This file is updated with new signature cards as new people are given authority, or authority is terminated.

In addition to knowing who can transact business for the corporation, banks keep records on the authority limits of each signer. The president, for example, may

### Situation

A retired couple is planning to take a lengthy vacation in their new recreational vehicle. They have arranged to have their pension checks automatically deposited into their checking account and want to give their daughter the ability to pay bills and otherwise manage the account while they are away. However, they also want access to cash from the account while they travel across the country. They give their daughter power of attorney over their checking account only and revoke the power of attorney when they return from their trip.

**Partnership agreement**— A legal agreement stating the contributions each partner has made to the business, the nature of the business, and the proportions in which each partner will share in profits or losses.

have unlimited authority, whereas the vice president of finance can sign checks up to a specific amount only. It is possible that several people will need to sign a check for it to be acceptable under the resolution. An example is shown below.

|  | *Individually* | *Combined (any two)* |
|---|---|---|
| Vice President | $5,000 | $10,000 |
| Comptroller | $5,000 | |
| Secretary | $5,000 | |

Unlike an individual or a partnership account, neither a corporate account nor the operation of the corporation is affected by the death of a stockholder, officer, or director.

### Government or Agency Ownership

A public funds account is opened by a unit of government to receive and disburse funds on behalf of communities and citizens. The unit of government officially appoints the banks with which it opens accounts. State and local laws usually prescribe the procedures that establish public funds accounts at banks.

Documentation generally consists of signature cards listing the authorized signers and an official letter or notice appointing the bank as a depository. The letter or notice typically is issued by the head of the unit of government. In general, these accounts are secured by segregated, specific assets held by the bank.

### Unincorporated Organization

Banks are asked to open deposit accounts for all sorts of unincorporated organizations, such as churches, bowling leagues, soccer teams, class reunions, and charitable relief funds. Although these are not "businesses" in the traditional sense, many banks treat them as business accounts.

When opening an account for an unincorporated organization, signature cards are required. Also, a taxpayer identification number is required, even if the organization does not pay taxes and is not designated formally as a nonprofit organization under tax laws. Each situation dictates what additional letters, forms, agreements, or special documents should be obtained. The bank's attorneys, compliance officers, and policy and procedures manual should be consulted when establishing account relationships with these organizations.

## OPENING A DEPOSIT ACCOUNT

A customer must open an account before the bank can accept items for deposit. The account-opening process entails much more than filling out forms at the new accounts desk. In opening the account, the bank
- establishes the identity of the person opening the account
- determines that the person has the legal capacity to open the account
- ensures that the person is authorized to open the account

By opening an account, a bank enters into a contractual relationship with the account holder and assumes risk. There is the risk that the customer will write checks for more than the amount in the account. There is the risk that deposited items will be returned. Bankers follow the same principle that applies to opening all accounts: know your customer!

## ESTABLISHING IDENTITY

As a protection against loss, a bank establishes the identity of the person opening the account. But can the bank truly verify identity? Unfortunately, there is no completely foolproof way. Forgers can counterfeit driver's licenses, auto registrations, credit cards, and other forms of identification. A passport is often regarded as ideal identification, but not everyone has a passport, and these documents are subject to fraud as well. Bankers must evaluate the identification that is offered according to the bank's customer identification program, and use good judgment.

### *Customer Identification Program*

The USA PATRIOT Act, which was introduced after the terrorist attacks of September 11, 2001, includes a provision requiring financial service providers, including banks, to establish a customer identification program (CIP) for new accounts. The intent was to stop terrorists from using the U.S. financial system for money laundering and to finance crimes.

Under rules that went into effect in 2003, a bank's written CIP must incorporate reasonable procedures to

- collect identifying information about individuals opening an account, such as name, date of birth, address, and an identifying number, such as a Social Security number or taxpayer identification number
- verify customer identification
- determine if a customer appears on any lists of known or suspected terrorists provided by any government agency
- maintain records of the information used to verify a customer's identity

The act also specifies minimum standards for the identification collected, requirements for verification, and requirements for record keeping.

## EVALUATING CAPACITY AND AUTHORITY

Despite a desire to attract new business, banks must be selective in opening accounts. A bank is not obligated to open an account if the potential customer fails to meet the requirements established by the bank.

### *Capacity*

Before opening an account, a bank determines that the person opening the account has the legal capacity to do so. Having legal capacity means that the person or organization is recognized under the law as being a legal entity with the right to open an account.

Most people have the capacity to open accounts, but a person who is considered a minor or incompetent normally does not have the legal capacity to do so. Although, minors can have checking accounts, the accounts are co-owned or otherwise guaranteed by a responsible adult. Organizations also are required to provide proof that the corporation, partnership, or unincorporated organization exists.

## Situation

Michael has three single accounts at the same insured bank: two accounts held in his name alone and one account held by his business, which is a sole proprietorship. Funds owned by a sole proprietorship are insured as the single ownership funds of the person who owns the business. Thus, the deposits in all three accounts are added together and the total balance, $125,000, is insured for $100,000, leaving $25,000 uninsured.

*Authority*

The person opening the account is asked to prove authority to open and use the account. Individuals opening an account in their own name need to prove their identity.

# DEPOSIT REGULATIONS

The federal government enacts laws designed to protect banks and those consumers and businesses that establish deposit relationships with banks. Federal bank regulatory agencies are responsible for supervising and enforcing these laws. State banking authorities also may supervise and enforce laws that define the deposit relationship.

When Congress passes a law, it usually delegates rule making authority to a banking agency like the Federal Reserve. Several examples of regulations that apply to deposit functions include Regulation D, known as Reserve Requirements for Depository Institutions; Regulation E, which implements the Electronic Fund Transfer Act; Regulation CC, which implements the Expedited Funds Availability Act; and Regulation DD, which implements the Truth in Savings Act.

## REGULATION D

Reserve Requirements for Depository Institutions, Regulation D, imposes uniform reserve requirements on all depository institutions with transaction accounts or nonpersonal time deposits. Regulation D defines such deposits and requires reports of deposits to the Federal Reserve. It establishes withdrawal penalties and transaction limits on deposit accounts, such as savings accounts and money market deposit accounts.

## REGULATION E

The Electronic Fund Transfer Act, implemented by Regulation E, establishes the rights, liabilities, and responsibilities of parties in electronic fund transfers (EFTs). It requires disclosures related to electronic fund transfers, including recurring credits to deposit accounts. For example, a bank must provide the customer with a notice when a preauthorized credit, such as a direct deposit of a Social Security check, has or has not been made as scheduled. Regulation E also outlines the customer's and bank's responsibilities for reporting and resolving disputed or erroneous EFTs.

## REGULATION CC

Regulation CC implements the Expedited Funds Availability Act and governs the availability of funds. Generally, the same availability schedule is applied whether the funds are deposited through a teller or through an ATM. Depending on the time of the deposit and the location of the ATM, however, funds deposited may be available later than if they were deposited at a teller window. Banks must alert customers to their funds availability policies, which are usually posted near the teller windows. The following types of deposits are made available on the first business day following the banking day of deposit (next-day availability):

- cash deposited in person
- electronic payments received for deposit in an account
- U.S. Treasury checks deposited in an account held by the payee, including those deposited at an ATM owned by the bank (a proprietary ATM)

- U.S. Postal Service money orders deposited in person into an account held by a payee of the check
- Federal Reserve Bank and Federal Home Loan Bank checks deposited in person into an account held by a payee
- state or local government checks deposited in person into an account held by a payee, if the institution is in the same state as the payor of the check
- cashier's, certified, or teller's checks deposited in person to an account held by a payee
- checks drawn on an account held by the drawee bank (on-us checks)

## REGULATION DD

The Truth in Savings Act, implemented by Regulation DD, requires banks to provide customers with information needed to compare deposit account features. Regulation DD requires banks to use one of two methods to calculate interest: daily balance method or average daily balance method. Banks must disclose at account opening the interest rate, **annual percentage yield** (APY), frequency of interest compounding, minimum balance requirements, fees, transaction limits, and other important information in the account agreement. The act requires periodic statements to disclose APY earned, amount of interest earned, fees imposed, and length of statement period. Customers must be given advance notice of changes in terms that would affect the account, such as the APY, fees, or maturity dates.

**Annual percentage yield**—A percentage rate reflecting the total amount of interest paid on a deposit account, based on the interest rate and the frequency of compounding for a 365-day period.

## FDIC INSURANCE PROTECTION

Deposit insurance comes into play when a bank fails and there are not enough assets to pay depositors. To be sure insurance funds are available when necessary, FDIC manages the Bank Insurance Fund and the Savings Association Insurance Fund.

FDIC insurance protection rules can be quite complex, and depositors have the ability to enjoy coverage over and above $100,000. The FDIC publishes Your Insured Deposit that outlines the basic concepts of ownership rights and capacities that determine how much coverage a depositor may have. FDIC also maintains the Electronic Deposit Insurance Estimator (EDIE) on its Web site that also can help individuals determine the amount of their deposits that are insured at any covered institution.

## SUMMARY

- Through the deposit function, banks provide a safe place for depositors to keep money and an economical method to pay checks written by a depositor. Deposit account services are easily accessible to customers through bank branches, ATMs, and the Internet.

- Banks offer a wide variety of deposit products and services. Deposits may be placed in a checking, savings, or time deposit account. Customers make checking account deposits because they intend to withdraw the funds at will to pay bills and meet expenses. Customers generally use savings and time deposit accounts to place funds they do not immediately need.

- Deposit account products offered to consumers include personal checking accounts, statement savings accounts, savings clubs, money market deposit accounts, CDs, retirement savings accounts, and health savings accounts. Deposit account products offered to businesses include checking and savings accounts, concentration accounts, CDs, and money market deposit accounts.

- Customers enjoy a number of deposit-related services, including the teller window, night depository, direct deposit, automated transfer service (ATS), electronic fund transfers (EFT), ATMs, wire transfer, mailing deposits, and courier or armored car services. Electronic access to deposit accounts and services is widely available. A rapidly growing number of customers bank on the Internet, performing such deposit account activities as balance inquiries, reviewing account history, account reconcilement, and account transfers. Debit cards, pin-only or signature based, are used for deposit transactions.

- Bank customers can deposit funds in a variety of ways, including in-person and electronically. Customers deposit coin and currency, cash items, and noncash items. Banks must collect cash and noncash items. Checks and substitute checks are examples of cash items. Checks in foreign currency are an example of a noncash item.

- The type of deposit account opened by a customer and the way in which the account is titled determines the ownership of the account, what identification is required, and what documentation is necessary to establish the capacity and the authority to open the account. An individual, more than one person (joint ownership), or one in a fiduciary capacity can open consumer accounts. Examples of fiduciary accounts include trust accounts, estate accounts, and guardianship accounts. Sole proprietorships, partnerships, corporations, public agencies, and unincorporated entities can open business accounts.

- Bank employees must exercise caution in opening accounts and ensuring that the customer provides the bank with proper identification. Before opening an account, the bank must determine that the person opening the account has the legal capacity and authority to do so. The USA PATRIOT ACT establishes minimum standards for a customer identification program.

- A number of Federal government regulations apply to deposit products and services offered by banks. These include Regulation D, known as Reserve Requirements for Depository Institutions; Regulation E, which implements the Electronic Fund Transfer Act; Regulation CC, which implements the Expedited Funds Availability Act; and Regulation DD, which implements the Truth in Savings Act. FDIC rules determine how deposits are insured.

**Learning Check**

# SELF CHECK & REVIEW

1. Why are deposits so important to banks?

2. What are the basic differences and similarities between a checking account and a savings account?

3. How do automatic transfer services benefit a customer?

4. What deposit account would you recommend to a customer who wants to earn interest and would also like the option of writing a small number of checks (three or less) per month?

5.  What options do customers have for making deposits into their accounts, other than going to their bank?

6.  How do account transactions differ for joint accounts held as joint tenancy versus tenants in common?

7.  When opening a deposit account, why is it important for a bank to establish the authority of the customer to use the account? What three steps does the bank take to accomplish this when opening an account?

8.  What types of deposit transactions are covered under Regulation E?

# ADDITIONAL RESOURCES

Resources

American Bankers Association, **www.aba.com**

*ABA Bank Compliance Magazine*, Washington D.C.: American Bankers Association, bimonthly magazine.

*ABA Bank Compliance Newsletter*, Washington D.C.: American Bankers Association, monthly publication.

*A Guide to IRS Information Reporting for Financial Institutions, Sixth Edition*, Washington D.C.: American Bankers Association.

CEDRIC Consumer & Economic Development Research & Information Center, Federal Reserve Bank of Chicago, **www.chicagofed.org/cedric/cedric_index.cfm**.

*Checking Accounts* brochure, ABA Education Foundation, Washington D.C.: American Bankers Association.

College and General Savings Calculator, ABA Education Foundation, American Bankers Association, **www.aba.com/aba/cgi-bia/comboNT.pl**.

Electronic Deposit Insurance Estimator (EDIE), **www2.FDIC.gov/edie/index.asp**.

*Financial Institutions Employee's Guide to Deposit Insurance*, Federal Deposit Insurance Corporation, **www.fdic.gov/deposit/deposits/financial/index.html**.

*Reference Guide to Regulatory Compliance*, Washington D.C.: American Bankers Association, 2004.

*Retail Banking Survey Report*, Washington D.C.: American Bankers Association, 2003.

*Teach Children to Save*, ABA Education Foundation, American Bankers Association, **www.aba.com**.

*Uninsured Investment Products: A Pocket Guide for Financial Institutions*, Federal Deposit Insurance Corporation, **www.fdic.gov/regulations/resources/financial/index.html**.

*Savings Accounts* brochure, ABA Education Foundation, Washington D.C.: American Bankers Association.

*Your Insured Deposit*, **www.fdic.gov/deposit/deposits/insured/index.html**

# Payments

# What You Will Learn

*After studying this chapter, you should be able to*

- describe the components of a check and what makes it a negotiable instrument
- identify the types of endorsements
- identify different types of bank checks
- explain the check payment process, including electronic innovations
- describe various electronic payment methods
- describe the care and distribution of coin and currency
- explain banking regulations related to payment processes
- define the bolded key terms that appear in the text

# Introduction

*Throughout history people have used countless items to facilitate the exchange of goods and to pay for services. Pharaohs of ancient Egypt, for example, used brass rings for money, and shark's teeth are still used in Micronesia. In today's industrial/technological society, payments are made through both simple and technologically sophisticated systems.*

*The payment system consists of instruments and procedures used to transfer money, make payments, and settle debts among consumers, businesses, and governments. In the United States, the three primary payment systems are checks, electronic payment systems, and cash. Legislation and related regulations govern the payment processes, to protect the economy, the banking industry, businesses, and consumers.*

## CHECKS AS A PAYMENT SYSTEM

Checks are a convenient and safe method of payment. Money can exchange hands by simply filling in blank spaces on a check. A completed check tells a bank how much money should be transferred, when it should be transferred, and to whom.

Checks are a universally accepted form of payment. A set of rules and practices governs their negotiability, the liability of the parties, and their processing.

### ELEMENTS OF NEGOTIABLE INSTRUMENTS

**Negotiable instrument—** An unconditional written order or promise to pay a certain sum of money. The document must be easily transferable from one party to another. Every negotiable instrument must meet all requirements of Article 3 of the Uniform Commercial Code.

A check is a **negotiable instrument** involving three parties: the person writing the check (the drawer), the person to whom the check is written (payee), and the bank that holds the checking account (the drawee) (see exhibit 5.1).

For the drawer, the check is a convenient way to pay for goods, services, or other obligations. For the payee, the expectation is that checks will be exchanged

### Exhibit 5.1: Parties to a Check

Payee  Drawer

ROBERT W. LARKIN
123 Main Street
Anywhere, U.S.A. 12345

2740

May 15, 20 XX     15-4
540 20

PAY TO THE ORDER OF   American Gas & Electric Co.     $ 61.79

Sixty-One and 79/100 - - - - - - - - - - - - - - - - - - - - - - - - DOLLARS

**LAST NATIONAL BANK**     SAMPLE  *Robert W. Larkin*

MEMO:

⑆054000043⑆   5 500 265⑈   2740

Drawee   Drawer

for cash at a teller window or credited to their bank accounts. The collection process and the governing laws are taken for granted.

As negotiable instruments, checks are governed by a set of legal requirements under Articles 3, Negotiable Instruments, and Article 4, Bank Deposits and Collections, of the **Uniform Commercial Code** (UCC). A check must have all the required components to be negotiable.

**Uniform Commercial Code**—A set of common laws adopted by all states to govern commercial and financial transactions between parties. Many states adopted their own amendments to the code.

---

### Exhibit 5.2: Elements of a Negotiable Check

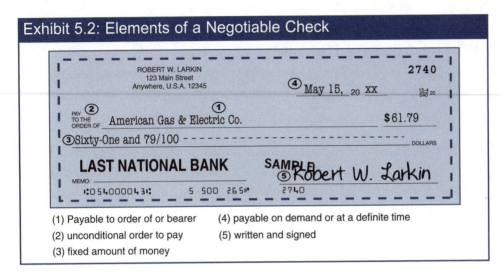

(1) Payable to order of or bearer
(2) unconditional order to pay
(3) fixed amount of money
(4) payable on demand or at a definite time
(5) written and signed

---

### Payable to Bearer or to Order

A negotiable instrument is payable to bearer or to order if the words "bearer" or "cash" are used, or if it otherwise indicates that the person in possession of it is entitled to payment. A check that is made payable to an identifiable person and endorsed by that person becomes a bearer instrument (see (1) of exhibit 5.2).

### Unconditional Order or Promise to Pay

A negotiable instrument is an unconditional order or promise to pay. Checks contain a written order to the bank to pay the amount of the check to the payee. This order cannot depend on any conditions—it must be unconditional (see (2) of exhibit 5.2). For example, a check may not contain the statement: "If he paints the house, pay to the order of Leonard." If an instrument contains a condition to payment, it is not a negotiable instrument.

### Fixed Amount of Money

The unconditional order or promise to pay must be for a fixed amount of money (see (3) of exhibit 5.2). The amount, which can be in U.S. dollars or in a foreign currency, must be specified clearly on the face of the instrument, in monetary terms. It may not be stated in terms of something of value that could be converted to money, such as the amount of one ounce of gold, even though the value of one ounce of gold can be easily determined.

### Payable on Demand or at a Definite Time

The stated date on the check determines when it is payable (see (4) of exhibit 5.2). A check may be postdated or antedated. If a check is not dated (either intentionally or unintentionally), the date of the check is considered to be the date it is issued.

**Negotiable Instruments** are
- payable to bearer or to order of
- payable without conditions
- payable for a specific, fixed, amount of money
- payable on demand or at a definite time
- in writing and signed by the issuer
- an order or promise to pay

### Written and Signed

To be a negotiable instrument, the check must be in writing and signed by the drawer (see (5) of exhibit 5.2). A negotiable instrument signed by a signature machine or stamped with an individual's signature is considered valid, as are "identifying marks" like Xs. Some banks may have specific policies and procedures about these types of signatures, and arrange for solutions ahead of time, often calling on the services of a **notary public**.

## OTHER TYPES OF CHECKS

Besides personal and business checks, banks provide cashier's checks, teller's checks, or certified checks for payment transactions.

### Cashier's Check

Cashier's checks are issued by a bank and drawn on that bank. Thus, the bank is both the drawer and the drawee. Often, banks use cashier's checks to pay their own obligations or to pay out loan proceeds. Banks also may sell these checks to customers who require an official instrument of the bank.

### Teller's Check

Similar to a cashier's check, a teller's check is issued by one bank and drawn on another bank or payer. The issuing bank's obligation for these checks is the same as for cashier's checks. In other words, even if the purchaser decides it does not want it paid after issuance, the bank is obligated to pay the check.

The payer bank supplies teller's checks and maintains the blank check stock, reconciles the teller's check account, stores the paid checks, and provides customer service to both the customer and the issuing bank.

### Certified Check

A certified check is accepted by the bank on which it is drawn. Essentially, it is a depositor's check stamped with the word "certified" and a signature and date. The original order to pay is transferred to the bank's promise to pay. Certified checks are legal liabilities of the bank.

Typically, a customer presents the personal check to be certified. The bank sets aside the funds for the check, debits the customer's account, and credits a 'certified checks outstanding' account. To complete the process, the bank places an official bank stamp and signature on the check. The magnetic ink character recognition (MICR) line is covered with the certified check account number or mutilated so that it will not pass through the customer's account.

## THE CHECK PAYMENT PROCESS

As illustrated in exhibit 5.3, the payment process starts when a check is transferred from one person or company to another person or company. The transfer is authorized by signing the bottom of the check. When the check is presented to a bank for payment, a collection process is initiated that results in the transfer of money from the check writer (drawer) to the check recipient (payee).

**Notary public—**A public officer who takes acknowledgment of or otherwise attests or certifies deeds and other writings or copies of them, usually under his or her official seal, to make them authentic.

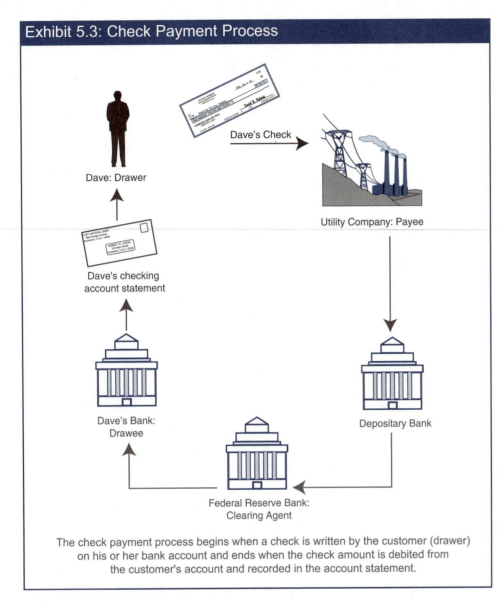

Dave: Drawer

Dave's Check

Utility Company: Payee

Dave's checking account statement

Dave's Bank: Drawee

Depositary Bank

Federal Reserve Bank: Clearing Agent

The check payment process begins when a check is written by the customer (drawer) on his or her bank account and ends when the check amount is debited from the customer's account and recorded in the account statement.

**Situation**

Franco and Lena are closing on a house tomorrow. The mortgage company will not accept a regular check for the closing for fear it will be dishonored. Franco and Lena do not want to bring a large amount of cash to the settlement, so they decide to purchase a cashier's check to pay for the down payment and closing costs.

## THE DRAWER

The first stage in the check payment process begins when the drawer writes a check on his or her account payable to an identifiable person, bearer, or cash.

### Checks Payable to an Identifiable Person

Negotiation of a check payable to an identifiable person (payee) requires endorsement by the identifiable person and delivery or transfer of the check. An identifiable person is an actual person or a legal entity such as a corporation.

If the endorsement of the payee is forged, then the negotiation is invalid. A depositary bank that takes a check with a forged endorsement is subject to a claim directly from the payee or a claim from the drawee bank.

### Checks Payable as "And" or "Or"

A check payable to joint payees (Bill and Betty) requires the endorsement of both payees. If one payee did not endorse the check and did not benefit from the proceeds, he or she may file a claim against the other. However, if the check is payable to one or the other payee (Bill or Betty), then either payee can negotiate the check.

### Checks Payable to Bearer

Instead of being made payable to an identifiable person, checks can be made payable to "cash" or "bearer." Negotiation is by delivery alone and does not require an endorsement. Thus, any person in possession of an instrument payable to bearer is the holder of the instrument.

If the bearer takes the check to a teller to obtain cash, most banks would require the check to be endorsed in order to identify the person to whom the cash was given. If the endorsed check is dishonored, the endorser, after being given timely notice, is obligated to take the check back.

### Holder in Due Course

The person in possession of a check is the **holder**. As checks proceed through the check processing system, they come into the possession of businesses, banks, and Federal Reserve banks. Individuals, businesses, and banks can accept a negotiable instrument, such as a check, without being liable for any claims and defenses, if they possess the check as a **holder in due course**.

## THE PAYEE

After the drawer writes the check, the next step is for the payee to accept the check. The payee can transfer the check to another person, convert it to cash, or deposit it to an account. What the payee intends to do with the check depends on how it is endorsed. The top one-fourth of the back of the check is reserved for endorsements. The principal types of endorsements are blank, special, and restrictive.

A *blank endorsement* (or an endorsement in blank), which is the most common endorsement, is the signature of the payee. A check endorsed in blank becomes a bearer instrument negotiated without other endorsement and used for any purpose.

A *special endorsement* names another designated person. The endorsement may state, "Pay to the order of," and then the payee signs under that statement. Only the designated person can negotiate the check. A special endorsement may be used if the payee is mailing the check to another person.

With a *restrictive endorsement*, the payee or other holder of a check restricts the purpose for which a check may be used. The most common restrictive endorsement, used for depositing an item to an account, is "For Deposit Only." Endorsed this way, the instrument can be used only for deposit to an account. Any other use is prohibited.

The endorser can cancel any endorsement, including a restrictive endorsement by deleting it or scratching through it and endorsing the check in another manner. The deletion, however, should bear the payee's or holder's initials.

---

**Holder**—A person who is in possession of an instrument and who is entitled to receive payment of the instrument.

**Holder in Due Course**— One who holds a negotiable instrument, such as a check, and who takes the instrument
- for value
- in good faith
- without notice that it is overdue or dishonored
- without knowledge that it has an unauthorized signature or is altered
- without knowledge of claims to the instrument or defenses against payment

## Bank-Provided Endorsement

Under Article 4 of the UCC, the bank automatically becomes a holder of an unendorsed instrument when it is accepted for deposit to the payee's account or other holder, or is cashed for the payee or holder. The bank becomes the holder of the instrument for all purposes, including becoming a holder in due course.

A bank can still supply a missing endorsement. If a customer failed to endorse an item, and the item itself did not require the personal endorsement of the payee, the bank could provide an endorsement that stated, "For deposit to the account of the within named payee." This endorsement usually is stamped on the item at the time it is deposited. The bank typically supplies the endorsement when items are received for deposit through the night depository, the mail, or an ATM.

## THE DEPOSITARY BANK

Continuing with the check payment process, the **depositary bank** then accepts the check, which has been endorsed by the payee. From there it is encoded, proofed, captured, sorted, and cleared for presentment to the drawee.

Most people think a check is being cashed when it is presented to a teller. However, the difference between paying and cashing a check is important.

### Paying Checks

A bank is obligated, to its own customers, to pay a check that is properly payable. When a person presents an **on-us check** to a teller, it is deposited in an account or paid over the counter. In either case, the teller is making final payment on the check. However, if it is paid or accepted by mistake, the check is deemed not to have been paid or accepted in spite of final payment.

Because making final payment on an on-us check presents a risk for the bank, it is important that the teller examine the check and the account on which the check is drawn to ensure

- the person presenting the item is properly identified
- no **stop payments** are on the check or holds on the account
- sufficient funds are in the account to cover the check

When inspecting a check, a teller can perform both visual and nonvisual tests (see exhibit 5.4).

**Depositary bank**—A bank in which a check is first deposited. The bank also may be the paying bank (drawee) if the check is drawn on, payable at, or payable through the bank.

**On-us check**—A check deposited or negotiated for cash at the bank on which it is drawn.

**Stop payment**—A depositor's instructions to his or her bank (the drawee) directing the bank not to pay a previously issued check or item.

**Paying Versus Cashing a Check**
- *Paying a check*: giving cash in exchange for an on-us check
- *Cashing a check*: giving cash for a check drawn on another bank

---

### Exhibit 5.4: Visual and Nonvisual Tests for Inspecting a Check

**Nonvisual Elements**
- Has a stop payment order been placed on the check?
- Has a hold been placed on the account?
- Is there sufficient balance to cover the check?
- Is the account balance available to the drawer?

**Visual Elements**
- Is the item an actual check drawn on the bank?
- Is the signature genuine and authorized?
- ❑ Has the check been altered?
- ❑ Is the check properly dated?
- ❑ Is the check properly endorsed?

• paying a check          ❑ cashing a check

## Wrongful Dishonor

A bank is liable for wrongful dishonor if it

- fails to pay an item drawn on sufficient collected funds
- pays a check subject to a stop payment order and then dishonors other checks that would otherwise have been paid
- places a hold order on the wrong account pursuant to an attachment order or IRS levy and then dishonors checks presented for payment
- mistakenly applies funds against an obligation not owed by the depositor, leading to the dishonor of checks
- closes its depositor's account without giving reasonable notice of the closure and dishonors checks that were outstanding before the account was closed

Online systems now allow tellers to view an image of the bank's record of the customer's signature so it can be compared to the actual signature on the check. This helps reduce instances of forged signatures. To ensure that the funds are available when the posting process is completed later that day, many banks also place a teller's hold on the funds when the check is paid.

A bank may pay a check on a customer's account only if the check is properly payable. Under Article 4, Bank Deposits and Collections, of the UCC, a check is properly payable if it is authorized by the customer and is in accordance with any agreement between the customer and the bank.

A bank is required to honor a check that is properly payable. Failing to do so, the bank could be liable to the customer for wrongful dishonor of the check. Unless the bank has an agreement to pay checks in overdraft, it is not liable for wrongful dishonor when it dishonors a check that would overdraw the account.

### Cashing Checks

A teller cashes a check by giving cash in exchange for a check drawn on another bank. Cashing checks has greater risk than paying checks. When cashing a check, the teller can verify only whether the check has been altered and was properly dated and endorsed.

Although there is additional risk with cashing a check, banks generally do so for at least two reasons. First, the person presenting the check usually has an account with the bank. Second, the drawer may have other relationships with the bank, such as loans.

If the bank cashes a check and it is not paid by the drawee, the bank may collect the amount of the check from the person who cashed the check or any other previous endorser. The bank also may look to the drawer for payment.

### Check Preparation

Once a check is accepted by the depositary bank for cash, payment, or deposit, it is processed for collection (see exhibit 5.5). The first step is preparation for proofing and encoding. Preparation includes removing staples, paper clips, and rubber bands. All checks are arranged face forward and right side up. Only checks to be captured are sent through the proof and encoding function.

### Proofing and Encoding

Most banks process checks in "batches" or bundles that may come from business customers to branch banks. In proofing, each transaction is checked to see that the dollar amount of the debits, such as checks, equals the dollar amount of the credits, such as deposit slips. This is where errors in addition, extra items not reflected on the deposit ticket, and items listed but not included are found. The proofing operator either balances the check or passes it on to another area in the proofing department to perform this function.

Encoding is the process of inscribing or imprinting magnetic ink character recognition (MICR) data on checks. High-speed reader-sorters then can read the MICR data and capture information such as the amount, account number, and check number, which expedites transaction posting and disposition of check clearing.

## Exhibit 5.5: Presenting Checks for Payment and Posting

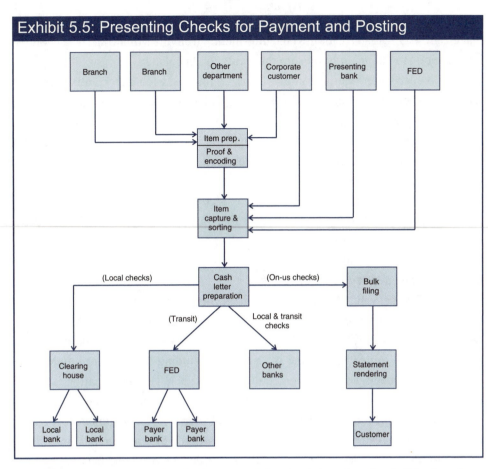

MICR data are printed at the bottom of the check in a line that is ⅝ inches deep. The line has five "fields": an auxiliary number field for commercial checks only, the routing number field, the account number field, the check number field, and the check amount field. The routing number field contains the Federal Reserve routing symbol, American Bankers Association's ABA institution identifier, and the check digit number.

When checks are ordered, most MICR encoding information is preprinted on the check. Proof operators use the same magnetic ink to add the check amount to the preprinted information on the MICR line.

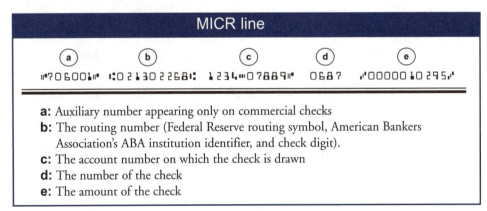

### MICR line

a: Auxiliary number appearing only on commercial checks
b: The routing number (Federal Reserve routing symbol, American Bankers Association's ABA institution identifier, and check digit).
c: The account number on which the check is drawn
d: The number of the check
e: The amount of the check

### Item Capture and Sorting

After being proofed and encoded, checks are sent to another area that reads (captures) the encoded information and sorts the checks and other items for further processing. The item capture and sorting department uses reader-sorter equipment that electronically reads (captures) the information from the MICR line. The captured information is read again to be sure the transactions balance.

The reader-sorter equipment also films, or images, each check and endorses it with the bank's information. It also sprays or stamps each check with a sequence number that identifies where the check is located in the bank's film or image archives. Some banks scan the entire image and convert it into a digitized format that is stored on computers and used for research, presented in courts of law, or as copies for customers.

Once the information is captured, the reader-sorter automatically sorts checks into bins or pockets. Sorting involves more than one pass or cycle. On the first pass, checks generally are sorted for **local**, **nonlocal**, and on-us checks. Other passes separate the checks from other paper documents and sort the checks by account number or statement-cycle cutoff dates.

In the first pass, the ABA institution identifier number on the check identifies the bank on which a check is drawn. For local clearing and transit items, the bank typically captures only the check amount and the ABA institution identifier. For on-us items, the entire MICR line is captured, including the account number, the amount of the check, and the sequential check number. This information is stored for processing later when debits and credits are posted to the accounts.

Local and non local checks are sorted and prepared for shipment to Federal Reserve banks, correspondent banks, local clearinghouses, or directly to drawee banks. As pockets in the reader-sorter fill, checks are removed and banded together into batches. Headers identify the dollar amount and list the items in the batch. Then a cash letter is completed with the dollar amount of checks in all batches. The **cash letter** generates the credit that is deposited into the depositary bank's account. Exhibit 5.6 illustrates the check sorting process.

Sometimes, during the first pass, the reader-sorter cannot read the checks because of an encoding error or a defect in the magnetic ink. "Rejects" are repaired and reentered in the system.

### *Clearing*

Local and nonlocal checks are presented to the drawee bank by sending them directly to the bank, by using a clearing house, or by using the services of the Federal Reserve bank or a correspondent bank. Most banks use a combination of these methods, taking into consideration availability, deadlines, price, and transportation. Correspondent relationships and services the clearing agent offers are considered as well. The clearing methods include:

**Direct presentment**     Bank messengers or local couriers carry local checks directly to local banks. Many banks agree to swap items free of charge. The settlement method could be by check, credit, debit due to and due from bank accounts, Fedwire, or credit to a Federal Reserve or correspondent bank account.

**Local check**—A deposited check drawn on another bank in the same Federal Reserve check processing region.

**Nonlocal checks**—A deposited check that is drawn on another bank located in a different Federal Reserve check processing region. Also a transit check.

**Cash letter**—An interbank transmittal form, resembling a deposit slip, used to accompany cash items sent from one bank to another.

# Exhibit 5.6: Check Sorting and Bundling

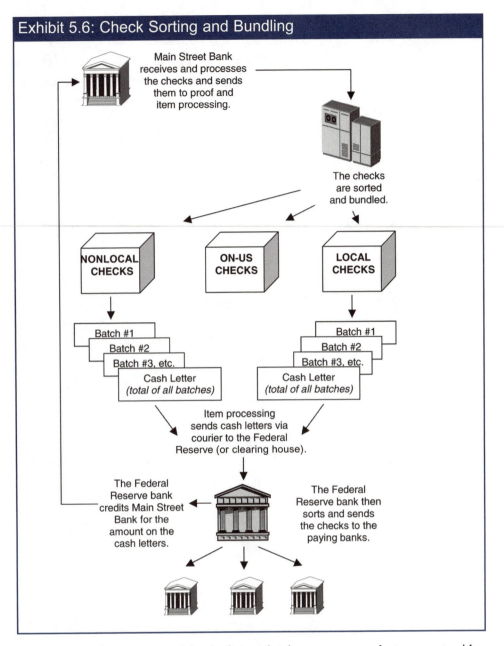

Main Street Bank receives and processes the checks and sends them to proof and item processing.

The checks are sorted and bundled.

NONLOCAL CHECKS

ON-US CHECKS

LOCAL CHECKS

Batch #1
Batch #2
Batch #3, etc.
Cash Letter
*(total of all batches)*

Batch #1
Batch #2
Batch #3, etc.
Cash Letter
*(total of all batches)*

Item processing sends cash letters via courier to the Federal Reserve (or clearing house).

The Federal Reserve bank credits Main Street Bank for the amount on the cash letters.

The Federal Reserve bank then sorts and sends the checks to the paying banks.

**Historical Fact**

Dr. Kenneth B. Eldredge, staff scientist at Stanford Research Institute, was awarded U.S. Patent Number 3,000,000 for his invention of the magnetic ink character reader machine. The machine and the magnetic-ink "common machine language" developed by the American Bankers Association in 1956 revolutionized check processing.

**Correspondent**   A bank that maintains a correspondent account with a larger bank often relies on it to present and collect checks. In processing and collecting checks, correspondent banks accept the day's deposited items, credit the sending bank's account, sort the items, and present them to drawees.

**Clearing houses**   Although clearing houses operate similarly to correspondent banks, a clearing house is an organization of banks in a city or region. Members do not pay each other for checks presented. Rather, they make one "net" payment to a clearing house that reflects the difference between total credits received and total credits due. A clearing house is established specifically to facilitate clearing checks written on accounts of participating banks.

**Historical Fact**

In 1899 to 1900, the Boston Clearinghouse began a uniform clearing procedure for clearing checks of all New England banks. Remittances would be at par, and any banks that refused to pay at par would be subject to an exchange charge.

**Federal Reserve**

The Federal Reserve Act established the first nationwide system for collecting nonlocal checks. Federal Reserve district banks serve as a center for check collection so that nonlocal checks flow efficiently among the districts. Efficiency is enhanced through Federal Reserve branch offices and regional check processing centers that supplement collection activities of the 12 reserve banks.

## THE DRAWEE

The drawee (paying bank) receives checks directly from other banks through a clearing house or from the Federal Reserve (a process called in-clearing capture). Regardless of how checks are received, banks must follow basically the same payment procedures.

### In-clearing Capture

When a bank or the Federal Reserve presents cash letters to the drawee, the drawee must prepare the checks for capture, capture the data, and settle the checks. In-clearing capture procedures are similar to the depositary bank's capture procedures, with one main difference. Because the checks are all drawn on the paying bank (drawee), the entire MICR line must be captured. If the reader-sorter cannot read the MICR characters, checks are rejected and the error is corrected for accurate posting.

Because the depositary bank did the encoding, the checks do not go through the encoding function. Instead, the checks are filmed with their assigned sequence numbers encoded and passed to the posting system.

### Posting

Data from capture runs, including items presented over the counter and from in-clearings, are stored throughout the day. At the end of the day, when the bank has completed all capture runs, transactions are posted to accounts.

Posting is the process of adding deposits to an account balance and subtracting checks and other withdrawals from that balance. Usually, deposits and other credits are posted first; then debits are posted.

### Exception Items

Checks rejected from the normal posting process require special handling. These checks commonly are referred to as exception items. Checks may require special handling for a number of reasons: nonsufficient funds (NSF); an uncollected balance may not leave enough funds to pay the check; a stop payment placed on the check; a hold placed on the account.

Each exception item requires an action. If a check is to be returned to the depositary bank, it is removed manually, stamped with the reason for the return, and sent back to the depositary bank. The depositary bank reviews the reason for the return and determines what to do. The check either is charged back (debited) from the customer's account or, if it was returned for **nonsufficient funds (NSF)**, it is redeposited and sent back through the system a second time for payment.

**Nonsufficient funds—** An expression indicating that a check or item drawn against an account exceeds the amount of collected funds in the account.

Banks place **holds** on customer accounts for a number of reasons. The bank may want to examine the signature on every check presented on a particular account because of a special situation or suspicion of some kind. Or the bank may have received a court order to freeze the funds in the account.

**Hold**—A restriction on the payment of all or any part of the balance in an account.

Whatever the reason, checks drawn on an account on which a hold is placed must be rejected, examined, paid, or returned. If a bank places a hold on an account with the intention of not honoring checks drawn on specific deposits, the bank must meet the requirements of Regulation CC, which governs banks' check collection and payment practices involving consumers.

## Document Examination and Filing

Most banks use bulk filing procedures for on-us checks. In a bulk file, checks are sorted daily by statement cycle and filed in bundles. If the bank examines the signatures, dates, or other details of the checks, they are sorted separately into account number sequence. Some banks use either film-based or image-based automated signature verification.

At statement-rendering time, checks are sorted into account number sequence, with dividers to separate accounts. Returned checks are taken to a statement preparation area to be processed.

## Statement Rendering

When a customer receives a statement in the mail listing the previous month's checking account deposits and debits, the check payments process has come full circle.

An account is assigned a statement cycle date, which is the date the statement is produced. In the typical statement rendering process, statements are printed in account number sequence and checks are sorted into account number sequence. Then a bar code showing the number of debit items that accompanied the statement is printed on the statement. Then checks are counted; and if the number matches the number on the statement, the envelope is sealed and stamped for postage. At this point, the statements are ready to be mailed.

On the account statement, the bank prints the date the check was paid, the amount of the check, and the check number. Customers can use this information to reconcile their account with their own records.

For large banks, operations described up to this point typically are done in operations centers apart from the bank. Consequently, the bank links its automated systems to its operations center.

---

### Reconciling a Bank Statement

$$\text{Statement Balance} + \text{Deposits} - \text{Checks} = \text{Checkbook Balance}$$

**By The Numbers**

1 2 3
4 5 6
7 8 9

Today is April 5th, and your checkbook shows an account balance of $254.75. You've just received your bank statement dated March 31 that shows an account balance of $360.90. On April 2nd, you made a deposit for $200.00 and wrote two checks in the amounts of $125.00 and $181.15. Does your bank statement balance reconcile with your checkbook balance?

| | |
|---|---|
| **Statement Balance 3/31** | **$360.90** |
| **ADD Deposit 4/2** | **+ $200.00** |
| **SUBTRACT checks** | **-$125.00** |
| | **-$181.15** |
| **TOTAL** | **$254.75** |

Yes, your bank statement and checkbook balances reconcile.

---

Some customers receive cancelled checks with their statements and are responsible for storage of those statements. As an alternative, customers may receive image statements. Traditionally, customers received separate statements for each checking and savings account they had with the bank. Now, many banks offer combined statements.

**Image statement**    Statement that contains an image of each paid check. An image scanner is used to scan checks and print the small images on regular statement paper, which is easier to store than actual checks. Imaged checks usually are available for on-line banking, whether or not a printed image is sent with the statement to the customer. Banks save on postage and handling expense, sorter passes, and statement preparation time.

**Combined statement**    Statement that combines the information from a number of accounts into a single statement. Statement may contain checking, savings, bank card, time deposits, and loan information. Regulations prohibit information about uninsured investment products, such as annuities, money market mutual funds, and other nontraditional types of accounts. Like image statements, combined statements may reduce bank processing costs.

## ELECTRONIC CHECK PROCESSING

**Substitute check—**
A paper reproduction of the original check that contains an image of the front and back. It bears the full MICR line as allowed by industry standards for such checks, conforms in paper stock and dimensions according to standards, and can be processed through automated check systems.

Many years ago, some people predicted that a "checkless" society was right around the corner. They thought electronic payments were superior to checks, and the physical collection and clearing process would soon become obsolete. However, bank customers resisted this change because they liked the convenience, security, and familiarity of checks.

In 2004, a new negotiable instrument was created to help overcome the obstacles to fully electronic check processing. The Check Clearing for the 21st Century Act—commonly known as "Check 21"—created the **substitute check** (see exhibit 5.7). The Federal Reserve issued amendments to Regulation CC to implement the changes. Adding Check 21 to existing electronic check processing technologies is

**Exhibit 5.7: Recognizing Substitute Checks**

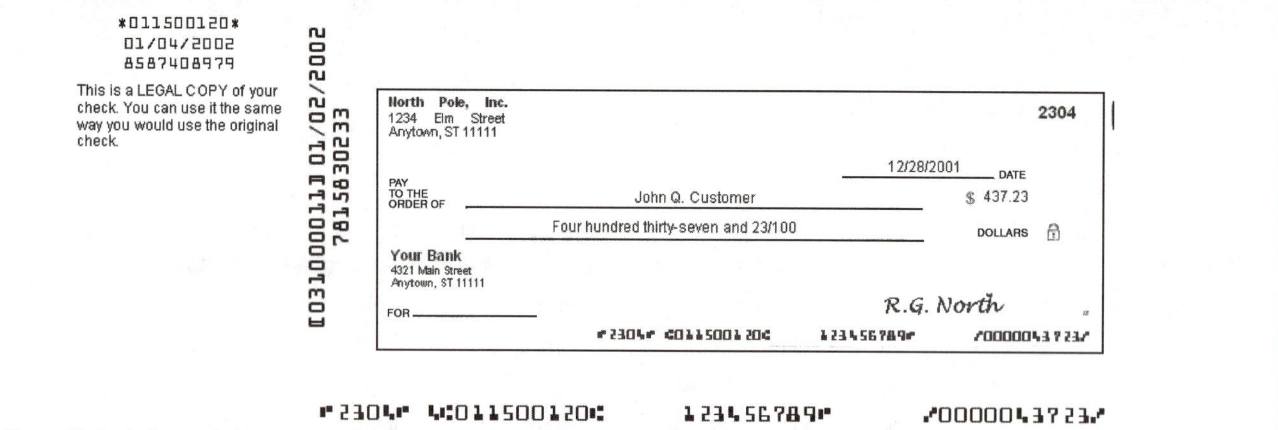

(Source: Wachovia Corporation)

stimulating greater interest in operational efficiencies that improve workflow, enabling remote image capture, truncation, and image check exchange. These new efficiencies generate substantial savings for banks.

To use the Check 21 process, a bank converts the paper check into an electronic image and then transfers the file, rather than the physical check, through the interbank collection process. If a bank somewhere along the processing chain does not exchange checks electronically, or if a customer wants a copy of the check, the electronic file can be converted back into a paper item at any point in the process. That paper item is the substitute check, and it is the legal equivalent of the original paper check. It can be processed through high-speed check processing equipment, and it is acceptable in a court of law and for all legal purposes.

Check 21 fosters innovation in the check clearing system without mandating the receipt of checks in electronic form. Creating a substitute check makes it possible for banks to **truncate** checks at any point in the collection process, regardless of state laws or agreements that may otherwise require delivery of the original paper check. Banks do not have to truncate checks for their own customers, but they are required to accept substitute checks from other banks that do truncate. When customers receive a substitute check in their monthly statement or when they request a copy of a check, they too must accept a substitute check as the legal equivalent of the original check.

**Truncation**—A generic term for the various banking systems designed to reduce the need to send or physically handle checks for customers' accounts.

# ELECTRONIC PAYMENT SYSTEMS

Electronic payment methods offer a convenient alternative to check writing. Card-based electronic payment methods include debit cards, stored value cards, and smart cards. Electronic Fund Transfers (EFTs) and Internet banking payments are also popular electronic payment methods.

## DEBIT CARDS

As a payment device, debit cards offer consumers a convenient alternative to paper checks at the point of sale (POS). Consumer use of debit cards for purchases has increased significantly over the past few years. For banks, the payment process has none of the labor costs associated with handling, sorting, and depositing checks. Debit cards have a magnetic strip that allows the customer to perform routine financial transactions, such as withdrawals, deposits, and transfers of funds between accounts, and to make payments.

There are two basic classes of debit cards: PIN-only debit cards and signature-based debit cards. For a PIN-only debit card, transactions are processed online and require a personal identification number (PIN) to authorize a transaction. Although customers still may call them ATM cards, their use has expanded to other POS merchant locations. Signature-based debit cards are used with either a PIN for online transactions or a signature for off-line transactions. They are used at ATMs and many more merchant locations. These debit cards may carry the MasterCard or VISA logo.

The payment process for card-based systems can be conducted either online or offline. With both transactions, funds are debited from the customer's bank account. An online transaction requires a PIN to authorize a transaction. The funds to pay for the transaction are immediately debited from the cardholder's bank account.

**Did You Know ...**

The number of consumers using debit cards to make in-store purchases increased from 48 percent in 1999 to 57 percent in 2003 (for PIN-based purchases) and from 42 percent to 54 percent (for signature-based debit purchases).

*(American Bankers Association and Dove Consulting)*

An offline debit card transaction uses the VISA and MasterCard credit card network to route the transaction to the issuing bank. Offline transactions require a customer signature rather than a PIN. Although the offline transaction is authorized online, the cardholder's checking account is not charged until the processing center makes the settlement for the transaction, which usually takes 24 to 48 hours. Exhibit 5.8 presents the basic steps in processing point-of-sale online and offline debit card transactions.

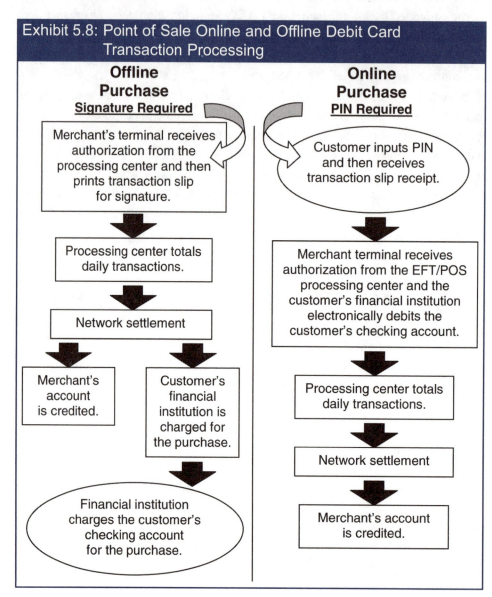

Exhibit 5.8: Point of Sale Online and Offline Debit Card Transaction Processing

## STORED VALUE CARDS

Stored value cards are sold by a wide variety of merchants, company payroll offices, and service providers, such as local mass transit systems. The card stores a specific value or amount of funds. When used the value is reduced by the amount of the purchase. Some cards are for one-time use, whereas others may be reloaded with value. Stored value cards are safer to use than cash or a check.

| Customer Service Tip: Debit Card Tips |
| --- |

- Check your statements immediately upon receipt. Make sure you made all listed card transactions.

- Keep your receipts. Check the receipts against your statement.

- If your card is lost, stolen, or subject to fraudulent use, immediately contact your bank.

- Memorize your PIN number. Never store the PIN number with your ATM or debit card.

- Know your cash withdrawal and purchase limits.

## SMART CARDS

Smart cards are an emerging card-based technology. Having the look of a debit card, the smart card contains a microprocessor chip that allows the card to compute and communicate information and store cardholder data. Potentially, one smart card, which can be coded to prevent fraudulent use, can function as a debit card, credit card, stored value card, driver's license, and medical ID card.

## EFT TRANSACTIONS AND THE AUTOMATED CLEARING HOUSE

The Automated Clearing House Association Network, begun in the 1970s to process large volumes of check transactions, was followed by the National Automated Clearing House (NACHA). NACHA develops the operating rules and business practices for electronic payments nationally. Electronic Fund Transfers (EFTs) are facilitated by the ACH network. The Federal Reserve Wire Network (FED wire) is another method used in electronic payments.

*Electronic Fund Transfers Using the ACH Network*

| *Direct Deposit Credits* | *Pre-Authorized Debits* |
| --- | --- |
| Payroll payments | Club or association dues |
| Social security payments | Utility payments |
| Interest payments | Insurance premiums |
| Pension payments | Tax payments |
| Dividend payments | Loan and credit card payments |
| | Mortgage loan payments |

The bank originating the ACH transaction is the originating depository financial institution (ODFI), and the bank receiving the transaction is the receiving depository financial institution (RDFI). The customer directs the ODFI bank to originate the transfer (pre-authorized transfer). This transfer is batched with others and sent to ACH. Banks, small businesses, corporations, and

## Banker Profile

**B.A. Donelson**
*Chairman, First State Bank, Stratford, Texas*

In 2003, B.A. Donelson was awarded the ABA Bruning Award, which recognizes individuals who dedicate their careers to providing credit and financial guidance to farmers, ranchers, and agricultural bankers. At the time of the award, he noted, "The greatest satisfaction I've had is in getting to know the people—both employees and customers."

B.A. Donelson rose through the ranks at First State Bank. In 36 years of banking, he has been a loan officer, trust officer, executive vice president, and president. "I'm not an X's and O's kind of guy. I am more interested in the people side of banking than the technical side." This belief helped Mr. Donelson start two community foundations, one that funds community improvement projects and another that funds innovative teaching opportunities.

Mr. Donelson is a graduate of Texas Tech University, Oklahoma Intermediate School of Banking, Southwestern Graduate School of Banking, and Harvard Senior Bank Officer School of Banking.

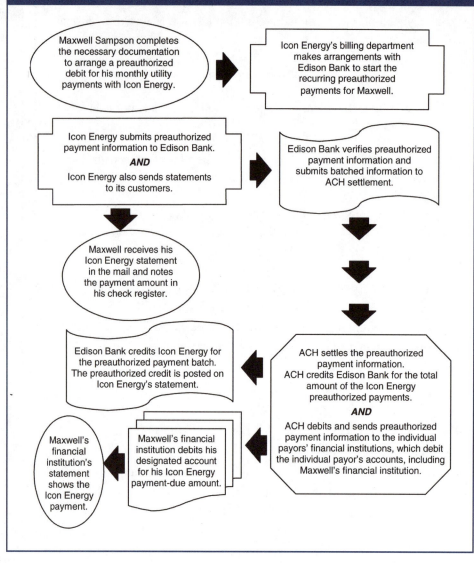

**Exhibit 5.9: Process Flow for Preauthorized Payment**

Maxwell Sampson completes the necessary documentation to arrange a preauthorized debit for his monthly utility payments with Icon Energy.

Icon Energy's billing department makes arrangements with Edison Bank to start the recurring preauthorized payments for Maxwell.

Icon Energy submits preauthorized payment information to Edison Bank.
**AND**
Icon Energy also sends statements to its customers.

Edison Bank verifies preauthorized payment information and submits batched information to ACH settlement.

Maxwell receives his Icon Energy statement in the mail and notes the payment amount in his check register.

Edison Bank credits Icon Energy for the preauthorized payment batch. The preauthorized credit is posted on Icon Energy's statement.

ACH settles the preauthorized payment information.
ACH credits Edison Bank for the total amount of the Icon Energy preauthorized payments.
**AND**
ACH debits and sends preauthorized payment information to the individual payors' financial institutions, which debit the individual payor's accounts, including Maxwell's financial institution.

Maxwell's financial institution's statement shows the Icon Energy payment.

Maxwell's financial institution debits his designated account for his Icon Energy payment-due amount.

government agencies, for various kinds of transactions noted, send batches to ACH. It then sorts, settles, and sends credits and debits to the RDFI for credit or debit to customer accounts (see exhibit 5.9).

## INTERNET BANKING PAYMENTS

Internet banking is an electronic delivery system of banking services. Through Internet banking sites, customers, using personal computers with internet access, can review account balances, make transfers between accounts, pay bills, order checks, and make online loan applications. Paying recurring bills is a service that uses ACH network capabilities.

Generally, a customer sets up a list of payees, companies, or persons the customer regularly pays and instructs the bank to make payments. Information may include: company's or person's name, accounts receiving the funds for deposit, the receiving depository's name, account from which funds are drawn, payment amount and date, payee's name, transaction type, and origination date. Businesses also may require the account or customer number.

The ODFI receives the customer's internet instructions for payment, consolidates all such payments going to particular company payees (such as utility companies), provides the payees with a list of amounts and payors included in the consolidated payment. Payments are then sent through the ACH to the RDFI, or if needed, checks are printed and mailed to the payees. The transaction will be listed on the originating customer's statement.

# CASH AS A PAYMENT SYSTEM

Cash is one payment system in our economy that everyone uses to some degree. Printing and distributing cash begins with the U.S. Treasury Bureau of Engraving and Printing. After printing, cash is processed through the Federal Reserve System to consumers and eventually back to the Federal Reserve Bank for destruction. For banks that are not members of the Federal Reserve System, distribution to and from correspondent banks serves as the intermediary connection (see exhibit 5.10).

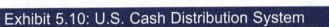

## Exhibit 5.10: U.S. Cash Distribution System

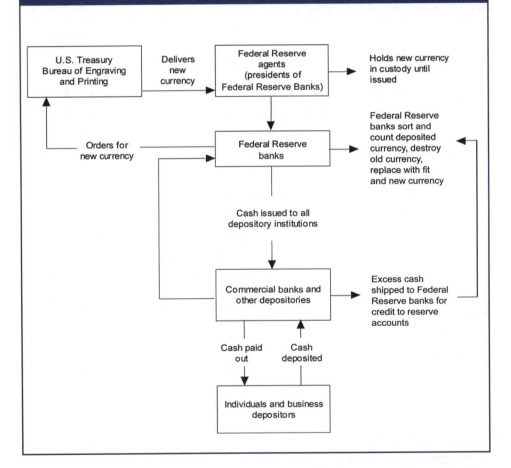

Currency shipments are prepared for and received in a **dual custody** procedure. When cash is received by the Fed, it is processed through high-speed sorting machines. Unfit currency is removed from circulation and shredded at the Federal Reserve Bank. Mutilated currency is routed to the U.S. Treasury for destruction.

**Did You Know ...**

In 2003, an estimated 1.5 billion bills were presented electronically—an increase of 300% over the previous year.

*(Council for Electronic Billing and Payment)*

**Dual custody (dual control)**—A security technique that uses two or more separate entities or people operating together to protect sensitive functions, information, or assets. Both entities are equally responsible for physically protecting materials involved in vulnerable transactions.

# LAWS AND REGULATIONS

The federal government has enacted a number of laws governing payment systems. Federal bank regulatory agencies have the responsibility to supervise and enforce these laws.

## BANK SECRECY ACT

The Bank Secrecy Act (BSA) places strict reporting requirements on banks for deposits, withdrawals or exchange of money that appears suspicious or exceeds $10,000. BSA also covers wire transfers through the travel rule, which requires banks with a wire transfer of $3,000 or more to include complete originator and beneficiary information with payment orders as the wire travels through the funds transfer systems.

## USA PATRIOT ACT

This law placed policy requirements into BSA regulations that grant permission to financial institutions to share specific information about people engaged in terrorist acts or money laundering activities. Financial institutions share this information with regulatory authorities and law enforcement officials.

## REGULATION E

Electronic Fund Transfer Act, Regulation E, provides protection and procedures for customers and banks transacting preauthorized EFT payments, as well as ATM and POS transactions. The regulation details the disclosures required when transactions are initiated, transferred, and are recurring. It also outlines customer and bank responsibilities for reporting and resolving disputed or erroneous electronic transactions and stop payments on preauthorized payments.

Regulation E places different limits on liability for unauthorized transfers, depending on how promptly the consumer notifies his or her bank. If a bank is notified within two days of learning of a loss or theft of a debit card, the consumer's liability for unauthorized transactions is no more than the amount of the unauthorized transaction, up to a total of $50. Waiting longer can add to the consumer's liability.

## REGULATION J

The Collection of Checks and Funds Transfers, Regulation J, covers check collection and returns, cash, and noncash items processed through Federal Reserve Banks, as well as funds transfers through Fedwire. Its purpose is to provide rules for collecting and returning items and settling balances.

## REGULATION CC

Expedited Funds Availability Act, implemented by Regulation CC, requires depository institutions to make funds deposited into transaction accounts available for withdrawal within a set availability schedule. The availability of the deposited items is based on the type of check involved (government, cashiers', or personal check) and on whether the check is local or nonlocal.

Banks may hold funds beyond the general funds availability schedule under certain "safeguard" exceptions, including funds in excess of $5,000 and funds from checks the bank has reasonable cause to believe are uncollectible. If a bank invokes an exception, it must notify the customer in writing.

Regulation CC requires the depositary to ensure its endorsement is placed in the proper location on the check; that the customer does not interfere with the area designated for the depositary's endorsement; and that the depositary accepts a returned check, even if delayed, because of improper placement of the endorsement or a customer obscured the endorsement.

Regulation CC was amended to include rules for Check 21. The rules require banks to

- educate customers about substitute checks and provide special customer notices in certain situations

- provide warranties and indemnities to protect the parties handling substitute checks

- establish a process by which customers may receive an expedited recredit of amounts paid if they believe a substitute check they received was incorrectly charged to their account

## Uniform Commercial Code (UCC)

The UCC sets up fair practice standards in commercial transactions. Individual states decide whether they will adopt the UCC standards. Article 3, Negotiable Instruments, and Article 4, Bank Deposits and Collections, of the UCC focus on the standards and definitions pertaining to negotiable items, such as checks, including endorsements and holder-in-due course actions, liabilities of all parties, and rules for presentment.

## SUMMARY

- A check is a negotiable instrument involving three parties: the person writing the check (drawer), the person to whom the check is written (payee), and the bank that holds the checking account (drawee). Articles 3 and 4 of the Uniform Commercial Code establish the legal requirements for negotiable instruments. Negotiable instruments are payable to the bearer or to order, contain an unconditional or promise to pay a fixed amount of money on demand or at a definite time, and are written and signed by the drawer.

- Besides personal and business checks, banks provide cashier's checks, teller checks, and certified checks.

- The check payment process begins when a check is written by the drawer on his or her account at a bank. The person in possession of a check is the holder. Individuals, businesses and banks can accept checks without liability for claims and defenses if they are a holder in due course.

   After the check is written, the next step in the check payment process is for the payee to accept the check. What the payee intends to do with the check depends on how it is endorsed. Principal types of endorsements are blank, special, and restrictive. The bank also endorses the check.

- The endorsed check is then accepted by a depositary bank. A bank is required to honor a check that is properly payable. Failing to do so, the bank could be liable to the customer for wrongful dishonor. A bank will pay an on-us check and may cash a check drawn on another bank, which carries more risk. Once a check is accepted by the depositary bank for cash, payment, or deposit, it is processed for collection. Checks are proofed, encoded, read (captured), sorted (as on-us, local, and nonlocal checks), batched, and, with a cash letter, presented to the drawee through the selected clearing arrangement (direct presentment, correspondent bank, clearing house, or Federal Reserve bank).

- The drawee receives checks for in-clearing capture. In preparing the checks, the full MICR line is captured. Data from capture runs are stored throughout the day and are posted to accounts at the end. Checks rejected during posting are exception items requiring special handling. Checks are sorted daily in bundles by statement cycle and filed. Once a month, customers receive account statements either with paper checks or with check images.

- The Check Clearing for the 21st Century Act (Check 21) created the substitute check. Banks in the clearing and payment chain can convert a paper check into an electronic image file for transfer and can reconvert the file back into a paper substitute check for further processing. The substitute check is the legal equivalent of the original paper check. Check 21 is helping banks move to fully electronic check processing.

- Other electronic payments systems include debit cards, stored value cards, smart cards, payments made through the Internet, and electronic funds transfers through the ACH network, including preauthorized payments.

- Cash still is used for payments today. Minted and printed by the Bureau of Engraving, coin and currency is disbursed through the Federal Reserve to banks. Damaged currency is collected through the same channels for destruction.

- Many laws and regulations govern the bank payment process. They include the Bank Secrecy Act, the USA PATRIOT Act, Regulation E (Electronic Fund Transfer), Regulation J (The Collection of Checks and Funds Transfers), and Regulation CC (Expedited Funds Availability Act), as well as Articles 3 and 4 of the Uniform Commercial Code.

**Learning Check**

# SELF CHECK & REVIEW

1. What five things make a check negotiable?

2. Who are the parties to a check?

3. Explain the difference between a blank endorsement and a special endorsement. Discuss when each is used.

4. What are the differences among a cashier's check, teller's check, and certified check?

5. In check preparation, proof, and encoding, the depositary bank performs what functions?

6. Give some examples of checks that might be rejected from the normal posting process and require handling as exception items.

7. Identify some differences and similarities between signature-based and PIN-only debit cards.

8. Define dual custody and provide one example of where it is used.

9. In reference to a stolen or lost ATM card, explain the cardholder's and bank's liability for unauthorized transactions.

Resources

# ADDITIONAL RESOURCES

American Bankers Association, **www.aba.com**

Banking Basics, Federal Reserve Bank of Boston,
   **www.bos.frb.org/genpubs/publicat.htm#genpub4**

*Check 21, Check Clearing for the 21st Century*, An ABA Toolbox, American Bankers Association, 2004. **www.aba.com/members+only/legislative/check21_toolbox.htm**

Federal Reserve Board of Governors for information about regulations.
   **www.federalreserve.gov**.

*Payment Systems Today*, Washington, D.C.: American Bankers Association, 2002.

*Study of Consumer Payment Preferences*, Washington D.C.: American Bankers Association, 2003/2004 edition.

*The Life of a Check*, Federal Reserve Bank of Boston,
   **www.kc.frb.org/fed101/services/check_sim.cfm**

Uniform Commercial Code **www.law.cornell.edu/ucc/ucc.table.html**

# *Lending*

# What You Will Learn _____

*After studying this chapter, you should be able to*

- explain the importance of the lending function
- describe lending products and services for consumers, businesses, and the government
- identify electronic lending services and processes
- describe the steps in the lending process
- explain the board of directors' role in governing loan policy
- describe laws and regulations that relate to lending
- define the bolded key terms that appear in the text

The word "bank" is derived from the Italian word "banca." One of the earliest and common forms of banking was exchanging one type of coinage for another. Money changers performed this role, often at benches or tables set up in or around public buildings. The Italian word "banca" means bench or counter. As transactions became more complex than simple exchanges of money across a counter, the word *banca* was extended to the institution itself.

# Introduction

*In adjusting to the changing economic, competitive, and regulatory environment, banks have diversified their businesses towards more investments and sales of other financial products and services. Yet, lending to consumers and businesses remains a bank's primary function.*

*Since the dawn of civilization, borrowing and lending money have been ongoing financial activities. In the ruins of ancient Babylon, for example, archeologists discovered written evidence of a loan made to a farmer, who promised to make payment with interest after he harvested and sold his crops. In the Middle Ages, goldsmiths, who held their clients' precious metals and other valuables in safekeeping, often made loans against the value of those assets. In the eighteenth century, two Continental Congresses financed the American Revolution in part through loan certificates. The federal government has borrowed to finance every subsequent war involving the United States.*

*Banks offer a wide variety of loans to consumers, businesses, and governments that provide financial flexibility and affordability. For the quality of a bank's loan portfolio to meet the objectives and requirements of a bank's loan policy, it is important that the bank carefully adhere to the lending process. Taking the application, matching the financial need to the appropriate product, establishing the customer's creditworthiness, proper loan documentation and careful rendering of a loan decision are all important aspects of the loan process. Following the requirements of laws and related regulations also ensures that the bank is balancing its overall operating objectives for liquidity, safety, and income.*

## THE LENDING FUNCTION

The lending function is important for many reasons, including the following:

- Of the three cornerstones of banking—the deposit, payment, and lending functions—the lending function represents a significant source of income.

- Lending is one of the most traditional elements in the relationship between a bank and its customers.

- Under the Community Reinvestment Act, banks are evaluated and given a public rating on their record of helping to meet the credit needs of low- to moderate-income customers in their communities, including home mortgage, small business, and small farm lending.

- The quality of a bank's loan portfolio often is critical to its survival.

- Loans are essential to the functioning of a healthy U.S. economy, for example, supplying financing for business operations, home and vehicle purchases, and college tuition.

## SOURCES OF CREDIT

| Short-Term Loan | vs. | Long-Term Loan |
|---|---|---|
| Repayable in one year or less. For businesses, used to finance current assets, such as inventory or accounts receivable. | | Repayable in more than one year. For businesses, used to finance fixed assets, such as equipment and real estate. |

Today, credit is available from many sources. Consumers can apply for credit from a finance company. They can borrow from an insurance company against their life insurance policies or from a brokerage firm against the value of their securities. They also can buy merchandise on credit from a retailer, obtain a home mortgage or home equity loan from savings or commercial banks, or from their credit union. As savings depositors, consumers may use their account balances as security for loans.

Commercial enterprises also may choose among many sources of credit. Although commercial banks traditionally have been the primary source of business loans, in recent decades, competitors have emerged. Savings banks now offer **commercial loans**. Commercial financing firms are another source of credit to businesses. One business may extend credit to another by selling merchandise in advance of payment. Insurance companies often make large, long-term loans for constructing shopping centers, office buildings, and factories. Many large corporations offer consumer and commercial loans through in-house financing companies, such as General Motors' GMAC Financial Services and General Electric's G.E. Capital Corporation.

Instead of borrowing from financial institutions, many large corporations with excellent credit ratings borrow in the money markets by issuing unsecured, short-term promissory notes known as **commercial paper**.

Federal, state, and local governments use a wide variety of short- and long-term borrowing techniques to raise funds. Banks themselves often borrow directly from one another, use Fed Funds, or use the facilities of the Federal Reserve to obtain short-term credit.

**Commercial loan**—A loan to a business to meet short- or long-term needs.

**Commercial paper**— Short-term, unsecured promissory notes issued by major corporations of unquestioned credit standing as a means of borrowing.

## BANKS' ROLE AS LENDERS

Although there are many sources of credit available, banks are a most important lending source. They offer attractive rates due to their efficiencies and cost of funds structures.

Small and large businesses, governments, and consumers take advantage of the variety of loan products banks offer. A typical bank loan term may be as short as 30 days or as long as 30 years. Although some loans are secured by collateral, many loans are made on an unsecured basis, with the bank relying on the borrower's written promise to repay.

## Types of consumer loans

- personal
- automobile (direct and indirect)
- automobile leases
- mobile home
- recreational Vehicle
- marine (boat)
- home improvement
- home equity or second mortgages
- home equity lines of credit
- bank card credit
- non-card revolving credit
- education
- unsecured lines of credit

**Consumer loan**—A loan extended to consumers, either individually or jointly, primarily for the purpose of buying goods and services for personal use.

**Secured loan**—A loan in which the borrower has pledged some form of collateral to protect the lender in case of default.

# LOAN CATEGORIES

Banks divide their loans into categories for reporting to government agencies and for internal management in monitoring and planning. The major categories include:

- consumer loans
- business loans
- real estate loans
- government-sponsored loans

Different operations centers may manage some loan types. Home equity loans and home equity lines of credit often are managed by the consumer loan department. Many banks classify commercial loans by industry so they can monitor how much of their portfolio is committed in certain sectors of the economy, such as petroleum, agriculture, or aerospace. If problems in an industry develop, an astute banker will be aware of the number and size of affected loans and will act to limit the bank's exposure to the troubled industry.

## CONSUMER LOANS

The demand for consumer loans continues to grow, prompting banks to direct more of their attention to serving this profitable market. **Consumer loans** have proven attractive to banks for several reasons:

- Banks may compete with other types of financial institutions and non-bank lenders.
- Interest income contributes to bank profits.
- Consumer loans are part of full-service banking.
- Most consumer loans are repaid as agreed.
- Other bank services such as deposit products are cross-sold to build customer relationships.

To meet the diverse needs of this segment, banks offer a broad assortment of consumer loan products. Consumer loans fall into two broad categories: open-end (revolving) credit and closed-end (installment) loans.

### Open-End Credit

In an open-end (revolving) line of credit, a borrower may draw on funds for an agreed-upon period and amount. The balance may fluctuate from zero up to the credit line's maximum amount. Two examples of open-end credit are a home equity line of credit and a credit card.

A home equity line of credit is secured by the borrower's residence. Because a home equity line of credit is **secured**, the interest rate typically is lower than for other types of open-end credit, and interest paid usually is tax deductible. The customer may borrow money at any time prior to the stated maturity date up to the amount of the credit line. Funds may be used for any purpose, including home remodeling, paying off high interest rate loans, taking a vacation, or purchasing a new car.

Credit cards are a flexible source of credit. The cardholder can control how and when to use credit. Instead of obtaining a single lump-sum loan up front, as in a personal closed-end loan, the cardholder can use the credit line as needed to travel, entertain, or purchase merchandise—and make payment later. Due to ease of use, credit cards are a preferred customer credit choice.

The customer receives a monthly statement from the bank containing a description of the purchases made that month. The customer has the option to pay the entire balance, make a minimum payment, or pay some amount in between. A few states require banks to give the customer a period of time, called a grace period, to pay the balance. If the entire outstanding balance is paid before the payment due date, generally the customer is not charged a finance charge. Credit cards carry a high amount of risk for the bank, such as fraudulent charges and stolen cards. Also, credit card debt generally is unsecured. For these reasons, credit cards typically carry a higher interest rate than other types of credit.

### Closed-End Credit

Closed-end (installment) loans have a specified amount, maturity date, and number of payments with due dates. The borrower receives a lump sum up front. Payments usually are scheduled monthly. For payment, the bank may automatically debit the customer's deposit account or provide coupons. The customer sends the coupon and the payment to the bank where it is credited to the loan account.

When using an automatic preauthorized debit, the bank charges the customer's checking account for the loan payment amount. The payment then is shown on the customer's checking account statement.

Closed-end loans are secured or unsecured. A purchased car, for example, may secure an auto loan, and the bank may hold the car title until the loan is paid. In making these loans, banks rely on the borrower's ability to repay as agreed in a signed **promissory note**.

A home equity loan is a secured closed-end loan. Like a home equity line of credit, a home equity loan is secured by the borrower's residence. The interest paid typically is tax deductible. Whereas a home equity line of credit may be used as the borrower needs funds, a home equity loan is for a one-time borrowing need. Both home equity loans and home equity lines of credit may offer a fixed interest rate with a fixed monthly payment or a variable rate with a variable monthly payment.

## REAL ESTATE LOANS

Real estate loans can be for both consumer and business purposes. Banks are involved primarily in two areas of real estate financing: short-term construction loans and longer-term mortgage loans.

### Construction Loans

Often a real estate developer requires funds to purchase, demolish, and clear existing property and begin erecting a new structure such as a shopping mall, an office park, or a residential development complex. Consumers also use construction loans when building a home. A bank can write a construction loan to accommodate the developer and consumer.

Construction loans are relatively short-term, with maturities consistent with the construction period. The borrower makes periodic payments on the loan, and at the end of the term, the bank may convert the loan to a mortgage loan. Frequently, a

### Situation

John and Nancy are shopping for a home equity line of credit. They have some credit card bills to pay off and also want money available to remodel their basement. John and Nancy have checking, saving, and retirement accounts at several banks. They are considering consolidating all of their accounts with one bank, if they can find a bank that meets all of their needs.

**Promissory note**—A written document with the borrower's promise to pay a certain sum of money to the bank, with or without interest, on demand or on a fixed or determinable future date.

bank provides the construction loan and another bank or combination of banks extend mortgage credit when the project is completed.

### *Mortgage Loans*

A mortgage loan is a closed-end, long–term loan credit with terms up to 30 years. To secure the loan, the borrower pledges the property for collateral. Banks extend mortgage loans on homes, office buildings, apartment houses, and shopping centers. As closed-end loans, scheduled payments include both interest and principal. Gradually the loan balance is reduced over time as payments are made.

The **adjustable-rate**, or variable-rate, loan has made the mortgage lending market attractive to both borrowers and lenders. A lender, in accordance with the promissory note, may adjust the interest rate on the mortgage during the loan term as rate conditions change. If interest rates decline, the borrower benefits from the lower rate. Interest for adjustable-rate loans is based on an index, such as **prime rate** plus a percentage. As the index rate changes, so will the loan's interest rate. Terms for most adjustable rate mortgages are between 5 and 15 years. Mortgages must be paid off or refinanced at the end of the term.

The pricing and availability of home mortgage loans are based on the borrower's income and creditworthiness and the home or commercial property's appraised value. Because mortgage loans are secured by the home or commercial property, if the borrower is unable to make the payments, the lender may proceed with **foreclosure** and sell the property at auction to recover the loan's unpaid balance.

## COMMERCIAL LOANS

Commercial loans are one of the largest components of a bank's total loan portfolio. Banks offer a wide variety of commercial loan products to meet the diverse financing needs of businesses. A garden nursery, for example, may need a seasonal line of credit to finance purchases of plants and other gardening equipment each spring, whereas an airplane manufacturer may need a term loan to expand a manufacturing facility. Secured or unsecured, commercial loans typically are categorized by type and by maturity—that is, as either a short-term or long-term loan.

The following are some of the most common types of commercial loans.

| Loan Type | Description |
|---|---|
| Working capital loan | A short-term loan (typically 90 days) used to provide immediate funds for a one-time need. For example, a toy manufacturer needing to buy raw materials to make toys in time for the holiday season. |
| Working capital line of credit | Similar to a consumer line of credit, this line of credit provides businesses with funds for recurring credit needs periodically during the year. Banks often require that the credit line be fully paid within at least 30 days during business's annual operating cycle. Rates typically are variable and based on the prime rate. |

**Adjustable-rate mortgage loan**—A mortgage on which the rate is subject to periodic adjustment. The rate usually is tied to a widely published market rate of interest or index.

**Prime rate**—A base rate a bank establishes that reflects its determination of cost of funds, overhead, loan portfolio risk, profit objectives, and other relevant factors.

**Foreclosure**—A legal procedure undertaken to permit a creditor to sell property that is collateral for a defaulted loan.

**Historical Fact**

The variable rate mortgage, also known as the adjustable-rate mortgage, was first introduced in California in 1975.

*(American Bankers Association)*

| | |
|---|---|
| Term loan | With typical maturities of one to five years, a term loan is used to purchase fixed assets other than real estate. Generally the payment schedule is tied to the useful life of the asset. Plant equipment, for example, is financed over a longer period than personal computers. |
| Participation loan | Loan made to a single borrower and shared by two or more banks. Common in commercial lending, usually shared loans are made when the loan amount exceeds one bank's loan policy or legal lending limit. |
| Indirect or third party loan | Loans made to customers of dealerships, such as automobile or appliance dealers. Banks work directly with the dealers and obtain loan applications from customers who purchase their products. These loans are a source of new consumer business for banks. |
| Floor plan loan | Loans to a dealer to finance consumer goods for display and sale. The consumer goods, such as automobiles or appliances, are collateral for the loan. |
| Letter of credit | An instrument issued by a bank that substitutes the bank's credit for the credit of the buyer of goods. By substituting a bank's credit for its own credit, the buyer is not required to pay in advance. |
| Lease financing | An arrangement whereby the bank owns the collateral and leases it to the customer for a specified period and monthly payment. Depending on the lease terms, ownership may transfer to the customer when the lease ends. |

**Situation**

ABC Manufacturing Company received an unusually large order from a new customer. ABC typically has enough funds to purchase the raw materials needed to fill orders, but does not have the cash available to purchase all the materials for this order. It appears that the new customer will be placing large orders several times a year. ABC is wondering if a working capital line of credit could be a solution for its periodic financing needs.

## GOVERNMENT AS BORROWER AND LOAN SUPPORTER

Just as consumers and businesses do, state and local governments borrow from banks. Tax revenues may not always be enough to finance their need to purchase road equipment or police cars or to meet other **working capital** needs.

Consequently, a government entity will seek approval from its board or elected oversight body to obtain a bank loan for a specific purpose. Governments often finance terms similar to loans made to businesses. Banks may provide a short-term loan based on the government's anticipated tax revenues to pay off the loan.

A second area of government activity in lending is through sponsored or support programs. Governments often institute legislative mandates through loan programs that support and promote social and economic objectives, including:

- *Affordable housing.* Through loan subsidies and guarantees, federal agencies, such as the Veterans Benefit Administration (VA) and the Federal

**Working capital**—The liquid funds available to a business or government for its current needs. It is current assets less current liabilities.

**Did You Know ...**

Since its founding on July 30, 1953, the U.S. Small Business Administration has delivered about 20 million loans, loan guarantees, contracts, counseling sessions, and other forms of assistance to small businesses.

*(U.S. Small Business Administration)*

**Secondary mortgage market**—Transactions involving selling and purchasing existing mortgages. Mortgage loans originate in the primary mortgage market. The sale of those loans occurs in the secondary market.

Housing Administration (FHA), make mortgages available to people who are otherwise unable to afford them. States may subsidize mortgage programs for low-income or first-time buyers.

- *Access to higher education*. The federal government provides student loans through Sallie Mae, for example. Student loan programs offer low-interest loans or fully subsidized interest loans, with repayment deferred until after graduation.

- *Small business development*. The Small Business Administration (SBA) guarantees some of the repayment of loans made to qualified small businesses, thus transferring some of the risk from the lender to the SBA.

A third area of activity is through government-sponsored enterprises, such as the Federal National Mortgage Association (Fannie Mae) and the Federal Home Loan Mortgage Corporation (Freddie Mac), which play an important role in the mortgage lending market. Through the **secondary mortgage market**, Fannie Mae and Freddie Mac buy mortgage loans granted by mortgage lenders and issue mortgage-backed securities for sale to investors.

The Government National Mortgage Association (GNMA or Ginnie Mae), a government corporation within the Department of Housing and Urban Development) guarantees the principal and interest of pools of residential loans insured by the FHA or guaranteed by the VA. GNMA-approved lenders that have a pool of such loans with similar rates and maturities can issue securities in the amount of the loan pool.

## THE LENDING PROCESS

Although banks differ in their credit standards and policies, all follow a general lending process (exhibit 6.1) that includes the loan application and interview, investigation, documentation, and management.

Every step in the lending process has a cost and risk to the bank. Larger loans require more detailed investigation, documentation, and management than smaller

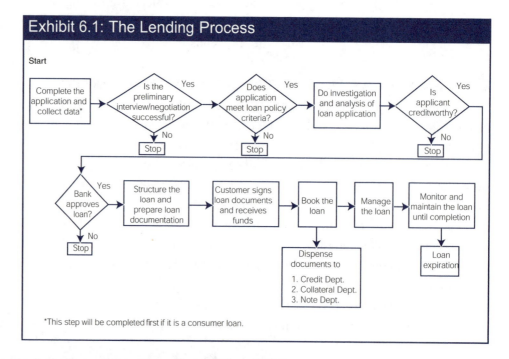

Exhibit 6.1: The Lending Process

loans. Lenders assess each request in terms of its risk, cost, and profitability, and apply the lending process according to that assessment.

Regardless of the type or size of credit, a proper lending process helps protect the bank against loss. There is, however, always some risk in lending. No formula or system positively guarantees full and timely repayment of loan principal and interest.

## THE APPLICATION AND INTERVIEW

The lending process begins with the loan application and the loan interview. The goal of this step is for the bank to understand the borrower's needs, gather initial supporting documentation, and assist the borrower in selecting the most appropriate loan product.

To gather preliminary information, most banks have the borrower complete a loan application. This information may be discussed during the loan interview, which may take place in person, over the phone, over the Internet, or through a third party.

The loan request's nature and level of detail determines the interview process. A loan officer may meet several times with a business owner, who is seeking a complicated commercial loan, in order to understand the company's financial situation. However, a car dealer (a third party) will interview a customer for a consumer automobile loan. Exhibit 6.2 lists some questions typically asked of a loan applicant during a loan interview.

After completing the application and interview process, the bank decides whether to continue with the loan request, ask for additional information, deny the loan request, or direct the customer to other financing sources. If the loan request is inconsistent with bank lending policy, it should be rejected. Loan

**Banker Profile**

**Richard G. Dorner**
*President and CEO, Ann Arbor Commerce Bank, Ann Arbor, Michigan*

In 1990, Richard Dorner was named the founding President & CEO of Ann Arbor Commerce Bank. His career prepared him for this undertaking. Starting at a community bank, Dorner moved on to regional banks for a diversified career in business lending, private banking, auditing, operations, branch management, credit card development, human resources, and marketing.

Mr. Dorner is very much involved in his community. "I believe bankers and their banks should serve a leadership role, not only in their profession, but also in their community." To that end, he serves on a number of civic boards in Ann Arbor.

Dorner promotes customer service in his bank. "Take care of the customer and the numbers take care of themselves." He also supports continuing education, through the American Bankers Association Professional Development Council and Commercial Lending School. "ABA does the best job in providing training for bankers."

---

### Exhibit 6.2: Sample Loan Interview Questions

How much money do you need?

How did you arrive at your loan request?

How will you use the loan proceeds?

What financing needs are you projecting?

What terms are you requesting?

How did you decide what terms are best for you?

How will you repay the loan?

What is your income?

Will personal assets be pledged as security for the loan?

Who owns the collateral?

Where is the collateral located?

How is the collateral valued?

Are there guarantors? If so, who are they, what is their relationship to you, and what is their financial strength?

What banks do you currently use?

Have you approached other banks with the loan request?

Do you have loans outstanding with other creditors?

What is the nature and extent of these loans?

**Did You Know ...**

Most credit reporting agencies provide credit scores, fraud detection, social security number discrepancies, and legal notices such as liens, lawsuits, and encumbrances.

officers must be aware of bank policy and lending regulations during this phase of the lending process. Consumer protection laws, such as the Equal Credit Opportunity Act and the Truth in Lending Act, impose specific requirements on lenders, beginning with loan solicitation and application.

### Lending Over the Internet

The Internet has revolutionized the delivery of loan products. Through interactive Web sites, banks offer both consumer and commercial loans to prospective borrowers across the country. Today, the entire lending process—from application to approval—can be conducted online. Most bank Web sites offer tools for customers to determine what type of loan they need, compare different loan terms and interest rates, calculate the loan payments, and determine whether they qualify for a loan. Then, the customer can complete and submit an online application and receive word on the loan request shortly thereafter. If the loan is made, the customer also can make the loan payments online or direct the bank to periodically withdraw the payment from a deposit account.

## THE INVESTIGATION

A credit investigation is conducted to evaluate a borrower's ability to repay debt. When making credit decisions, banks obtain and evaluate available information and balance this information against the potential cost of making the loan. An incomplete credit investigation can increase the bank's risk for loan loss.

### Consumer Credit Investigations

Credit investigations usually consist of verifying the applicant's employment, income, credit history, and existing debt. Most lenders subscribe to a basic standard when credit is evaluated, especially when analyzing the creditworthiness of consumer loan applicants. The standard is known as the five Cs of credit: character, capacity, collateral, capital, and conditions (see exhibit 6.3)

A first step in credit investigation is to check appropriate bank records. Banks also rely on credit reporting agencies as a source of information. Credit reporting

**Types of credit information**
- credit history
- income
- employment
- residence
- collateral value

**Sources of credit information**
- application
- bank's internal files
- directly from other financial institutions
- credit reporting agencies
- public records

---

**Exhibit 6.3: Five C's of Credit**

*Character:* The borrower's willingness and determination to repay the loan. Usually considered the most important of the Five C's of Credit.

*Capacity:* The borrower's ability to repay the loan—that is, to generate enough funds and manage those funds to make loan payments.

*Collateral:* The assets the borrower pledges as a source of loan repayment in case of loan default. It usually is viewed as a secondary source of repayment only.

*Capital:* Other assets that may be used to pay the loan. For commercial borrowers, capital often consists of the equity owner's have in the business.

*Conditions:* External factors that may affect the borrower's ability to repay the loan, such as a change in employment.

---

agencies maintain detailed records on consumers' credit histories and activities. These agencies can provide a bank with daily input on new loan applications, repayments, rejected requests for credit, and delinquencies. Information the applicant provides is cross-checked with agency reports to determine its accuracy.

If a bank declines a consumer loan request on the basis of unfavorable credit information, the bank is required to inform the consumer that a credit report was used to make the decision. Creditors also must provide the reason for the denial or a statement that the consumer may request the reason.

Banks often rely on credit scoring to improve the efficiency and fairness of a credit investigation. A credit score relies on a mathematical formula to determine the likelihood that a borrower will repay a loan, given adverse circumstances. Many factors are considered, including amount and type of outstanding credit, repayment patterns, and credit history.

Credit scoring also is used with electronic underwriting. The electronically generated score determines whether the applicant profile falls within the bank's acceptable range. This procedure allows the bank to process large numbers of loan applications and refers only those that fall into a pre-defined "gray" area to a loan officer for further evaluation.

### Business Credit Investigations

Because of the larger loan amounts and complexities of commercial loans, the investigative process is more detailed for commercial loans than for consumer loans. Many sources of information are used, including:

- *Loan analysis (credit) department.* Credit files maintained on each business account and borrower provide a history of the bank's relationships with its customers. They contain reports of interviews; copies of correspondence; financial statements supplied by the borrower; internal memos, including previous credit analyses; and data on average balances, previous loans, overdrafts, and loan approval documentation.

- *Credit agencies.* Credit agencies such as Dun & Bradstreet publish regular business reports, which provide current financial information on a company and include the firm's history, management structure, products, scope of operations, and borrowing history with suppliers.

- *Suppliers.* Because most merchandise is sold with credit terms, it is important that a bank know a company's track record in paying its suppliers. This information can be found in credit agency reports or through direct contact with suppliers.

- *Internet.* A growing number of companies have their own Web sites. These sites often contain annual reports and information about a company's products, services, and history that may be helpful in the investigation.

- *Tax returns and financial statements.* Tax returns and financial statements are a good source of information about growth and earnings, industry trends, and repayment sources.

## Situation

Cindy and George both have stable jobs that provide them with a comfortable income. Three years ago, they finished paying off loans for their children's education. With the exception of a home mortgage, which they have paid monthly for 20 years, they are debt-free. When Cindy and George applied to a bank for a home-improvement loan, they were surprised to have their request rejected on the basis of a negative credit report from a credit reporting agency. They contacted the credit reporting agency and discovered that the college loans they had paid were incorrectly listed as being delinquent. After their credit report was corrected, their loan request was approved.

## Credit files contain:

- copies of loan documents
- financial information
- credit inquires and reports
- collateral information
- correspondence and memos
- other borrower information such as annual reports for businesses

## Sample loan documentation for a home equity line of credit

- promissory note with disclosure of credit
- mortgage agreement (deed of trust)
- insurance binder
- title search
- appraisal
- flood determination (flood plain check)
- rescission notice

**Security interest**—The right a lender has to obtain possession of the collateral, sell it, and retain the proceeds (up to the amount of the remaining debt) in the event the borrower is unable to repay the loan.

# LOAN DOCUMENTATION

Loan documentation begins at the time of application. After loan approval, loan documentation involves obtaining and completing all necessary forms to secure the lender's interest and comply with federal and state requirements.

The purpose of loan documentation is to have a written, legally enforceable understanding of the lender's and borrower's obligations under the lending arrangement. Failure to properly document the loan could make the loan agreement unenforceable. Proper loan documentation is an important responsibility for the lender because it helps to

- protect the bank's investment
- ensure that the borrower understands the loan terms
- prevent litigation against the bank
- prevent loan loss for the bank
- prevent compliance violation penalties

Loan documentation is a detailed process. All documents required by federal and state law must be completed. The loan officer ensures that all sections are complete, calculations and collateral description are correct, signatures and dates are obtained and witnessed (if necessary), and any alterations are initialed by all parties.

Lenders also use documentation to meet their obligation to inform borrowers about the major components of the loan. Federal law, most notably the Truth-in-Lending Act, requires that consumer borrowers be informed of the repayment program, annual percentage rate (APR), total cost of the loan, consequences of not paying on time, and information about collateral. Lenders provide disclosure forms and other informative documents during this stage.

The documentation required is dependent on the loan type and the bank's location. Different types of loans require different types of documentation. Documentation requirements also vary from bank to bank and from state to state.

## *Collateral*

The documentation of collateral is governed by many federal and state statutes, in part because of the various assets that can be pledged as security for a loan. Government obligations, securities, savings account balances, residential or commercial property, and vehicles are among the assets that can be used as collateral for a loan.

A bank can take physical possession of some types of collateral, such as stocks, bonds, or certificates of deposit. If so, the bank provides for safekeeping and control of the collateral.

Other types of collateral, such as a vehicle or house, cannot be held by the bank. Therefore, the bank's right to the collateral must be in writing, rather than actual possession. A security agreement is the standard document for establishing that right. A security agreement creates or provides a **security interest** in the collateral. State law will dictate how the security agreement must be registered and made available to the public.

Although it should never be the sole reason for approving a loan, collateral may strengthen a borrowing situation. A bank does not succeed by foreclosing, repossessing, or seizing real estate, automobiles, or factories. Usually, a bank incurs additional costs associated with foreclosure or repossession.

## LOAN DECISION

In deciding about whether to approve an application for credit, a bank evaluates all the information collected—from credit reports to financial statements analyses. If at any time during the lending process it becomes clear that the purpose, amount, or terms of the loan do not meet the bank's lending standards, then the loan request should be rejected. The bank may want to offer an alternative credit arrangement or direct the applicant to another lender.

If the decision is made to reject the loan, the bank is required, under the Equal Credit Opportunity Act and Regulation B, to provide the applicant with a written "adverse action" notice explaining the reasons for the denial of the request.

## LOAN ADMINISTRATION

The loan is finalized when all documents are complete, appropriate forms are signed, funds disbursed, and documentation filed. At this point, the loan moves into the administration phase. Loan administration includes

- mailing regular statements

- receiving and posting agreed-upon payments

- maintaining current address information

- ensuring that the bank's security interest is recorded, filed, and returned to the bank

- answering customer inquiries

- reporting the loan to various credit reporting agencies

- maintaining files and documentation for review and examination by internal and external auditors and by regulatory agencies

- taking the loan off the books when the final payment is received

After it has been approved and placed in the bank's loan portfolio, the bank monitors the loan to ensure it does not become a problem loan; that is, a loan in which the borrower is not living up to the terms of the loan agreement. For business loans, the loan officer monitors the company's financial performance and usually maintains contact with the company to stay informed about developments that could affect loan repayment. Consumer loans also are monitored for signs that the loan is becoming a problem.

## LOAN REVIEW AND ASSET RECOVERY

Because interest income on loans represents a large source of bank revenue and the loan portfolio quality is vital for overall asset quality within the bank, loan losses and underperforming loans are a source of serious concern to stockholders and directors.

**Historical Fact**

The Tax Reform Act of 1986, which made interest on home equity loans up to $100,000 tax deductible for most borrowers, opened up even wider the rapidly growing field of home equity loans. Now home equity loans and home equity lines of credit are significant loan types in consumer loan portfolios.

*(American Bankers Association)*

**Loan review**—The function of examining loan documents to ensure accuracy, completeness, and conformity with the bank's loan policies and regulatory requirements.

**Loan review** gives management and directors assurance that

- lending officers have stayed within their authority
- lending policies and procedures have been followed
- the investigation and analysis process was adequate
- all necessary documentation on each loan has been obtained and properly filed

If the size of the bank's portfolio warrants, the review may cover unsecured and secured loans, loans made previously, and new loans.

Inevitably, some loans become problem loans. In such cases, asset recovery departments help prevent losses by taking timely action to collect late payments and, if necessary, by restructuring the terms of a loan for the benefit of both bank and borrower. Asset recovery officers watch for any indications of poorly performing loans. They examine all loans that have late payments, identify existing or potential problems, and recommend corrective action, including a potential increase in the bank's loan loss reserve.

---

### Customer Service Tip: Credit Warning Signs

- paying only the minimum mandatory amount month after month
- being out of cash constantly
- being late in making important payments, such as rent or mortgage
- taking longer and longer to pay off balances
- borrowing from one lender to pay another

---

# LOAN POLICY

As the governing body of the bank, the board of directors, along with the bank's chief financial officers and credit policy officers, establishes the bank's loan policy and oversees the bank's lending function.

A loan policy contains all the information applicable to the bank's lending practices. As the guiding document for all bank employees, it covers areas such as:

- the organization of the bank's lending function
- lending objectives
- loan criteria and standards
- loan risk rating standards
- levels of loan authority
- review and charge-off procedures
- policy on loans to bank officers and directors

The board of directors reviews and approves the loan policy annually. Directors, usually through membership on a loan committee, are actively involved in the following loan activities:

- determining the types of loans the bank will consider or refuse to make
- tightening overall credit standards when conditions warrant

**Collection and Recovery Objectives**
- maintain delinquencies and losses within acceptable limits
- generate loss recovery at desired levels
- counsel clients who have difficulty managing debt
- ensure adherence to bank objectives
- manage collection and recovery efficiently

- establishing and monitoring legal lending limits as well as minimum loan amounts

- determining policies that define loan collateral and loan maturities, outline maximum lending to certain business sectors, and set standards for down payments on automobiles or residences

- assigning lending authority to the bank's loan officers so that they know the maximum amount they can approve individually and the combinations of higher authority needed for larger amounts

- authorizing loans above a stipulated amount, that is loans that exceed the authority of any combination of officers' lending authority

- reviewing the bank's portfolio of outstanding loans to ensure that the bank is meeting the credit needs of its customers and community in compliance with the Community Reinvestment Act

- conducting periodic reviews (audits) of the bank's loan portfolio to ensure proper procedures are followed and undue risks are not taken

# LEGAL REQUIREMENTS

State banking departments and federal agencies, such as the Office of the Comptroller of the Currency, the Federal Deposit Insurance Corporation, and the Office of Thrift Supervision ensure that loans comply with applicable regulations and periodically monitor the quality of bank loan portfolios.

Bank lending is especially subject to regulation. There are laws and regulations to ensure depositors' funds are lent wisely, borrowers are given appropriate information, credit applicants are not improperly discriminated against, loans are made to the community, and loans to bank "insiders" are restricted.

Banks are limited as to the maximum amount they can lend to any single borrower. Instead, banks are encouraged to offer many borrowers the benefit of lending programs. The requirement also enables banks to participate with other banks when offering large loans.

## Equal Credit Opportunity Act (Regulation B)

The Equal Credit Opportunity Act (ECOA) of 1974 (Regulation B) prohibits lenders from denying a loan based on personal characteristics or conduct unrelated to credit-worthiness. Specifically, lenders are prohibited from discriminating against credit applicants on the basis of age, race, color, religion, national origin, sex, marital status, or receipt of income from public assistance programs. Regulation B requires lenders to give consumer applicants in writing the reason a loan application was rejected or a statement that they may request the reason. Similar rules apply for business loans.

## Truth in Lending Act (Regulation Z)

The Truth in Lending Act (Regulation Z), a consumer protection law, applies to loans "primarily for personal, family, or household purposes" and not commercial loans. There are times, however, when a loan made to a commercial customer could be construed as a personal loan and thus subject to the regulation.

Regulation Z prescribes uniform methods for computing the cost of credit, for disclosing credit terms, and for resolving errors on certain types of credit accounts. Disclosures for these loans include the cost to the consumer for the credit (the finance charge, the **annual percentage rate**, and the calculations used to derive these), the credit terms, the consumer's right to rescind in certain types of credit transactions (like home equity loans), and the consumer's fair credit billing rights (for open-ended credit).

**Annual percentage rate (APR)**—The finance charge expressed as an annual percentage of the funds borrowed. It results from an equation that considers the amount financed, the finance charge, and the term of the loan. APR allows a comparison of credit costs regardless of the dollar amount of the costs or the length of time over which payments are made.

**Redlining**—Excluding potential borrowers because they are from a certain geographic area, regardless of whether they otherwise meet all other criteria of creditworthiness.

## THE COMMUNITY REINVESTMENT ACT (REGULATION BB)

Enacted in 1977, The Community Reinvestment Act (CRA) addresses what Congress perceived to be unfair treatment of prospective borrowers by financial institutions on the basis of arbitrary considerations, such as geographic location. For example, some institutions were accused of **redlining**.

CRA affirms that every financial institution has an obligation, consistent with safe and sound practice, to help meet the credit needs of its entire community, including individuals and businesses in low- and moderate-income neighborhoods. Although CRA is often thought of as a consumer-related law, commercial loans also are taken into account when assessing a bank's compliance efforts.

CRA gives regulatory agencies the authority to assess a financial institution's record of meeting the needs of its entire community and then take that record into account in evaluating its future applications for mergers, acquisitions, and branches. To be in compliance with CRA, banks must demonstrate that they are lending actively in their communities, including low- and moderate-income areas.

## LOANS TO BANK INSIDERS (REGULATION O)

Regulation O implements the insider transaction restrictions of the Federal Reserve Act, and later the Financial Institutions Regulatory and Interest Rate Control Act of 1978. Regulation O places tight restrictions on Federal Reserve member banks extending credit to its executive officers, directors, and principal shareholders. FDIC regulations implement Regulation O provisions for banks that are not members of the Federal Reserve.

## HOME MORTGAGE DISCLOSURE ACT (REGULATION C)

Regulation C implements the Home Mortgage Disclosure Act (HMDA). HMDA requires banks to keep records of mortgage and home improvement mortgage lending activity by geographical area. The purpose of the law is to allow the public to determine whether banks are serving the housing credit needs of the neighborhoods and communities in which they are located.

## REAL ESTATE SETTLEMENT PROCEDURES ACT (REGULATION X)

Real Estate Settlement Procedures Act (RESPA) (Regulation X) of the Department of Housing and Urban Development (HUD) provides borrowers with information about expenses involved in residential real estate settlement processes. Under RESPA, good faith estimate of closing costs and HUD-1 settlement statement disclosures generally are required at the time of loan application and closing, respectively. RESPA also contains broad prohibitions against kickbacks and unearned fees. For example, a bank cannot accept a fee for services in connection with the settlement of a mortgage loan, unless the bank provided the services itself.

## FAIR CREDIT REPORTING ACT

The Fair Credit Reporting Act, passed in 1970, ensures fair and accurate credit reporting and protects consumers' rights to privacy concerning their credit reports. The act was amended in 1996 and again in 2003 by the Fair and Accurate Credit Transactions Act, with one objective being to increase the accuracy of credit reports. FCRA amendments provide for one free credit report per year from credit reporting agencies and allow consumers access to credit scores at a reasonable fee. Also, any bank that may submit negative information to a national credit reporting agency must give consumers a one-time written notice that they have done so or may do so.

Banks are prohibited from reporting inaccurate information if the furnisher of the information knows or has reasonable cause to believe the information was inaccurate. Banks must investigate claims that the information they furnished was inaccurate. FCRA requires banks involved in risk-based pricing to provide special notices when they respond to applicants with a counteroffer containing terms that are less favorable than originally offered.

## THE FAIR DEBT COLLECTION PRACTICES ACT

Enacted in 1977, The Fair Debt Collection Practices Act eliminates abusive and deceptive practices in credit collection without putting reputable debt collectors at an unfair disadvantage. The Federal Trade Commission has been given the authority to enforce the act. There are no regulations that implement it.

## BANK LENDING LIMITS

The purpose of bank lending limits is to prevent a bank from placing too much of its capital in loans to any one borrower. Placing limits on loans to a single borrower safeguards the depositor's funds by spreading a bank's loans among a larger group of borrowers. In 1982, the Garn-St Germain Depository Institutions Act imposed new lending limits. The Office of the Comptroller of the Currency (OCC) issued regulations to implement the requirements of the act. The Office of Thrift Supervision (OTS) published rules that adopted the national bank limits.

# SUMMARY

- Loans contribute a significant portion of a bank's income. Therefore, the profitability of any bank depends to a large extent on the quality of its loan portfolio. Bank loans also serve a valuable economic need, providing an essential source of financing for individuals, businesses, and the government.
- Most banks divide loan operations into categories that reflect their primary customer bases: consumer loans, commercial loans, real estate loans, and government loans. To meet the diverse credit needs of these customers, banks

offer an assortment of loan products. Consumer loans are either open-end (revolving) credit or closed-end (installment) loans. These loans may be unsecured, such as credit cards, or secured, such as a home mortgage.

Commercial loans, which make up a large proportion of a bank's total loan portfolio, are lines of credit, short- and long-term loans, secured and unsecured. State and local governments borrow from banks to meet working capital needs that tax revenues cannot finance. Banks also offer a variety of loan products in conjunction with government-sponsored or government-supported programs.

- The loan process begins with the loan application and the loan interview. The bank then decides whether to continue with the loan request. A decision to decline a loan may be made at any time during the loan process, in which case the customer must be provided an adverse action notice. If the bank continues with the loan request, the next step is to conduct a credit investigation, which includes obtaining a credit report for consumer loans and extended inquiries and analysis for business loans. Loan documentation begins at the time of application and includes obtaining and completing all the necessary forms to secure the lender's interest and to comply with federal and state requirements. After the loan is properly documented and closed, it moves into the loan administration phase. Loan administration includes activities such as posting payments and maintaining files and documentation. Loans are periodically reviewed to ensure a quality performing loan portfolio. Asset recovery specialists monitor the loans for potential problems and take action when needed to prevent loan losses.

- The board of directors, along with bank executive management, establishes the bank's loan policy and oversees the bank's lending function. The board's responsibilities include reviewing the bank's loan portfolio, assigning lending authorities, and adjusting credit standards.

- Lending is a highly regulated bank activity. Some of the laws or regulations include the Equal Credit Opportunity Act (Regulation B), Truth in Lending Act (Regulation Z), Community Reinvestment Act (Regulation BB), insider lending restrictions (Regulation O), Home Mortgage Disclosure Act (Regulation C), Real Estate Settlement Procedures Act (Regulation X), Fair Credit Reporting Act, and Fair Debt Collection Practices Act.

**Learning Check**

## SELF CHECK & REVIEW

1. List the reasons why the lending function is so important to the bank.

2. What is the difference between open-end credit and closed-end credit? Give some examples of open-end and closed-end consumer loans.

3. Why are home equity loans and home equity lines of credit popular with consumers?

4. If a business wants to purchase a piece of equipment, what loan type is appropriate—working capital loan or term loan? Why?

5. Name the five "C's" of credit. Is collateral the most important "C"? Why or why not?

6.  What are some electronic advancements in loan services and loan processing?

7.  What are some activities involved in loan administration?

8.  What roles do bank directors play in the overall lending function?

9.  What laws should a loan officer be aware of when making a mortgage loan?

# ADDITIONAL RESOURCES

**Resources**

American Bankers Association, **www.aba.com**

*Commercial Lending*, Washington D.C.: American Bankers Association, 2004.

*Consumer Credit Delinquency Bulletin*, Washington D.C.: American Bankers Association, published quarterly.

*Consumer Lending*, Washington D.C.: American Bankers Association, 2001.

Federal Home Loan Mortgage Corporation, **www.freddiemac.com**

Federal National Mortgage Association, **www.fanniemae.com**

Federal Reserve Board, **www.federalreserve.gov**

*Get Smart About Credit*, Washington D.C.: ABA Education Foundation.

Government National Mortgage Association, **www.ginniemae.gov**

*Home Equity Lending Survey*, Washington D.C.: American Bankers Association, 2002.

*Installment Credit Survey Report*, Washington D.C.: American Bankers Association, 2002.

*Reference Guide to Regulatory Compliance,* Washington D.C.: American Bankers Association, 2004.

Risk Management Association, **www.rmahq.org**

*Side by Side: A Guide to Fair Lending*, Federal Deposit Insurance Corporation. **www.fdic.gov/regulations/resources/side/index.html**

*Shop, The credit card you pick can save you money*, Federal Reserve Board. **www.federalreserve.gov/pubs/shop**

Small Business Administration, **www.sba.com**

*The Bankcard Business—Today and Tomorrow*, Washington D.C.: American Bankers Association, 2003.

*When your Home is on the Line: What you should know about Home Equity Lines of Credit*, Federal Reserve Board. **www.federalreserve.gov/pubs/HomeLine**

# *Specialized Products and Services*

**7**

# What You Will Learn

*After studying this chapter, you should be able to*

- describe trust department products and services
- discuss selling and delivering investment products and services
- identify cash management services for collecting and disbursing commercial payments
- describe capital markets products and services
- identify insurance products sold to consumers and businesses
- describe global banking services that help foreign trade
- define the bolded key terms that appear in the text

# Introduction

*Traditionally, banks provided customers with checking, savings, and loan accounts. Banks now seek a full customer relationship and serve the customer's total financial needs. With the provisions of the Gramm-Leach-Bliley Act and technological advances in payment and Internet information systems, banks have become full service providers.*

*For consumers, this means personal financial planning or wealth management advisory services are available now. Consumers now have access to checking, savings, investments, insurance, credit, estate planning, and related delivery systems through their bank. For business customers, it means payment, investment, cash management, loan services with related delivery systems, and financial expertise appropriate for the nature, size, and scope of the business are conveniently provided by their bank.*

*Nondeposit consumer and business products, in a full service environment, include trust, investments, insurance, capital markets, and global banking. Banks offer these products and services in different combinations, directly or in partnership or through subsidiaries or affiliates.*

# TRUST SERVICES

**Trust**—A relationship in which one party holds property for another party, based on a trust agreement and fiduciary principles of law.

**Indenture**—A contract underlying a bond issue that is signed by the issuing corporation and by the trustee acting for the bondholders. It sets forth the rights and responsibilities of the corporation, trustee, and bondholders, and the terms of the security issue.

In the early years of U.S. banking, **trust** services were offered by trust companies only. In time, trust companies assumed commercial bank functions; they accepted deposits, extended credit, and obtained state banking charters to become bank and trust companies. With the Federal Reserve Act of 1913, national banks were allowed to offer trust services.

Trust departments offer both individuals and corporations specialized and personalized services. A trust department may manage a portfolio of stocks and bonds and, in most cases, have full authority to make investment decisions on behalf of beneficiaries requiring the expertise of a trained investment manager. Trust department employees may specialize in fields unrelated to banking. A trust department, for example, may manage real property with significant natural resources, such as timber. Trust specialists manage assets solely for the benefit of customers and beneficiaries.

A bank may serve as a corporate trustee for a corporate or municipal bond issue. In that capacity, a bank monitors compliance with the **indenture** agreement between bond issuer and bondholders, often handles periodic interest payments to bondholders, and protects the interests of bondholders if the issuer defaults.

Trust services complement other banking services and facilitate a total financial relationship with individual and corporate customers. To offer trust services, a bank's federal or state charter must accord it trust powers. Many banks in recent years have applied for and received trust powers so they can serve the growing wealth management market.

As trust services providers, banks act in the capacity of a fiduciary. Banks are required by law and regulation to adhere to fiduciary principles, such as acting in the sole interests of the beneficiaries, avoiding conflicts of interests, and carrying out their duties with prudence, loyalty, and care.

There are four participants in a trust:

| | |
|---|---|
| **Trust** | Property (cash, stocks, bonds, real estate, or any other item of value) for which the trust is created. |
| **Trustor** | Person creating the trust. |
| **Trustee** | Person or entity that takes control of the trust property and administers the trust. |
| **Beneficiary** | Person for whose benefit the trust was established. |

Banks, in their role as trustee, must observe the following.

| | |
|---|---|
| **Prudent investor principle** | Requires banks to act with caution, skill, diligence, and a sense of responsibility. Standard applied to total portfolio and not to isolated investments. Part of an overall investment strategy. Bank has duty to diversify investments unless not **prudent** to do so. Bank must be loyal, impartial, delegate authority, and select supervising agents. Bank must incur only costs that are reasonable in amount and appropriate for the services provided. |
| **Segregation of trust assets** | Assets of each trust kept separate from other trusts and from bank's own assets. Trust departments usually are segregated from the rest of the bank, with their own vaults, data processing equipment, and other facilities. |
| **Prevention of conflicts of interest** | Bank should have no personal interest whatsoever in investments bought or sold for trust funds. Bank should not purchase or benefit in any way from property or other assets held in trust. |

## PERSONAL TRUST SERVICES

Depending on the needs of its market and the volume of business it is able to produce, a bank may offer personal trust services such as estate settlement, trust administration, guardianships, and personal agency services.

**Did You Know ...**

At the end of 2003, depository institutions nationwide held a total of almost $13 trillion in fiduciary and related assets.

*(Federal Deposit Insurance Corporation)*

**Prudent investor**—An investor, and in the case of trusts, a trustee, who acts with caution, skill, diligence, and sense of responsibility in managing the investments in a customer's portfolio.

## Estate Settlement

When a person dies, a trust officer will help settle the deceased person's estate. Outstanding debts or taxes may need to be paid, and assets of the **estate** must be distributed to the decedent's heirs.

A trust department's estate planner usually advises customers to leave a will that describes the property owned and its location. A will should designate the beneficiaries to whom the property will be left and the person or entity that will settle the estate. The person designated in the will to settle the estate is referred to as the executor or, in some states, personal representative. The executor can be a relative, one of the heirs of the estate, the bank, a lawyer, or some combination thereof.

If the decedent did not have a will, or if the will is invalid, the estate is distributed in accordance with the laws of the state. The court appoints an administrator to carry out the terms of the will, if the executor cannot or will not serve.

Basically, duties of executors and administrators are the same:

- Take inventory to determine the exact value of the estate. Itemize and show a dollar value for every asset of the decedent.
- As necessary, take control of some or all of the assets.
- File federal and state tax returns and pay all taxes on the basis of the value of the estate.
- Settle all debts and claims against the estate.
- Distribute the remaining assets, either according to the terms of the will or as directed by state laws.

When a bank acts as administrator or executor, it is legally liable for maintaining detailed records and is accountable to the court and beneficiaries for all its actions.

## Trust Administration

The most common types of trust funds administered by banks are testamentary trusts, living trusts, and charitable and institutional trusts.

| | |
|---|---|
| **Testamentary trust** | Trusts created under the terms of a decedent's will. As trustee, a bank is responsible for managing assets turned over to it by the executor or administrator and for paying income to the beneficiaries, as specified in the will. |
| **Living trust** | Trusts created voluntarily by a living individual who executes a trust agreement and transfers property to the trust. Individuals often want to avoid the details of probate or maintain privacy of the transfer. Sometimes, individuals no longer wish to manage their affairs because of sickness, extensive traveling, or lack of financial expertise. The trustee then manages the assets for the trust. |
| **Charitable and institutional trust** | Established when an individual or an institution such as a university or hospital, or a charitable organization turns over cash, securities, or property to the bank. The bank then manages the investments that have been and will continue to be made. |

---

**Estate**—The sum total, as determined by a complete inventory, of all the assets of a decedent.

## Situation

Adam, a retired business-man wants to revise his will. Ten years earlier he had named his son as executor. However, in the past decade, his assets have grown considerably, and he has acquired works of art and overseas real estate. Although he still wants his son involved in settling his estate after he dies, he would like the services of a professional also. He solves his problem by naming his son and his bank trust department as co-executors in his will.

## Guardianships

A guardianship (sometimes called conservatorship) is established by court order for the benefit of a minor or incapacitated person, the **ward**. A trust department is appointed to hold in safekeeping and manage the property for the minor or incompetent person. To prove that all the proceeds are being used for the person's benefit, the trust department periodically provides an accounting to the court.

## Personal Agency Services

In addition to trust services, trust departments offer agency services. There is a legal difference between the role of agent and that of trustee. Trustees assume legal title to property turned over to them, whereas agents do not. Instead, an individual who retains legal title to the asset gives specific authority to an agent. Safekeeping, custody, investment advisor, and investment manager are the most common agency services for individuals. A bank functioning as an investment advisor or manager acts in a fiduciary capacity and in accordance with the highest fiduciary standards.

**Ward**—A person who by reason of minority, mental incompetence, or other incapacity is under a court's protection either directly or through a guardian or another party.

| | |
|---|---|
| **Safekeeping** | Bank accepts, holds, and returns upon request stocks, bonds, or other assets. |
| **Custody** | Bank safekeeps the assets and collects income. Custodians buy and sell securities when specifically instructed to do so by the customer or appointed agent. Banks provide custody services for individuals, correspondent banks, and government agencies. |
| **Investment advisor** | Bank performs the duties of a custodian plus other responsibilities granted to it by the individual. In handling securities, bank may review investments and suggest retention, sale, exchange, conversion, or new securities purchases. As investment advisors, banks may handle real estate. Banks act in an agency capacity to collect rental income, pay property taxes, provide for upkeep and maintenance, and disburse any net income as directed by the owner. |
| **Investment manager** | In addition to the above duties, an investment manager makes financial decisions on the customer's behalf, based on previously established investment parameters. |

## CORPORATE FIDUCIARY SERVICES

Corporations also need expert safekeeping and administration of company assets. Banks traditionally have served businesses in this fiduciary role. Two main lines of business are corporate agency services and employee benefit services.

**Historical Fact**

Continuing a project begun by the New York Clearing House, the ABA formed the Committee on Uniform Security Identification Procedures (CUSIP) in July 1964, under the direction of John L. Gibbons. The committee developed a standard numbering system of nine digits for identifying securities and announced its results in January 1967.

*(American Bankers Association)*

### Corporate Agency Services

For corporations and agencies of government, banks provide transfer agent, registrar, and paying agent services.

| | |
|---|---|
| **Transfer agent** | Bank is responsible for changing title of ownership on corporation's shares of stock, as required when shares change hands. Old shares are canceled and new shares are issued in the name of the new stockholder. |
| **Registrar** | Bank maintains records of shares canceled and reissued so that an overissuance does not occur. Corporation establishes maximum number of shares of stock that may be issued. |
| **Paying agent** | Bank, as paying agent or dividend disbursing agent, is responsible for making interest or dividend payments to holders of stock or bonds a corporation or government unit issues. A paying agent also is responsible for redeeming debt issues as they mature. |

### Employee Benefit Services

Managing trust funds for paying pension and other benefits to employees of corporations, universities, and state and local governments is one of the fastest growing and most competitive areas of trust services. Basically, a business establishes a defined-benefit plan trust or profit-sharing trust and makes regular contributions into the trust fund. The bank's duties, whether for its own employees or those of another entity, are to receive regular contributions from the employer and the participants, invest the contributions, maintain detailed records to show the accrued value for each employee, make disbursements, and provide detailed data on transactions.

Another employee benefit service is managing a defined contribution plan, such as 401(k) plans. These are salary deferral plans to which employees contribute a percentage of their wages. Employees choose their own investments from a list of approved investment options. Companies also may contribute funds on their employees' behalf. Plans are managed by the trust department for its own employees or for other entities. Fund managers handle contributions, direct investments according to participants' instructions, file tax reports, manage year-end accounting and reporting, arrange payouts, and complete disbursements.

## INVESTMENT SERVICES

Bank subsidiaries or holding companies' affiliates may offer investment and brokerage services through a number of organizational structures, including third-party, joint ventures, and in-house.

| | |
|---|---|
| **Third-party** | A licensed brokerage firm operates on the bank's premises, and the bank is paid a fee. Banks earn less in fees this way than from performing the service themselves. However, the bank has few responsibilities relative to the service while making it available to its customers. |
| **Joint ventures** | Banks arrange with broker-dealers to sell securities. Employees work for both the bank and the broker-dealer. Employees working for a broker-dealer generally are licensed and registered representatives who have taken all qualifying exams. A licensed broker-dealer must supervise brokerage functions performed by bank employees. |
| **In-house** | Banks sell brokerage products through their own discount or full-service brokerages, formed either as bank subsidiaries or as holding company affiliates. Discount brokerages sell investment products and services but do not offer investment advice; they are typically less expensive than a full-service brokerage. Full-service brokerages sell securities and offer investment advisory services. They may perform the same services as large non-affiliated brokerage houses, including underwriting and dealing in equity securities. |

Investment products, such as stocks, bonds, annuities, and mutual funds, are not bank deposits and thus are not insured by the Federal Deposit Insurance Corporation (FDIC). Bank regulators want to ensure that bank customers do not assume that investment products are insured and will not lose value. Consequently, banks selling investment products must take several precautions, including:

- Marketing nondeposit investments in a manner that does not mislead or confuse customers about the products or the risks. Banks should separate the retail deposit-taking and retail nondeposit sales functions.

- Prohibiting bank employees, particularly tellers, from offering investment advice.

- Refraining from offering uninsured retail investment products with a product name identical to the bank's name.

- Conspicuously disclosing that investment products are not FDIC insured, are not obligations of or guaranteed by the bank, and carry investment risk and possible loss of principal.

## Banker Profile

**Denise McClelland**
*Senior Vice President, Wells Fargo Private Client Services, Long Beach, California*

Denise McClelland began her career practicing law In San Francisco. Later she joined the financial world first in Denver and then in Los Angeles.

Ms. McClelland pioneered change in trust administration around technology, work and process flow, and product specialization. "Our clients' exposure to financial planning techniques, alternative investment strategies, and trust and investment services are, today, a few mouse clicks away."

Ms. McClelland serves on the Institute of Certified Bankers Certified Trust and Financial Advisor (CTFA) Advisory Board. "With increasing client sophistication, it is imperative to have trust and investment professionals trained on the most current estate planning and wealth management issues."

Ms. McClelland, who holds a Bachelor of Arts and Juris Doctorate, is licensed to practice law in California and Colorado. She is a Certified Trust and Financial Advisor and a licensed principal (Series 9 and 10).

# INVESTMENT PRODUCT OFFERINGS

Many banks offer customers an assortment of investment products, including stocks, bonds, mutual funds, and annuities.

### Stocks

A share of stock represents an ownership interest in a company. Stocks can provide capital growth for the issuing company and dividend and other forms of income for stockholders. Because it can lose value, stock is a higher risk investment than an insured bank product like a certificate of deposit. When stock is sold, it may be worth more or less than its original purchase price. Historically, however, the return on stocks has outpaced many other investment types, making them a good investment choice over the long term.

### Bonds

Corporations or municipal authorities issue bonds. By purchasing bonds, investors are loaning money to these entities to carry out some purpose, such as building a school. In exchange for the loan, bondholders earn interest. Interest is usually paid on a regular basis, and the principal amount of the bond is repaid on a predetermined maturity date. Income generated from tax-free bonds is exempt from federal, state, or local income taxes.

Risks associated with bond investments arise from the quality of the issuer and the fluctuation in interest rates. Municipal or corporate bonds carry varying degrees of risk, depending on the issuer's fiscal soundness and the nature of the funded project. Like stock, a bond can lose or gain value. This happens when a bond's interest rate is less than or more than the prevailing interest rates for similar bonds.

### Mutual Funds

Mutual funds are a collection of stocks, bonds, and other investments owned by a group of investors and managed by a professional investment company. They are popular because they give investors access to professional management and investment diversification with a relatively low required initial investment. Risk is spread over all the stocks, bonds, and other investments in the portfolio.

Dividends and interest earned are divided among investors. Because the investors' money is pooled, the investment company has more buying power than it would if it were investing separately for each individual.

### Annuities

Insurance companies issue annuities. The primary objective of an annuity is to pay financial benefits to annuitants during their lifetime. There are two basic kinds of annuities: deferred annuity and immediate annuity. The deferred annuity (pay-in) is for accumulation of capital that will be used later. An immediate annuity (pay-out) is for disbursing funds to an annuitant, usually periodically and usually for a lifetime or set period.

Annuities are structured in a number of ways, including with fixed or variable rates. Like other kinds of nondeposit investment products, FDIC does not insure annuities.

**Historical Fact**

The United States entered World War I, and Federal Reserve policy shifted to support of U.S. war borrowing. Banks raised more than $21 billion for the World War I effort alone.

*(American Bankers Association)*

# INVESTMENT MANAGEMENT

Most banks do more than just sell investment products. Through holding company affiliates or non-affiliated broker-dealers, banks provide investment management services and advice to both individuals and corporations.

## *Asset Management Accounts*

Asset management accounts provide a convenient way for a bank customer to consolidate investments, which can be accessed via check or a debit card. Typically, there is a minimum initial investment and a fee that may be waived if a required minimum balance is maintained. In return, the customer is provided with up-to-date account information online or monthly statements, an annual summary statement that recaps all account activity, a daily **sweep** of credit balances, direct deposit, and dividend reinvestment.

**Sweep**—A prearranged automatic transfer of funds in an account, above a specified amount, to an investment pool, an interest earning account, or to pay a line of credit.

## *Trading Accounts*

Trading accounts allow customers to research and place trades either online or through a bank-affiliated financial consultant. Access to proprietary research, such as third-party stock research and mutual fund profiles, typically are offered. Customers may trade in a wide array of investments, including stocks, bonds, and mutual funds. Trades are subject to commissions and fees and may be waived for active traders and customers who maintain high balances in bank-affiliated investment or deposit accounts. Customers usually have online access to trade confirmations, account history, balances, and positions.

## *Investment Advice and Financial Planning*

Banks also serve as investment advisers and financial planners for consumers (particularly the affluent), corporations, pension plans, endowments, and public agencies. In this capacity, banks provide advice on investments, purchasing, and selling securities. Through a mix of investment products, banks help customers achieve investment objectives, such as maintaining liquidity, preserving capital, minimizing risk, or generating income.

An investment strategy usually has three levels of risk. The balance and types of investments within each level reflect the customer's tolerance for, or aversion to, risk.

**Safe assets (low risk)**

Safe assets are traditional bank products like checking, savings accounts, money market accounts, and certificates of deposit. They are used to meet everyday life expenses and often provide a small investment return. Many of these products are FDIC insured and are liquid.

**Income assets (moderate risk)**

Income assets provide greater income-earning potential. They are not meant to provide growth in the investment's value. Rather, they provide a regular income stream for the investor. These investments are not FDIC insured, and the income generated can be taxable or tax deferred. Bonds or fixed income mutual funds are examples.

| Growth assets (higher risk) | Growth assets are purchased for their potential to increase in value. Stock and stock mutual funds are common examples. These products, offered through third-party or affiliated broker-dealers, are not FDIC insured. |
| --- | --- |

# CASH MANAGEMENT

Banks offer cash management services to businesses as well as consumers. Cash management services help businesses collect income and payments quickly, manage and reconcile outgoing payments efficiently, and obtain timely and complete information on their bank accounts.

Cash management services are attractive to corporations and small businesses with significant billings and payments and the need to put their money to work instead of leaving balances in noninterest-bearing demand deposit accounts.

## CASH VAULT SERVICES

Cash vault services help businesses safely deposit funds, while maximizing funds availability. Deposits are delivered directly from the business to the bank's cash vault. To ensure the safety of deposits in transit, banks offer safeguards such as tamper-evident deposit bags, video surveillance, and dual custody processing. Company employees are not put at risk because they do not carry cash to the bank. Customers receive expedited deposit processing, and deposits received by the deposit deadlines are given same-day credit.

## LOCKBOX SERVICES

Lockbox services help companies access their money faster. Before the advent of lockbox services, a customer would mail a payment directly to a business, a government unit, a correspondent bank, or a university. These payments were subject to delays in the mail, processing, deposit, and collection.

With lockbox services, payments are sent directly to a post office box managed by the bank. The bank retrieves payments directly from the lockbox, deposits them immediately, wires the funds to the payee, and sends the payee a record of the customers who made payments. Because checks do not pass first through the company, delays in deposit and collection are eliminated. Bank fees are offset by improved funds availability, making the company's net cost lower.

## DIRECT DEPOSIT

Direct-deposit transactions processed electronically through an automated clearing house (ACH) enable businesses to deposit net pay, reimbursements, commissions, retirement plan payments, pension benefits, dividends and other payments into the checking or savings accounts of employees, retirees, and shareholders. For businesses, direct-deposit services eliminate the cost of creating and distributing paper checks and reduce exposure to check fraud. For recipients, direct deposit expedites funds access and offers the convenience and security of having payments posted electronically to a bank account, thus avoiding a trip to the bank to endorse and deposit a paper check.

## CONTROLLED DISBURSEMENT

A controlled disbursement account is drawn on an affiliate or branch of the primary bank and processed at another check processing facility. The paying bank accumulates totals throughout the processing day of checks presented for payment and advises the customer of the amount that will be paid on the account that processing night. With a controlled disbursement account, a customer can make payments by transferring money from concentration (investment) accounts or by directing the bank to fund the account from the company's line of credit.

## CASH CONCENTRATION

In cash concentration, businesses have disbursement accounts at numerous banks and pool balances in one account, the concentration account. Pooled account balances then can be invested for a higher return than would be possible in separate accounts. To pool the funds, the business initiates ACH debits to the various disbursement accounts and credits the concentration account.

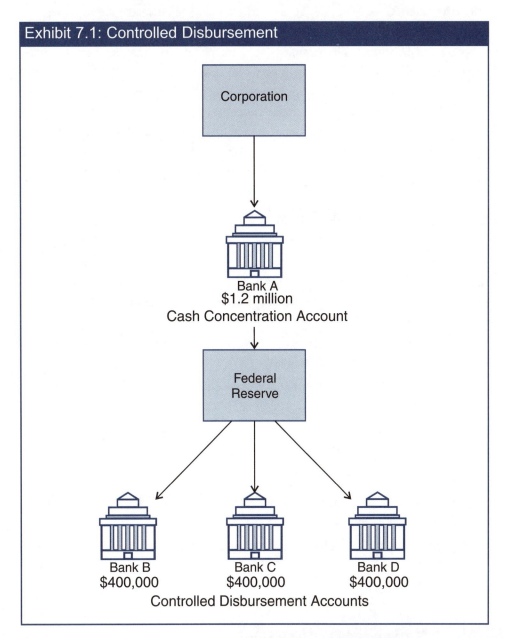

Exhibit 7.1: Controlled Disbursement

Corporation

Bank A
$1.2 million
Cash Concentration Account

Federal Reserve

Bank B
$400,000

Bank C
$400,000

Bank D
$400,000

Controlled Disbursement Accounts

## Zero-Balance Accounts

Zero-balance accounts are demand deposit accounts, or controlled disbursement accounts, that maintain a zero balance. They are linked to a concentration account or a line of credit. As checks are presented for payment, the bank automatically transfers funds from the concentration (or investment) account or line of credit to maintain the checking account balance at zero. A positive balance in the account is transferred to the concentration (investment) account to earn interest or to the line of credit to pay the outstanding balance.

## Merchant Card Services

Banks provide merchants with the capability to accept customer payments by credit or debit card or electronic check. The market for merchant card services includes retailers, online businesses, and telephone and mail order companies.

Banks that offer merchant card services provide businesses with the equipment to process transactions, including card terminals and receipt printers. Customer card information is received by swiping a card through a card reader or by taking the information down over the telephone. When the information is verified, the transaction is accepted or declined. The business has an account with the merchant bankcard processor, which provides settlement services. If the transaction is approved, funds are debited from the customer's credit card or deposit account and credited to the business's deposit account. The bank processor receives a fee for the service, usually a percentage of each customer transaction. Merchant card services provide immediate approval of transactions, reduce the risk of returned payments, reduce labor costs associated with check handling, and reduce time for funds availability.

# CAPITAL MARKETS

Banks offer a variety of services to assist companies in raising money for their operations by accessing public and private equity and debt markets. Many of these services may be required to be offered through an affiliated broker-dealer. The capital market services provided to corporate clients range from specialized lending and asset management to advisory services. This includes

**Securitization**—Packaging loans as a unit to be sold to outside investors. The loans are no longer assets to the bank, although the bank may still continue to service them for investors.

- structuring and distributing debt securities supported by company assets (asset-backed **securitizations**)
- underwriting and distributing corporate equity and debt and preferred stock
- structuring and syndicating loans
- providing assistance on structuring and negotiating the sale or purchase of business assets in mergers and acquisitions
- structuring and distributing private placement transactions
- underwriting and distributing debt securities of government, municipalities, and other institutions
- providing financing to specialized businesses, for example, real estate developers

## MERCHANT BANKING

The Gramm-Leach-Bliley Act (GLBA) permits nonbank affiliates of financial holding companies to offer merchant banking services. Merchant banking services are broad in scope and may include direct investment by a financial holding company in nonfinancial companies. Under GLBA, these investments are referred to as "merchant banking investments." In this capacity, a financial holding company is an actual investor and may assume an active role in the company in which it has invested, including board participation. In addition to providing capital, merchant banking may extend to corporate lending, leveraged finance, investment banking, and other corporate financing solutions.

# INSURANCE SERVICES

The financial modernization provisions of the Gramm-Leach-Bliley Act permit banks to engage in sales of a full range of insurance products. Banks also may act as brokers by offering product lines from different insurance companies.

The financial modernization law also permits bank holding companies to underwrite insurance and annuities, either directly through the parent holding company or through a nonbank affiliate of the holding company. To engage in insurance **underwriting**, a bank holding company must qualify as an FHC.

Insurance products tied to investments, such as whole and variable life insurance policies and annuities, are considered nondeposit investment products. As a result, insurance products are subject to the same marketing and sales restrictions that apply to stocks, bonds, and other investment vehicles.

Some of the insurance products that banks now offer include life insurance, credit life insurance, disability insurance, long-term care insurance, health insurance, property insurance, and liability insurance.

## LIFE INSURANCE

Life insurance provides a monetary payment to survivors upon the death of the insured. Many types of life insurance are sold. Two basic categories of insurance products are term life and whole life.

With term life insurance, the purchaser pays a specific amount of money for a specific amount of life insurance for a period from 1 to 30 years. At the end of the chosen period, no excess premium remains and the contract terminates.

Whole life insurance is both an insurance product and an investment vehicle that provides income to the insured. Whole life insurance premiums are invested in an account portfolio held by the insurance company. Depending on the features of the whole life insurance product, premiums can be invested in stocks, bonds, money market instruments, or other assets, and pay a fixed or variable return. The policy owner may borrow funds from the accumulated cash value in the whole life insurance policy. Other types of life insurance products include **variable life insurance** and **universal life insurance**.

**Underwriting**—The assumption of a risk for a fee such as for insurance or investments. Insurance underwriting guarantees cash payment in the event of a loss or casualty. Firm commitment investment underwriting, as opposed to a best effort investment underwriting, guarantees the sale of a securities issue.

**Variable life insurance**—A form of life insurance in which the cash value of the policy may fluctuate according to the investment performance of separate account funds. The policy owner chooses among various funds offered by the insurer.

**Universal life insurance**—Life insurance that gives policy owners the ability to set and vary their own premium levels, payment schedules, and death benefits, within certain limits.

### CREDIT LIFE INSURANCE

Credit life insurance pays off the insured loan if the borrower dies while the loan is still outstanding. Banks traditionally have sold credit life insurance in conjunction with making loans.

### DISABILITY INSURANCE

Disability insurance provides a source of income to workers if they become disabled or sick for an extended period. Because the chances of becoming disabled increase with age, disability insurance is most attractive to older workers in the years before retirement. Employers often offer group disability income insurance coverage to their employees. Personal disability insurance policies also can be sold to individuals.

### LONG-TERM CARE INSURANCE

Long-term care insurance provides coverage for services that an insured may need when unable to walk, bathe, dress, or perform other basic daily living activities. Services include home health care, care in assisted living facilities and nursing homes, respite care, and hospice care. Long-term care policies are issued typically to individuals between ages 30 and 85. As the U.S. population ages, the percentage of people needing long-term care increases. Consequently, long-term care policies have become a popular form of insurance.

### HEALTH INSURANCE

Health insurance covers the cost of physician and hospital care. Companies are the biggest purchasers of health insurance. If employer-provided health insurance is not available, people seeking health insurance may apply directly to an insurance company for an individually issued policy. Retirees also purchase health insurance to supplement their Medicare hospital and medical care coverage. The health insurance business is flourishing, and policies are sold that cover vision, dental care, and prescription drugs.

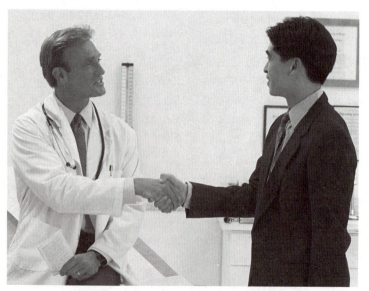

### PROPERTY INSURANCE

Property insurance protects the value of anything owned by consumers—homes, boats, jewelry, silverware, money, and so forth—that can be lost from fire, theft, lawsuits, or other events. Businesses insure assets such as computers against loss.

### LIABILITY INSURANCE

Liability or casualty insurance protects an individual or business against losses resulting from liability for bodily injury or property damage to other persons. Such policies normally cover legal expenses and attorney's fee, medical expenses, and funeral expenses, incurred by persons who are injured, and the cost of repairing or replacing damaged property. Professional liability insurance protects the insured against claims arising out of the practice of professional services.

## VEHICLE INSURANCE

Vehicle insurance covers the risk associated with owning and operating vehicles such as automobiles, motorcycles, all-terrain vehicles, and snowmobiles. Vehicle insurance policies provide liability coverage for pain and suffering to those who have been injured and for damaged property. Collision coverage protects against losses arising from damage to a covered automobile or another object.

## TITLE INSURANCE

Title insurance protects homebuyers from financial loss due to questions about ownership of the property. Title insurance differs from property insurance in that it protects the title of the property rather than the property itself. If someone came forward with a valid claim on property that was surveyed incorrectly, title insurance would reimburse the owner for losses.

## KEY PERSON INSURANCE

A company purchases key person insurance on an employee or employees whose loss, either by death or from disability, would financially hurt the company. Executives and other employees with specific managerial or technical expertise usually are insured. Small businesses, which are more susceptible than larger enterprises to adverse impact from the loss of a key employee, are ideal candidates for such insurance policies.

Proceeds from a key person insurance policy can be used to recruit and train a replacement, help replace profits the company may have earned had the employee not died, and help assure creditors and suppliers about the continuity of the business.

# GLOBAL BANKING

Global banking services meet the needs of businesses operating in a world where countries are increasingly dependent on one another, and money flows with no regard for geographic boundaries. Each day, billions of dollars are transferred electronically among international money centers such as Hong Kong, London, Tokyo, Paris, Frankfurt, and New York.

Many major U.S. banks have global banking departments. Even in banks where the volume of international business does not require the facilities of an independent department, the demand for foreign transaction services grows each year along with international trade. Although major U.S. banks typically have fully staffed global banking departments, smaller banks may rely on a larger bank to act as a correspondent to provide specialized services, such as letters of credit, banker acceptances, and foreign exchange.

**Historical Fact**

The Society for Worldwide Interbank Financial Telecommunications (S.W.I.F.T.), founded in 1973 by a group of 250 European and North American banks, is a mutually owned organization headquartered in Brussels, Belgium. The society's objective is to maintain a cost-effective, high quality, responsive and secure international payment financial messaging system.

*(American Bankers Association)*

## LETTERS OF CREDIT

A buyer of goods often requires assurance that the merchandise being bought will conform exactly to specifications, whereas a seller of goods often requires assurance of payment after the goods have been shipped. Often, without some independent guarantee that the right merchandise will be sent and that payment will be made, importers and exporters would be hesitant to trade.

Letters of credit satisfy the requirements of both parties and minimize the risks of international trade. A letter of credit is an instrument issued by a bank, substituting the credit standing of the bank for the credit standing of the importer (buyer) of goods. It guarantees that the bank will pay the exporter (seller) if all the terms of the contract are met. At the same time, it protects the buyer by assuring that no payment will be made until the contract has been fulfilled. With a reputable bank in the middle, both parties are willing to trade.

Most letters of credit are irrevocable. An irrevocable letter of credit stipulates that no changes can be made without the full consent of both the buyer and the seller. Revocable letters of credit, which can be canceled or changed solely at the buyer's request, are less common. Another type of letter of credit is a standby letter of credit, which is paid when something does not happen. Normally, they are not drawn against and have a period of one year when they may be renewed. They are used to reinforce the customer's credit standing.

### Situation

S.F. Machine Tools Corporation has negotiated with a firm in Germany to purchase a quantity of machine tools at a specific price. The U.S. firm wants to make sure the contract is fulfilled before it pays for the merchandise, but the German company wants to be sure it will be paid before it ships the merchandise. A letter of credit satisfies the requirements of both parties.

Letters of Credit

IMPORTER
Letter of Credit

EXPORTER
Goods

## BANKERS' ACCEPTANCES

Bankers' acceptances are **drafts** drawn by a company upon a bank and "accepted" by the bank. The drafts instruct the bank to pay a designated party a certain sum of money at a specified time in the future. Thus, the bank that accepts the draft assumes the obligation of making payment at the maturity of the acceptance. Bankers' acceptances generally mature in 30 to 180 days. Bankers' acceptances are typically used in international trade in a similar way that a check is used in domestic trade.

**Draft**—A signed order by one party (the drawer) addressed to another (the drawee) directing the drawee to pay, in the future, a specified sum of money to the order of a third person, a payee.

## FOREIGN EXCHANGE SERVICES

**Foreign exchange** services are another global banking service large banks make available to corporations operating in markets around the world. International commerce cannot occur unless money can be exchanged easily from one currency to another. U.S. banks that offer foreign exchange services send and receive payments in all of the major currencies worldwide.

Global banking departments offer corporate customers the ability to send and receive payments in dozens of currencies worldwide. Payment can be made via wire, international ACH, draft, traveler's checks, foreign currency banknotes (cash), or through other channels and financial instruments. A key function of global banking departments is to monitor the exchange rates of the world's currencies in order to know what the U.S. dollar is worth in euros, yen, or some other currency. Exchange rates then can be calculated immediately for international transactions.

**Foreign exchange**—Trading in or exchange of foreign currencies for U.S. funds or other foreign currencies.

**By The Numbers**

*Currency Conversion*

$$\text{Foreign Currency} \times \text{U.S Dollar Exchange Rate} = \text{U.S. Dollars}$$

Your company is importing widgets from Canada. Each widget costs $150 Canadian dollars. The current exchange rate is $1 Canadian dollar = $0.75 U.S. dollars. How much does each widget cost in U.S. dollars?

**$150 x 0.75 = $112.50 U.S. dollars**

## SUMMARY

- In addition to the basic banking products, such as checking and savings accounts and loans, banks offer an array of specialized services. These services include trust, investment and brokerage, cash management, capital markets, insurance, and global banking.

- Banks offer trust and agency services to individuals and corporations. They offer estate settlement, trust administration, guardianships, and personal and corporate agency services, such as safekeeping, custody, investment advisor, investment manager, transfer agent, registrar, and paying agent. Trust administration services include testamentary trust, living trusts, and charitable and institutional trusts. Bank trust departments also manage employee benefit programs such as pension plans and 401 (k) plans. In its role as trustee, a bank trust department takes on fiduciary duties and must act in the sole interests of the trust customer and beneficiaries, following the prudent investor principle, segregating trust assets and avoiding conflicts of interests.

- Bank subsidiaries and affiliates offer products that compete directly with other financial services providers, such as brokerage and investment firms. However, in selling and marketing these nondeposit investment products, banks are required by law to provide clear disclosures to customers, including that the products are not bank deposits and are not insured by the FDIC. Investment products include stocks, bonds, mutual funds, and annuities. Services include asset management, trading accounts, investment advice, and financial planning. Banks also offer investment services through third-party providers, in joint ventures, in-house discount brokerage programs, and broker-dealer affiliates.

- Cash management services help individuals and businesses collect income and payments quickly, manage and reconcile outgoing payments efficiently, and obtain timely and complete information on their bank accounts. Bank products and services that help businesses achieve these objectives include cash vault services, lockbox services, direct deposit, controlled disbursement services that use cash concentration and controlled disbursement accounts such as zero-balance accounts, and merchant card services.

- By accessing public and private equity and debt markets, large banks offer a variety of services to assist companies in raising money for their operations. Capital market services provided to corporate clients include specialized lending, structuring, distributing and underwriting debt, merchant banking, and assisting asset sales in mergers and acquisition.

- As a result of the Gramm-Leach-Bliley Act, banking organizations can offer insurance products to their customers. Banks sell life, credit life, disability, long-term care, health, property, liability, vehicle, title, and key person insurance. The law also permits certain bank holding companies that have elected financial holding company status to underwrite insurance products.

- More than ever before, banking involves a worldwide market. To remain competitive, banks offer services to their customers that transact international business. Letters of credit, bankers' acceptance, and foreign exchange services help protect the interests of both the buyer and the seller of goods in the international marketplace.

**Learning Check**

# SELF CHECK & REVIEW

1. What are the basic legal obligations of a trustee?

2. What personal (individual) trust services do banks typically provide?

3. What corporate trust services do banks typically provide?

4. What is the primary difference between a testamentary trust and a living trust?

5. What are nondeposit investment products?

6. What types of cash management services help a corporate customer optimize the interest earned by deposits or reduce the interest expense of loans?

7. What types of customers need capital market services? What are some examples of capital market services that banks provide?

8. What types of insurance could be sold to a customer who has just taken out a mortgage loan?

9. How does a letter of credit protect the interests of both the buyer and the seller of goods?

10. Your company is importing widgets from Europe. Each widget costs €100 euros. The current exchange rate is: €1 = $1.15. How much does each widget cost in U.S. dollars?

# ADDITIONAL RESOURCES

**Resources**

American Bankers Association, **www.aba.com**

ABA Insurance Association, **www.aba.com/ABAIA/default.htm**

ABA Securities Association, **www.aba.com/ABASA/default.htm**

American Bankers Association, **www.aba.com**

*Bank Insurance Survey Report*. Washington, D.C.: American Bankers
 Association, 2003.

Currency Converter, **www.xe.com/ucc/**

*Fiduciary Law and Trust Activities Guide*, Washington D.C.: American
 Bankers Association, 2004.

*Insurance Management Guide*, Washington D.C.: American Bankers
 Association, 2004.

*Investment Management Guide*, Washington, D.C.: American Bankers
 Association, 2004.

*Personal Financial Planning Guide*, Washington, D.C.: American Bankers
 Association, 2004.

*Retail Banking Survey Report*, Washington, D.C.: American Bankers
 Association, 2003.

*Tax Law Guide*, Washington D.C.: American Bankers Association, 2004.

Uniform Prudent Investor Act **www.law.upenn.edu/bll/ulc/fnact99/1990s/upia94.pdf**

*Uninsured Investment Products: A Pocket Guide for Financial Institutions*:
 Federal Deposit Insurance Corporation,
 **www.fdic.gov/regulations/resources/financial/index.html**

# Building Relationships: Sales and Customer Service

**8**

# What You Will Learn

*After studying this chapter, you should be able to*

- explain how sales, marketing, and customer service help build customer relationships
- discuss the components of the marketing concept
- identify what customers expect from bankers
- discuss the nature and importance of cross-selling and referrals
- explain how a customer makes a purchase decision
- identify the components of effective product development
- define the bolded key terms that appear in the text

# Introduction

*Like other businesses in today's economy, banks focus on building relationships with customers, providing excellent customer service, and developing and selling services that meet customer needs and expectations. Their fiduciary relationship to customers is important. Everyday banks must demonstrate that the money held in their care is safe, well-managed, and accessible. They also must demonstrate that caring for the customer is important.*

*Sales, marketing, and customer service are important in today's financial services environment, and building long-term relationships with customers is key to bank profitability and success. Every bank employee plays a role in relationship building. Customers have specific expectations for the service they receive, and all employees can serve to meet these expectations. In developing and selling products and services, banks follow processes that incorporate their understanding of customer needs and expectations and how purchase decisions are made.*

## Situation

Newlyweds Jim and Carlene open a checking and savings account at the bank. They are pleased with the service and the friendly bank employees. As a result, when they decide to buy a second car, they consider the bank first for an automobile loan. Later, when they need a home loan, a credit card, insurance, and an individual retirement account, they automatically think of their bank. In time, they have several accounts. When they have their first child, they naturally talk to a bank officer about saving for college. Eventually, Jim and Carlene will want investment or trust services. Because of their long-term relationship with the bank, they will talk to the wealth manager at their bank.

# SELLING IN TODAY'S ENVIRONMENT

A customer in a long-term relationship with a bank may regard the bank as the primary, and even lifelong, source of financial services. For good customer relationships to be formed and sustained over time, all employees need to practice a customer-centered philosophy on their jobs.

## SALES, MARKETING, AND CUSTOMER SERVICE

Many banks have a marketing department or officer responsible for promoting products and services and projecting an image of strength and trust to the community. Some banks, usually smaller banks, may outsource the marketing function.

Marketing plays a fundamental role in relationship building. Through advertising, the marketing department ensures that both existing and prospective customers are aware of the bank's products and services that will help them meet their personal goals or solve financial problems. Typically, the marketing function includes public relations responsibilities, for example, charitable and sponsorship activities that help a bank fulfill its role as a community partner.

Banks also engage in sales and business development. A bank's CEO and president frequently play a prominent role in selling the bank's products and services to community leaders. Members of the board may bring in new customers and accounts through their ties in the business community. Although larger banks often employ business development officers whose job entails finding opportunities for the bank's financial services in the marketplace, most banks require all bank officers to seek these opportunities. Officers in lending, trust, commercial services, and retail banking employ sales strategies to ensure the bank captures and maintains adequate **market share**.

If a customer's everyday experience with a bank is unsatisfactory, the bank's marketing and sales efforts are wasted. An employee's most important job is to help the bank build long-term customer relationships. Employees keep this in mind whenever they work with a customer. When handling an important transaction, care, accuracy, and professionalism ensure the customer will want to return to the bank. Smiling, remembering a customer's name, taking time to understand and answer a question, or expressing genuine appreciation for the customer's business may seem like small gestures, but they are powerful incentives for customers to continue their banking relationship.

Even if a job does not involve face-to-face contact with customers, employees are very important in the relationship-building process. A bank will have difficulty convincing customers that it cares about their business, for example, if it regularly makes errors when posting transactions. A loan approval that takes too long is not likely to please a borrower.

## THE MARKETING CONCEPT

The **marketing concept**, which is fundamental to bank customer relationships, applies to all types of companies. It is broader than advertising and promotional activities most often associated with marketing. The marketing concept holds that a business's objectives are best reached by first identifying customer needs and wants and fulfilling them through an efficient, organization-wide and management-supported effort.

In banking, it is an organizational philosophy that influences and directs all operations. The four pillars of the marketing concept are total company effort, customer satisfaction, profitability, and social responsibility.

### *Total Company Effort*

To customers, bank employees are the bank. Every time a customer interacts with an employee, the bank markets (sells) itself. If a teller or call center employee is rude to a customer, then as far as the customer is concerned, the bank is rude. If a proof operator habitually makes mistakes, as far as the customer is concerned, the bank is careless and untrustworthy. No matter what an employee's job is, marketing is inherent to the job. By doing the job well, the employee is marketing (selling) the bank, and thus its products, services, and standard of customer service.

In an organization that operates according to the marketing concept, every department sees itself as serving the bank's customers in some way. Employees understand that, if they are not serving the customer directly, they are serving someone in the bank who is serving the customer. For that reason, employees also regard other employees in the bank as their internal customers. They treat each other as professionals, all working toward the same goal of serving customers with care and distinction.

**Market Share**—One seller's portion of the total sales of a product, usually measured as a percentage.

**Marketing concept**—An organizational philosophy that influences and directs all bank operations. It consists of customer satisfaction, total company effort, profit, and social responsibility.

**To be a successful salesperson**
- know your customer
- know your bank's products and services
- match your bank's products and services to your customer's needs
- demonstrate the benefits
- anticipate questions and be prepared to answer
- ask for the business

**Historical Fact**

In 1946, Exchange National Bank of Chicago offered the first drive-in banking service.

*(American Bankers Association)*

## Banker Profile

**Sandra J. Pattie**
*Executive Vice President
and Chief Operating Officer,
BankNewport, Newport,
Rhode Island*

Sandra Pattie is a community banker
in the fullest sense. Throughout her
career, she has served both the
banking industry and communities in
Rhode Island.

Beginning with BankNewport as a
consumer lender, Ms. Pattie has
managed operations, marketing,
human resources, and retail banking.
Today, she is responsible for planning,
communicating, implementing,
and directing the activities of
BankNewport.

Serving her community, Ms. Pattie
is a foundation trustee of Community
College of Rhode Island (CCRI) and
was recently honored as "Outstanding
Alumni." She is a dedicated member
of United Way of Rhode Island. "The
agencies supported by the United
Way do such fantastic work, it's hard
to visit a women's shelter or the
Salvation Army without feeling moved
and wishing I could do more."

Ms. Pattie exemplifies commitment to
continuing education. After graduating
from Providence College, she kept
studying and became a Certified
Financial Planner.™

### Customer Satisfaction

The marketing concept recognizes that customer satisfaction is the "business" of banking. Without customer satisfaction, the bank will not only lose customers, it will fail to build broader relationships with the customers who stay. Customer retention and relationship-building depend on customers perceiving that the bank values their business.

Retaining customers costs less than attracting new ones. More marketing dollars are needed to advertise in newspapers, television, and the radio than to convey targeted messages to existing customers. The very best and least costly way to promote the bank is to provide excellent customer service.

Customer satisfaction should drive bank operations. In fact, customer satisfaction is achievable only when the bank organizes its processes to serve the interests and convenience of its customers. Although certain forms, disclosures, and account opening procedures are required by bank law and regulation, how they are processed and how the customer is treated during the transaction makes a difference.

Many banks put the customer, not the paperwork, at the center of each transaction. One example is the universal account agreement in which information about the customer is kept on file. Later, when another account is opened, the customer has less paperwork to complete. To make banking more convenient, banks have changed their hours and locations. Lobby and drive-in hours have been extended, for example, to include weekends and evenings.

Electronic banking services, including Internet banking, provide the ultimate in customer convenience. They allow customers to handle bank transactions from the comfort of their home, their work place, or from another remote computer.

Bank employees are taught to be discrete when addressing a customer's private banking needs. Within bank procedures or management approval, employees are encouraged to take the initiative when seeking solutions to a customer's banking requirements.

### Profitability

Profitability is an important part of the marketing concept. Without profits, the bank will not have the capital and resources to maintain and grow its business. Furthermore, profitability and customer satisfaction are not mutually exclusive. Indeed, the marketing concept holds that profit objectives can best be met by providing customer satisfaction.

Customer satisfaction has a direct bearing on pricing for services. Customers who are satisfied with their bank are less price-sensitive than customers who are dissatisfied. This is important because banks charge fees that reflect the true cost of services. Experience has shown that a satisfied customer gladly will pay a reasonable fee for high-quality, attentive service. A dissatisfied customer, on the other hand, is likely to seek competitive pricing for products and services.

Consistent with customers' needs, a successful organization seeks ways to use resources efficiently. It prices products and services to provide value to the customer while earning a profit for the bank. For example, banks set loan interest rates that are attractive to borrowers and contribute to earnings while covering costs and risks. Banks that build value into products and services attract more customers at higher prices than competitors who offer less value. **Value** leads to customer satisfaction, which in turn improves bank earnings by enlarging the customer base, increasing deposit balances, and raising interest and fee income.

**Value**—The worth of a product or service.

### *Social Responsibility*

Although they are private businesses, banks are expected and required to preserve and promote the well-being of their communities, especially low-to-moderate income customers. The vast majority of banks have built their success by assuming a prominent role in their community's economy, providing financial resources for individuals, families, small businesses, and others to grow and prosper.

Banks also serve the nation. They act as fiscal agents of the federal government and collect federal tax deposits from businesses. They work with the federal government to help implement the nation's monetary policies and keep the economy strong.

Bankers themselves are unique in the sense that so many of them are involved in civic affairs and local service organizations. Many banks give their employees time off for volunteer and civic activities, and they frequently recruit employees to help in disaster relief efforts, public events, and other community activities. In addition, through their community relations programs, many banks support the arts, philanthropic causes, scholastic achievement, public school programs, and amateur sports. Still other banks assume an educational role by, for example, opening branches in schools where young people can learn how to handle personal finances.

# MEETING CUSTOMER EXPECTATIONS

In building and maintaining customer relationships, bankers must be mindful of customer expectations. These expectations are the standards by which bankers develop their skills for effective customer service and sales. When asked what they want in a bank, customer responses mostly fall into the following categories:

- responsive service
- competent staff
- customer perspective
- courteous treatment
- reliable service
- viable products and services
- professional appearance
- accessibility to funds and staff
- financial privacy

## RESPONSIVE SERVICE

Customers want their bankers to be ready and willing to serve them. Responsive service makes it clear that the bank wants and values the customer's business.

**Did You Know ...**

Bilingual advertising, flexible underwriting standards, financial education seminars, and effective community partnerships are among the effective strategies that can be used to reach out to America's 31 million-member immigrant community.

*(American Bankers Association)*

**Did You Know ...**

Committed, personal service has been credited with keeping community banks strong even as consolidation in the banking industry is reducing the number of banks overall. The reason is that community banks perform highly important roles as providers of relationship-based banking services.

*("The Role of Community Banks in the U.S. Economy," Federal Reserve Bank of Kansas, 2002)*

Responsiveness involves:

- acknowledging customers as they approach

- being ready to help customers

- listening carefully to understand customer needs

- taking responsibility for the problems customers present

- functioning as a team member with other bank employees to solve problems and serve customers

- solving problems promptly and accurately

- being friendly and caring when resolving special problems

## COMPETENT STAFF

Customers expect bank employees to have the skills and knowledge needed to explain the bank's products and services and answer questions clearly. They expect to be directed to the products and services that will be most useful to them. Demonstrated competency reassures customers that their money is in good hands.

## CUSTOMER PERSPECTIVE

In all interactions with customers, it is important to recognize and understand their perspective. Both written and spoken communication should be in clear, concise language articulated with the customer's, not the bank's, point of view in mind. "Preauthorized automatic transfers are available with this account" may be operationally correct, but the following shows a customer perspective: "You may arrange to have funds automatically transferred from your checking account to your money market savings account, making regular saving easier for you."

Similarly, bank employees should avoid bank jargon when dealing with customers. Terms such as "truncation," "demand deposit," "foreign bank," and "amortizing" may be familiar and important to bank employees, but they are not to the average bank customer. Acronyms like PMI, APY, and even CD may draw blank stares from customers. Unless absolutely necessary for regulatory compliance purposes, avoid technical terms and acronyms when a simple explanation will suffice. When technical terms are required, they should be explained using language the customer can understand.

## COURTEOUS TREATMENT

Customers want to be treated in a friendly, thoughtful, efficient, and respectful manner. When customers believe they have been treated discourteously, they conclude that they and their business are unimportant to the bank. They may feel uncomfortable interacting with bank employees and ultimately take their business elsewhere. In contrast, satisfied

customers feel valued and believe that the bank wants their business. Courteous behavior is conveyed in a variety of ways.

## Banker Profile

**Steve Martin**
*Vice President, Marketing, Canandaigua National Bank & Trust, Canandaigua, New York*

Steve Martin knows that life need not be a complex endeavor. Enthusiasm and involvement are all that's needed. "Successful people are advocates, with excellent interpersonal skills," he says.

As Vice President of Marketing, Steve communicates to his community about his bank and bank's services. He also serves as an involved advocate in his community, coaching youth in sports and serving as a board member for the American Red Cross and the Rochester Broadway Theatre League.

Continuing education is important to Steve. "Career bankers are inspired learners. Not just classroom learners, they are motivated to direct their own learning." Steve, a graduate of the ABA School of Bank Marketing and a Certified Marketing Professional through the Institute of Certified Bankers, is a Trustee on ABA's National Education Foundation Council. As an inspired learner, he continues to inspire others.

| | |
|---|---|
| **Making eye contact** | Looking customers in the eye as they approach lets them know they are important. |
| **Smiling** | A smile communicates warmth. When employees smile, customers are left with the impression that the bank is happy to serve them. |
| **Acknowledging and greeting the customer** | Customers expect to be acknowledged and greeted promptly when they approach. Bankers should stand, shake hands, and initiate introductions. This makes customers feel welcome and comfortable stating their business. |
| **Using the customer's name** | Calling customers by name makes them feel at home and familiar. It raises the interaction to a more personal level. |
| **Using expressions of courtesy** | "Please," "thank you," and "excuse me" should be used liberally in all customer contact situations. |
| **Having a positive attitude** | Employees always should respond to customers in a helpful, cheerful, and interested manner. Even when customers are upset or angry, bank employees should show their willingness to listen calmly. |

## RELIABLE SERVICE

Customers understandably expect a high level of service from banks. They expect statements to arrive on time and to be accurate; they expect renewal notices for certificates of deposit; they expect electronic banking services to be available when needed; and they expect problems to be resolved quickly. Reliable service means meeting and exceeding customer expectations.

## VIABLE PRODUCTS AND SERVICES

Customers expect banks to have a variety of banking products, and they expect each product to have specific benefits that address financial needs. Listed below are four basic financial needs and some examples of appropriate bank products and services addressing those needs.

| *Financial Need* | *Product/Service* |
|---|---|
| Save money | Savings account, money market deposit account, certificate of deposit, investment advisory services |

## Situation

Elva, widow of a small business owner, comes to her local community bank to seek a loan. She is older and has little experience in banking transactions. It is a very busy day, and the banker has a number of loan applications that need his review before sending them on to credit investigation. Anthony, the banker, notices the woman struggle with completing the loan application package. Instead of hurrying her along, he focuses first on assisting the widow, the customer, and then the paperwork.

| | |
|---|---|
| Borrow money | Auto loan, mortgage, home equity loan/line of credit, credit cards |
| Move money | Checking account, automatic transfer, direct deposit, internet banking, telephone banking, ATMs, wire transfers |
| Protect assets | Trust services, insurance services, FDIC insurance |

## PROFESSIONAL APPEARANCE

Customer attitudes are shaped in part by the appearance of the bank facility and its employees. Drab or disorganized facilities and unprofessionally attired staff erode confidence. Customers expect the office where they bank to look like a safe place to put their money. Banks have long designed their facilities to project an appearance of trust and strength. Today, many bank lobbies are being redesigned to project a more modern, retail-oriented atmosphere.

Moreover, when employees dress professionally, customers feel more confident about the bank. Most banks require employees who interact with the public to dress in business attire. Business casual is often allowed in areas that do not have direct customer contact. Many banks also issue policy expectations to employees about other aspects of personal appearance, as long as such guidelines do not discriminate against a protected group of employees. Professional appearance gives the impression that employees respect themselves and their customers, and, in turn, deserve customers' respect.

## ACCESSIBILITY TO FUNDS AND STAFF

Customers expect services and employees to be available when and where needed. Internet banking, automated teller machines (ATMs), and telephone banking are examples of how banks have employed technology to deliver bank products and services to customers at any hour of the day. Customers have access to their funds when they need them. Banks also have extended branch banking hours to meet customer needs for services that require direct employee interaction. This "customer first" attitude is reflected also by employees who are accessible and demonstrate a willingness to help. Accessibility applies not only to employees with customer contact responsibilities. Every employee has an obligation to be of assistance to their coworkers.

## FINANCIAL PRIVACY

Bank customers expect their accounts to be handled in complete privacy. As the amount of personal information stored and transmitted electronically grows, so does consumer anxiety about financial confidentiality. Banks, more than most other businesses, have in their files and databases a great deal of confidential information about their customers. Bank employees must observe the bank's privacy policies and never discuss accounts or transactions with friends or neighbors.

With the Gramm-Leach-Bliley Act (GLBA), Congress included provisions requiring financial institutions to protect the privacy of customers' personal information. The act requires banks to disclose whether they share customer information with third parties and to refrain from sharing such information if the customer objects. Whereas banks always have placed a priority on protecting customer account information, GLBA privacy provisions provide additional assurance that the banking industry is committed to protecting customers' personal, private financial information.

# CROSS-SELLING AND REFERRALS

Bank marketing studies show that on average the more products and services a customer uses, the more likely the customer will remain loyal to the bank—and provide the bank with a profitable customer relationship.

The best way bank employees can build additional product and service relationships with customers is through cross-selling and **referrals**. Cross-selling is the practice of recommending the benefits of additional products or services to current customers. Referrals usually are made when a bank employee does not have the expertise or authority to sell a product or service, or the product or service is offered by another department or a bank affiliate. Referrals involve suggesting to customers that they speak to someone in the bank or bank affiliate who can explain a bank product or service that would be appropriate for them. In both cases, listening to customers to recognize and learn their needs is the important first step.

**Referral**—Directing a potential customer from one area of the bank, such as consumer lending, to another area, such as insurance, to help the customer obtain information about or purchase another product or service.

A bank that effectively cross-sells additional products and refers business to other departments or affiliates expands its customer relationships, helps customers meet their financial goals, and sells more products, both immediately and over the long-term. Also, when employees cross-sell and make referrals, customers feel appreciated and realize that the bank values their business and has their financial interests in mind.

To cross-sell and make referrals, bankers must be aware constantly of marketing and sales opportunities. For example:

- A teller who notices a customer with a large balance in her savings account should suggest a money market account or a certificate of deposit (cross-selling) or the bank's investment services (referral).

- A loan officer who helps a customer finance a new car should suggest opening a checking account and arranging for the automatic loan payment service (cross-sell) and an insurance review with the bank's insurance subsidiary (referral).

- A call center employee should suggest Internet banking or telephone banking to a customer who inquires about an account statement or current history (cross-sell).

- A commercial loan officer should recommend cash management services for a small business (cross-sell) and private banking services (referral) for the owner who has an established credit relationship with the bank.

**Did You Know ...**

Psychologist Abraham Maslow identified five levels of need that motivate human behavior: physiological need, the need for a sense of security, the need to belong, the need for a sense of self esteem, and the need for self-actualization.

Identify
Needs

Postpurchase
Assessment

Prepurchase
Searching

Purchase
Decision

# THE PURCHASING PROCESS

Understanding how a customer proceeds to make a purchase is essential to building customer relationships. The customer purchasing process is influenced by every transaction, communication, and experience with the bank. Knowing the steps in the process helps bankers facilitate customer decisions to obtain a product or service. The purchasing process usually happens in four phases: needs identification, prepurchase searching, the purchase decision, and postpurchase assessment (see exhibit 8.1).

## NEEDS IDENTIFICATION

The starting point for any purchase is an unsatisfied need. Two types of needs are involved.

**Recognized needs**    The customer is aware of recognized needs. For example, a young college graduate who has gained employment in his profession realizes that he needs to establish credit. A regular savings account customer realizes that she could be earning more interest by investing in a certificate of deposit.

**Unrecognized needs**    The customer is unaware of these needs. The college graduate turned professional may not know the credit options and financial planning services available to him. The savings account customer may not realize that she could grow her savings faster by investing in the equities market or purchasing an annuity.

Bank employees play a key role in the needs identification process. Most customers welcome advice on how their bank can serve them better. For employees to offer advice, they must know their customers and have a good understanding of their bank's products and services. In short, bank employees should be alert for opportunities to recommend a product to a customer.

## PREPURCHASE SEARCHING

Once a need is identified, the customer begins to search for the best way to satisfy the need. The level of effort expended in this search depends on the cost, durability, and complexity of the product or service being sought. When purchasing a savings product, the customer may look through newspaper ads to compare the rates offered by competing financial institutions. When shopping for a mortgage loan or a home equity line of credit, customers may search longer and carefully because mortgage products are complicated and require knowledge about the various terms and conditions available on the market.

Although prepurchase searching often includes talking to other people, reading consumer information pamphlets, or requesting a loan application, the most important source of information is a bank's employees. Often a prospective customer will call the bank or approach an employee in person to solicit information about financial products, offering an opportunity to sell a bank product or service. An employee who shows interest in the customer's needs, conveys enthusiasm about the bank's products and exhibits knowledge and capability, is more effective than any promotional material in selling a bank's products.

### Features and Benefits

Much of the customer's prepurchase activity involves information gathering around **features** and **benefits** of possible product solutions. As discussed, customers have basic financial needs: save money, borrow money, move money, and protect assets. Product benefits address those basic financial needs.

The following is an example of common bank products and related features and benefits.

| Product | Feature | Benefit |
|---------|---------|---------|
| Home equity line of credit | Revolving line of credit | Customer can use funds as needed, pay interest only on outstanding balance, save time and money |
| Money market deposit account | A higher yield than statement savings accounts; no fixed maturity date | Customers earn more money than with statement savings accounts, and can move money more freely than with time deposits |

**Benefit**—The value the product or service features give to customers to meet their needs, such as earn money, save money, save time, provide convenience, or provide security.

**Feature**—A characteristic of the product or service. For example, the interest rate or maturity period.

**Purchase decision**—In the buying process, the culmination of prepurchase activity, in which information gathered to reduce the risk associated with a decision about a product is assessed and the purchase is then made.

When discussing product features and benefits with the customer, bankers translate product features into benefits the customer will appreciate. For example, "With Internet banking you can pay bills online. What that means to you is time saved writing out bills and money saved in postage. You are also assured the bill will be paid on time."

## PURCHASE DECISION

When deciding to make a purchase, the customer uses information gathered during the prepurchase phase to weigh the advantages and disadvantages of the product or service, compare the relative merits of alternatives, and select among various features. In the context of banking, this may mean choosing the most appropriate type of individual retirement account or applying for a fixed-rate versus an adjustable-rate mortgage. The **purchase decision** is often the result of an informed choice, and the choice becomes more complex as the product or service becomes more complex. Bankers play an important sales and service role by answering any questions the customer may have, and either moving to close a sale, if possible, or referring the customer to other bank personnel who provide the product or service.

## POSTPURCHASE ASSESSMENT

After customers make a purchase, an assessment of the purchase decision inevitably ensues. Customers want assurance that they made the right choice. Many customers experience anxiety, especially if the purchase decision was difficult or attractive alternatives were rejected. Was the decision the right one? Were the most appropriate features selected? Such questions occur to most customers as they reevaluate a product or service following its purchase.

Bankers, aware of this stage in the purchasing process, take steps to ease customers' anxieties and offer evidence that the decision was good. They know that a customer generally needs continuing support after making a purchase. In the banking world, reassuring new customers may entail:

- sending them welcome letters
- calling to thank them for their business and offering further assistance
- answering questions after they deposit their money or sign loan papers

# PRODUCT DEVELOPMENT

Banks not only market and sell existing products, they also evaluate and introduce new ones. The financial modernization reforms under the GLBA broadened the scope of products and services that banks may offer, and today many customers demand more products to meet their financial goals.

Developing new products is a multiphase process (see exhibit 8.2). It begins with conducting market research, profiling the market, soliciting new product ideas, testing the concept, and conducting a business analysis. The product is then developed and test marketed before being introduced to the marketplace. Finally, the effectiveness of the product is evaluated relative to its objectives.

In most banks, the product development process is a joint effort among the marketing officer, department management, and senior management. Compliance or risk management officers are also frequently part of the team because many new products have regulatory or risk implications.

**Conducting market research**

**Marketing customer information file**—A software program that can sort and analyze customer information and that can serve as a customer information database.

Up-to-date information about customers, the market, and competitors is drawn from internal records such as the **marketing customer information file**; local contacts such as the chamber of commerce; regulatory agency reports; the Internet such as bank Web sites; surveys such as those about customer preferences; secondary sources such as lists of new home development sites.

## Exhibit 8.2: New Product Development

**Conduct Market Research**
Obtain current information on customers, market, and competitors.

↓

**Profile Customers, Market, and Competitors**
Aggregate data for meaningful analysis.

↓

**Getting New Product Ideas**
What is the need in the marketplace?

↓

**Screening New Products**
What is the initial reaction against the bank's objectives,
other products, and company resources?
Are there regulatory constraints?

↓

**Testing the Concept**
What do the small focus groups say?

↓

**Business Analysis**
Is there sufficient demand for the product?
Does it fit with the bank's goals and objectives?

↓

**Developing the Product**
What will the features be?
How will the bank promote, distribute, and price the new product?

↓

**Test Marketing the Product**
What target markets will the bank test the product in?
How will the bank promote the product in those markets?

↓

**Introducing the Product**
How will the bank introduce the product?
What impact will this product have on the existing product line?

↓

**Evaluating the Product**
How does the progress of the new product meet the company's goals?
What adjustments are necessary?

**Did You Know ...**

Nearly two-thirds of community banks require their employees to return e-mails and voice-mails the same day they are received, according to the 2003 Community Bank Competitiveness Survey.

*(ABA Banking Journal and the ABA Community Bankers Council)*

---

**Profiling customers, the market, and competitors**

A bank's **profile** of its consumer customers may include information about age distribution, occupation, educational level, income, and geographic location. A market profile may describe the number and value of housing units, population data, and demographic information in the bank's geographic area. A competitive profile may include information on competitors' market share and the types and prices of services they offer.

**Profiling**—Identifying relevant characteristics to gain insight about the need for a product in the marketplace.

**Soliciting new ideas** Ideas for new products come from many sources including market research, management or employees, or as author-

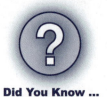

**Did You Know ...**

Effectiveness of
Communication:
7% of meaning is in the
words that are spoken
38% of meaning is in
the tone of voice
55% of meaning is in
body language

ized by laws and regulators, such as health savings accounts, insurance, and investments.

| | |
|---|---|
| **Screening the product** | New product ideas are screened against the bank's product objectives, policies, resources, and the probable effect on existing products. Then, the bank decides whether to pursue the product. |
| **Testing the concept** | The product idea is tested in the market place through customer focus groups or customer surveys. |
| **Performing a business analysis** | Market and business analysis techniques determine market share, product demand and compatibility with bank goals, and objectives. Then, product objectives, target market, and strategy are defined. |
| **Developing the product** | The product is defined, including features and benefits, pricing, processes, and procedures to support the product, distribution, and promotion strategies. |
| **Testing and marketing the product** | The product is tested in one or more bank geographic markets, using different features, distribution methods, and promotion strategies. |
| **Introducing the product** | Introducing a new banking product requires a substantial investment in advertising, sales promotions, and employee training. Customer-contact employees should understand thoroughly product features and customer benefits. |
| **Monitoring the product** | Monitoring product performance helps identify needed adjustments, effect on other product lines, and other product development opportunities. |

## SUMMARY

- The most successful banks build long-term relationships with their customers. For good customer relationships to be formed and sustained over time, the entire bank—systems, procedures, and people—must adopt a customer-centered philosophy of doing business. Every employee, including those who do not have daily contact with customers, can build customer relationships. Sales, marketing, and customer service are all part of building customer relationships and fulfilling the marketing concept.

- The marketing concept is fundamental to a bank's customer relationship orientation. The broad concept of marketing holds that the objectives of an organization are best reached by identifying the needs and wants of its customers and meeting those needs and wants through an integrated, efficient, organization-wide effort supported by management. The pillars of the marketing concept include total company effort, customer satisfaction, profitability, and social responsibility.

- To succeed in today's sales-oriented banking environment, employees must be personally and professionally skilled. Customers have a right to expect responsive service, competence, courteous treatment, reliable service, professional demeanor, and privacy in their interactions with employees. They have a right to expect the employee to understand their customer perspective and that the products and services will meet their needs.

- The best prospects for new sales are current customers. This is the underlying principle behind cross-selling— that is, getting users of one or more services to buy or use additional services. To cross-sell, bankers must constantly be aware of sales opportunities and provide the best service at all times so customers want to buy products in the future. Referrals involve listening for customers' needs and then arranging for the customer to talk to another knowledgeable staff member or authorized bank affiliate employee for more information about the product or service.

- In keeping with a customer-oriented philosophy, bank employees should understand the stages a customer goes through when purchasing a product. There are four stages to the purchasing process: needs identification, prepurchase searching, the purchase decision, and postpurchase assessment. As they interact with customers during these stages, bank employees have opportunities to build customer relationships.

- Banks must not only successfully market and sell existing products, they must continually introduce new ones as well. Developing a new product begins with conducting market research and developing a market profile. New product ideas can come from many sources, including employees. Product ideas are screened and tested. If a business analysis indicates that consumer acceptance is likely, the product is developed and test marketed before being introduced to the marketplace.

# SELF CHECK & REVIEW

**Learning Check**

1. Do employees who rarely interact with bank customers have a role in building customer relationships? Why or why not?

2. What are some of the ways a bank employee can demonstrate responsiveness to customer needs?

3. What are the benefits of cross-selling and referrals?

4. What are some of the things customers do in anticipation of making a purchase?

5. What is the difference between a product feature and product benefit?

6. What steps are involved in bringing a new product to market?

# ADDITIONAL RESOURCES

*ABA Bank Marketing Magazine*. Washington, D.C.: American Bankers Association.

*ABA Bank Marketing Planning Survey Report*, Washington, D.C., American Bankers Association, 2003.

*ABA Bank Marketing Survey Report*, Washington, D.C.: American Bankers Association, 2002.

*ABA Banking Journal*, **www.banking.com/aba**

ABA Marketing Network. **www.aba.com/MarketingNetwork**

*ABA Retail Banking Survey Report*, Washington, D.C.: American Bankers Association, 2003.

"Best Practices in Immigrant Lending" Compiled for the American Bankers Association by ShoreBank Advisory Services, Chicago, 2004. **www.aba.com/aba/pdf/ImmigrantLending_May2004.pdf**

Federal Deposit Insurance Corporation statistical reports for bankers, **www.fdic.gov**

*The Drive for Quality and CRM, The Evolution of Financial Services Call Centers*, Volume V, Washington, D.C.: American Bankers Association, 2002.

# Safeguarding Customers, Bank Assets, and the Nation

# What You Will Learn

*After studying this chapter, you should be able to*

- describe how banks safeguard customer information and privacy
- discuss identity theft and other financial crimes against bank customers
- describe roles of the board of directors, bank committees, officers, and employees in safeguarding bank assets
- identify typical check fraud schemes, currency counterfeiting techniques, and prevention efforts
- identify steps employees can take to deter a robbery
- describe how banks assist in safeguarding the nation
- define the bolded key terms that appear in the text

# Introduction

*Banks are unique in the business world. They have a very special steward relationship with their customers and communities, and they play a pivotal role in the national economy. Banks are not just about profits. They provide vital services to customers and are expected to safeguard customer assets entrusted to them. At the same time, bank stockholders and the public assume that banks will protect their own financial assets so that loan and investment funds will be available to keep local economies strong and vibrant. Banks also occupy a unique position in the nation's economic life by providing fiscal and agency services to the government, helping to carry out the nation's monetary policies, and financing economic development. Furthermore, banks contribute to our country's foreign policy and national security goals.*

*With all these critical roles to fulfill, banks have a special duty to protect customer information, safeguard customer and bank assets, deter financial crimes, and help protect the nation's financial system against misuse and corruption. It is for these reasons that banking has been called a "public trust." Bank employees should understand their role in helping safeguard customers, bank assets, and the nation.*

# SAFEGUARDING CUSTOMERS

Banks are considered to be safe repositories for people's money. Just as important, a bank is a repository for customer information that, in this electronic age, can be more valuable than money and cause great injury to the customer if misused. Bank employees have an obligation to safeguard customer information and to ensure customers are not victimized by financial fraud.

### INFORMATION SECURITY

Banks always have recognized their responsibility to protect the confidentiality and security of customer information, while ensuring customers' access to their accounts and account information. In the late 1990s, however, banks confronted an unusual but critical challenge to information safekeeping, security, and availability. As the year 2000 approached, banks around the world faced the prospect that their computer systems would crash or critical information suddenly would become unavailable unless software was updated to reflect the date change to a new millennium.

In addition, the Gramm-Leach-Bliley Act (GLBA) legally mandated banks and other financial institutions to develop security policies and procedures designed to protect customer account information and financial data. Title V of GLBA requires banks to improve the safeguards that keep confidential customer information secure. The banking agencies issued guidelines specifying the steps bankers should take to protect against anticipated threats or hazards to the security or integrity of customer records and guard against the unauthorized use of records or information that could result in substantial harm or inconvenience to any customer.

In response, virtually all banks have updated or instituted physical, technical, and administrative safeguards for protecting computer systems that store customer account and financial data.

## CUSTOMER INFORMATION PRIVACY

GLBA also includes provisions that give customers some control over how their personal information is used. Banks are required to disclose their privacy policies to customers and to give customers a reasonable opportunity to elect not to have their "nonpublic personal information" shared with third parties for marketing. This ability is called the "opt-out" privilege. If customers do not opt out, banks are permitted to share certain customer information with third parties.

The Fair Credit Reporting Act also places restrictions on sharing information with affiliated parties. Among other things, banks must allow their customers to opt-out of having certain information shared with affiliates.

States also have privacy laws, and some of them are more restrictive than federal laws. For example, some states require customers to "opt-in" to information sharing. This means that banks operating in those states must ask every customer whether they affirmatively give their consent to having their customer information shared with third parties or affiliates. Federal law may preempt some state laws.

## COMPUTER ATTACKS

Because banks store sensitive customer financial information on computers, illegal attempts to gain access to private accounts are a special concern for information technology specialists. Computer attacks can come from inside the bank—perpetrated by disgruntled employees who are knowledgeable about the bank's computer security systems, or outside the bank—perpetrated by hackers.

Typically, hackers attack computer systems with a virus that can destroy data or crash the system. Most computer viruses are spread through e-mail messages and Internet use. When the recipient of the e-mail downloads an attachment, for example, the virus is released to other computers on the network through the victim's e-mail distribution list. Computer viruses also can infect computers through Internet browsing, file downloading, and disk and CD exchanging. The extent of damage varies. Viruses can affect the operation of an individual personal computer or shut down a bank's entire computer network or Web site.

The danger of virus-infected material entering a bank employee's computer is greater than ever. If it happens, a bank can lose critical customer information and incur the cost it takes to restore data. In some cases, information is permanently lost.

Many banks have installed virus protection software centrally. Nevertheless, because the stakes are so high, all bank employees should be aware of how their actions can affect the bank's systems adversely. Employees can help safeguard the customer and bank from computer attacks by installing virus protection software at home. At work, and as directed at the bank, they can maintain backup files, practice safe Internet and e-mail usage habits, and otherwise follow bank policy regarding secure use of computers.

## IDENTITY THEFT

Identity theft is one of the fastest growing financial crimes. Bank regulatory agencies have issued guidelines calling on banks to institute safeguards against identity theft. In doing so, the Office of Comptroller of the Currency wrote, "This growing crime has a devastating effect on financial institution customers and a detrimental impact on the banks."[1]

Identity theft involves stealing a customer's personal information and using it for illegal purposes, such as to gain access to bank accounts, apply for loans or credit cards, or purchase merchandise. Personal information commonly stolen and used to commit identity theft includes:

- name
- address
- date of birth
- mother's maiden name
- Social Security number
- financial account numbers and name of bank
- place of employment
- children's names
- drivers license number

Identity thieves obtain information in a variety of ways. The flood of applications and forms that people receive requesting personal information provides a cover for identity thieves. People are accustomed to giving out their personal information. Transactions conducted over the telephone often require consumers to give personal

**Did You Know ...**

Identity theft is the most common consumer complaint. Of over 500,000 complaints the Federal Trade Commission received in 2003, 42 percent were identity theft reports.

*(Federal Trade Commission)*

---

**Customer Service Tip: Cell Phone Photographs**

Watch out for people holding cell phones standing near you at retail stores, restaurants, and grocery stores. With the new camera cell phones, they can take a picture of your credit card, which gives them your name, number, and expiration date.

*(American Bankers Association, Bank Risk News)*

## Customer Service Tip: Safeguarding Your Information

- Don't give your Social Security number or other personal credit information to anyone who calls you.

- Tear up or shred receipts, bank statements, and unused credit card offers before throwing them away.

- Check for any missing mail.

- Review your monthly accounts for unauthorized charges.

- To ensure accuracy, order copies of your credit report once a year.

- Choose to do business with reputable companies, particularly when making purchases online.

- When conducting business online, ensure the browser's padlock or key icon is active.

- Do not open e-mail from unknown sources, and use virus detection software.

- Protect your PINs and passwords (do not carry them in your wallet).

- Use a combination of letters and numbers for your passwords and change them periodically.

- Report any suspicions of fraud to your bank and the fraud unit's credit reporting agencies immediately.

*(ABA Education Foundation)*

## Situation

Bob is a senior citizen who banks over the Internet for the convenience it offers. One day Bob received a telephone call from someone claiming to be an auditor from his bank. The caller tells Bob that there has been a security breach and that everyone who has an online banking account should change their password. The caller asks Bob for his password to effect the change. Bob remembers advice in a bank brochure about identity theft that recommended never giving personal or account information over the phone. Bob declines the caller's request and reports the incident to his bank.

information. The Internet provides identity thieves with an easy way to obtain information by searching Web sites. In a practice called "dumpster diving," identity thieves retrieve cancelled checks and financial statements from the trash. Discarded records contain enough information to allow a person to assume the identity of an unsuspecting customer and cause financial havoc.

In short, numerous opportunities present themselves every day for identity theft to occur, and unfortunately, bank employees are sometimes unwitting accomplices. Too many bank employees have been victimized by a scam known as "pretext calling". A pretext caller will ask for personal and account information over the telephone by impersonating a customer and making up a story about losing or forgetting account numbers and other sensitive information. The trusting bank employee divulges the information to help the "unfortunate" customer, not knowing that the caller was an identity thief.

### Identity Theft Deterrence

The best deterrents to identity theft are vigilant employees and informed customers. All employees have a role to play in curbing identity theft, especially front-line tellers and customer service representatives who receive, or are asked to provide, account information or who accept applications. Bank employees also can remind customers how to safeguard their own information.

By law, every bank is required to have comprehensive information about security procedures. These procedures define appropriate employee conduct for handling customer information, and employees should abide by them. Banks have strict guide-

## Banker Profile

**Dianne E. Kolb, CFSSP**
*Vice President and Director of Security, Fulton Financial Corporation, Lancaster, Pennsylvania*

As vice president and director of security, Dianne Kolb is responsible for compliance in all aspects of the Bank Protection Act, including its security program, securing all facilities, OFFAC monitoring, managing the bank's emergency recovery program, and training employees on security matters.

"Technology has both enhanced conveniences for customers and opportunities for criminals. The challenge for bankers is to continue to enhance services while also being good stewards of the trust that customers bestow on us."

Ms. Kolb holds degrees in psychology and sociology. She maintains membership in professional organizations, including the Institute of Certified Bankers, where as a Certified Financial Services Security Professional (CFSSP), she serves on the ICB Certification Council.

Her advice to new bankers: "Continue to educate yourself. Expose yourself to many banking areas from a variety of sources and you'll learn where your own talents and interests lie."

lines when communicating with customers seeking information on their account or a third party, such as another bank, seeking to verify the authenticity of an individual's account. Never should an employee provide customer information without the caller first providing a personal identification number (PIN), password, or some other identifier known only to the customer, such as answers to these questions: "What is the name of your first pet?" or "Where were you born?" Such secure identifiers normally are established when the account is opened.

When another financial institution or merchant calls seeking information, banks often use caller-ID or a call-back to the institution or merchant to verify the caller's identity. Some banks prohibit releasing some customer information over the telephone under any circumstances.

## BANK CARD FRAUD

Bank card fraud involves a criminal stealing a credit or debit card or number and then purchasing goods or services fraudulently. The potential for loss is high because a criminal often can make purchases before the victim knows the card is missing.

Criminals obtain bank card information in a number of ways, including:

- taking a card from a stolen wallet or handbag
- stealing a card or statement from a mailbox or from within the postal delivery service
- copying of information by sales associates or servers from a card presented for a legitimate transaction
- buying account information sold by dishonest card issuer employees
- stealing statements from files or trash cans

Under Regulation E, consumer liability from debit card fraud is limited to $50, if the customer notifies the bank in a timely fashion (generally within two days) of learning of the unauthorized transaction. Similar rules apply to credit card transactions outlined in Regulation Z. Because of the caps on consumer liability, card issuers absorb the bulk of the losses resulting from fraudulent transactions. Banks employ the following safeguards to counter unauthorized transactions.

- To thwart mailbox theft, customers must call a toll-free number to activate their cards. This call is made to confirm that the legitimate cardholder, not a thief, possesses the card. Often, the issuer will send a follow-up notice stating that the card has been sent and needs to be activated. If the card was not received, the intended recipient may alert the issuer.
- To have a transaction approved, a customer's card must have a current expiration date and account number.
- So merchants can compare signatures at the point of purchase, card-holders must sign the backs of their cards. Merchants should verify that the signature on the receipt and card match.
- Cards feature a gold or silver hologram showing clear, three-dimensional images that appear to move when the card is tilted.

- The account number, expiration date, and cardholder's name are printed across the face of the card in raised letters.

- Most banks set limits on the amount of cash customers can obtain through ATMs.

- Many card issuers use sophisticated software to monitor account activity. Unusual increases in activity, such as an uncharacteristically high spending volume, increases in mail orders, or use in atypical parts of the country or world, initiate a warning on the account. Until transactions are verified, the card issuer may freeze or flag the account. Some card issuers contact the cardholder when suspicious account activity appears.

## CONSUMER SCAMS

For every scam that is exposed and addressed through customer and employee education, another one surfaces. Federal regulators frequently issue advisories alerting banks and bank customers to these schemes. Bank employees must pay attention to these advisories and follow bank procedures for handling schemes. Phishing, advance fee fraud, and credit card protection fraud are three examples of scams.

### "Phishing"

"Phishing" (pronounced "fishing"), a relatively new type of fraud, has become common. Phishing involves sending customers seemingly legitimate e-mail requests over the Internet. Customers are directed to a phony "customer service" site and asked to provide personal account information. Basically, the customer is tricked into providing account numbers, Social Security numbers, or passwords. The illegally obtained confidential information is then used in identity theft, credit card fraud, and Internet-based frauds.

Like all frauds of this type, the most effective remedies are educated customers and alert, helpful bank employees. Banks can combat phishing by:

- providing notices on bank Web sites reminding customers that the bank never requests confidential information through e-mail and to report any such requests to the bank

- restricting electronic communications with customers through an e-mail system available through the bank's secure Internet banking application only

- printing warnings and notices on customer statements or other paper mailings

- using authentication methods and procedures

- explaining how customers can authenticate the bank's web pages

- sending customers educational brochures

### Advance Fee Fraud

"Advance fee" fraud victimizes banks and their customers. The average loss per person is over $6,000.

The scam often begins with the intended victim receiving an unsolicited letter, fax, or e-mail allegedly from a foreign national who claims to be a high-level civil servant. The "official" requests assistance in depositing millions of dollars that the

## Situation

In looking over her monthly bank card statement, Chris notices several charges for purchases at a store called Bill's Fertilizer Depot. Chris is a city dweller and does not recognize the store. She calls her bank card company. After investigating the matter, the bank card company discovers that Chris is a victim of bank card fraud. Chris's bank card account is closed, and she is not charged for the unauthorized purchases.

## Customer Service Tip: Phishing Protection

- Never give out your personal financial information in response to an unsolicited phone call, fax, or email, no matter how official it may seem.

- Do not respond to email that may warn of dire consequences unless you validate your information immediately.

- Check your credit card and bank account statements regularly and look for unauthorized transactions, even small ones. Report discrepancies immediately.

- Secure your Internet transaction. When submitting financial information to a Web site, look for the padlock or key icon at the bottom of your browser, and make sure the Internet address begins with "http."

- Report suspicious activity to the Internet Fraud Complaint Center, a partnership between the FBI and the National White Collar Crime Center.

- If you have responded to an email, contact your bank immediately so they can protect your account and your identity.

*(ABA Education Foundation)*

"official's" government overpaid on a contract. Other fraudulent requests may involve disbursements from wills, proceeds from real estate sales, converting hard currency, or selling crude oil at below market prices.

For assisting in the funds transfer, the recipient of the correspondence (the fraud victim) is promised a large commission. The victim is instructed to provide company letterheads and pro forma invoicing to show completion of the contract, which upon approval by a bank in the "official's" country, will result in the funds being remitted to the victim's account. Inevitably, something arises to threaten the deal, such as an unforeseen tax or fee that must be paid.

Bank employees should be alert to questions from customers who have been contacted by such "officials" concerning financial ventures. Banks must contact appropriate law enforcement officials and bank regulatory agencies whenever there is information of advance fee fraud or any other type of bank fraud.

### *Credit Card Protection Fraud*

With offers of credit card "protection" services, illicit telemarketers claim that they are calling on behalf of a credit card issuer or a government agency. The caller claims that criminals are using the Internet to steal credit card numbers and that consumers are liable for any unsubstantiated charges made by online thieves. The sales pitch concludes with an offer of a credit card "protection" package that covers unsubstantiated charges, along with an unconditional money-back guarantee. During the call, the telemarketer obtains the consumer's credit card number and other information, and charges for the "protection" package, whether or not the consumer agreed to purchase the protection.

Bank employees should advise cardholders that, under federal law, they are liable for up to $50 of unauthorized charges made to their credit cards. Thus, there is little need for credit card "insurance."

# SAFEGUARDING BANK ASSETS

In addition to helping customers avoid financial fraud and information breaches, banks must take steps to prevent their own victimization and monetary losses. Banks are obligated to their stockholders, employees, and customers to safeguard assets by adopting good corporate governance controls and deterring financial crimes.

## CORPORATE GOVERNANCE AND ETHICAL BEHAVIOR

Corporate governance is the manner in which a company is managed and its assets accounted for and reported to the public. Corporate governance is the responsibility of a company's board of directors and senior management.

Lax or dishonest corporate governance practices have resulted in the failures of several major corporations. Although the banking industry has not been implicated directly in any of the scandals of the 1990s, the corporate governance crisis eroded public confidence in the accounting and reporting practices of all businesses.

In 2002, to improve corporate governance practices, Congress enacted the Sarbanes-Oxley Act. The act imposes significant new responsibilities on boards of directors, corporate executives, audit committees, and external auditors of public companies. Corporate executives now are required to attest to the completeness and accuracy of the information contained in company financial reports. Also, to ensure that the board of directors independently exercises its oversight responsibility, members of the audit committee cannot be members of management. These are just two ways the Sarbanes-Oxley Act improves corporate governance responsibilities.

Banks are subject to federal laws and regulations that impose high standards of corporate accountability and ethical behavior, and the Sarbanes-Oxley Act parallels some requirements already in place for banks. Soon after the Sarbanes-Oxley Act became law, bank regulatory agencies issued guidelines that clarified how the law applied specifically to banks.

### Board of Directors and Management Responsibilities

All bank employees must observe the highest ethical standards and be committed to doing the right thing when a choice presents itself. The conduct and practices of several parties, however, are especially important to good corporate governance.

| | |
|---|---|
| **Board of Directors** | Responsible for setting the bank's policies and directives, and ensuring that management carries them out. Primarily responsible for establishing and maintaining procedures for controlling risks. Ultimately responsible for ensuring depositor funds are protected and public confidence in the bank remains high. |

| | |
|---|---|
| **Audit committee** | Monitors bank management and staff compliance with board policies and with the applicable laws and regulations. Selects internal and external auditors; oversees internal audit function; reviews and approves audit scope and frequency; receives audit reports and reviews the conclusions with management; ensures that management takes necessary corrective actions. |
| **Other board committees** | Play an important role in safeguarding the bank and its assets: the loan committee approves major loans, reviews problem loans, and assists in internal loan examinations; the trust committee oversees bank's trust activities. |
| **Senior management** | Their words, attitudes, and actions define and reinforce ethical behavior. Avoid policies and practices that encourage inappropriate behavior such as undue emphasis on short-term performance, performance-dependent compensation, ineffective segregation of duties that may tempt misuse of resources or conceal poor performance, and insignificant or overly onerous penalties for improper behavior. |

### *Employee Responsibilities*

The bank's expectations for employee conduct, both professionally and personally, are communicated in a code of ethics. A code of ethics helps employees decide what is in the best interests of the bank versus their own personal interests. Employees should review the bank's code of ethics periodically.

## CHECK FRAUD

Check fraud is a major cause of financial loss for banks. The amount of loss continues to grow even as check use declines. Criminals find novel ways to defraud others.

The broad term "check fraud" encompasses a variety of schemes, including counterfeiting and alteration, forgery, paperhanging, and check kiting.

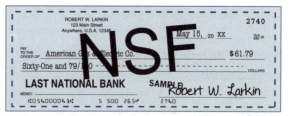

| | |
|---|---|
| **Check counterfeiting** | May entail stealing a blank check, retrieving a discarded canceled check, or removing a check used to pay a bill from a mailbox. A personal computer, software, scanner, laser printer, or high-resolution photocopier may counterfeit checks as well. |
| **Check alteration** | Checks can be **altered** by removing the payee's name or dollar amount but leaving the authorized signature. Information on the check can be erased through check |

**Altered check**—A check on which a material change, such as the dollar amount, has been made. Banks are expected to detect alterations and are responsible for paying checks only as originally drawn.

washing. Payee's name, dollar amount, check serial number, and date are changed, but the authorized signature remains.

**Check forgery**     A common type of check fraud. Typically, a criminal steals check, endorses it, and presents it for payment at a teller window or a store, using bogus personal identification.

**Paperhanging**     Checks intentionally written on closed accounts. Criminal fraudulently obtains blank checks or reorders checks on closed accounts.

**Check kiting**     Opening two or more checking accounts and drawing against nonexistent balances. Criminal opens several checking accounts in different banks, often in different areas of the country and often with a cashier's check or with cash. Checks then written to transfer funds from one account to another. Transfers occur so frequently that actual funds do not exist in a given account when a check is written. At this point, the customer usually leaves town with more money than originally deposited. By using "float time," check kiters create fraudulent balances.

### Bank Efforts to Combat Check Fraud

One of the best weapons in the war against check fraud continues to be vigilant tellers and other bank employees. Knowing some of the indicators of check fraud helps bank employees thwart a fraudulent transaction. To identify a bogus check, bank employees inspect for the following:

- Check lacks perforations, is stained or discolored, or has an odd "feel." Most check paper has the same weight and texture.

- Check number is either missing, does not change, or is low (between 100 and 500). Ninety percent of returned checks have low check numbers. Low check numbers indicate a recently opened account and, therefore, a potentially more risky check.

- Font used to print the customer's name looks visibly different from the font used to print the address.

- Additions to the check are hand written.

- Customer's address or bank's address is missing.

- Evidence of erasures or alterations.

- MICR numbers are missing or are shiny. Fraudulent checks often substitute regular toner or ink for magnetic ink.

- MICR encoding does not match the check number, the bank district, or the routing symbol in the upper right-hand corner of the check.

**Historical Fact**

Under contract to the ABA, the Union Pacific Railroad, and the Great Northern Express Company, the Pinkerton National Detective Agency identified and hunted down the "Wild Bunch" gang. By September 1902, the Pinkerton Agency believed that only three members of the gang remained alive: George Parker, alias "Butch" Cassidy, Harry Longbaugh, alias the "Sundance Kid," and William Cruzans.

*(American Bankers Association)*

- Name of the payee appears to have been printed by a typewriter. Most payroll, expense and dividend checks are printed by computer.
- Word VOID appears across the check.
- Check lacks an authorized signature.

Technology also is helping banks stem losses from check fraud. Modern check processing technology has reduced float time therefore making it more difficult for check kiters to exploit processing delays to obtain funds. Beginning in late 2004, under the Check Clearing for the 21st Century Act ("Check 21"), checks can be converted into electronic image files. This action will further deter check kiting because check clearing and settlement will not require a physical inspection before payment. The reduction or absence of physical checks from the payment system will reduce opportunities for check fraud as well.

## BANK ROBBERY

Although banks suffer greater losses from check fraud, bank robbery is a serious concern because of its potential for personal trauma, injury, and loss of life. According to Federal Bureau of Investigation (FBI) statistics, thousands of bank robberies occur in the United States each year. In almost half of those robberies, tellers or other bank employees are physically threatened or attacked.

Although banks have a basic responsibility to protect depositors' funds, the primary objective during a bank robbery is to ensure the safety of employees, customers, and law enforcement officers. Limiting losses and helping to identify and prosecute offenders are secondary objectives.

During a holdup, tellers and other bank employees should not resist. Resistance places their personal safety and the safety of others at risk. FBI statistics show that, in nearly two-thirds of robberies, weapons were observed (usually handguns).

Although bank robberies may not be prevented, their numbers can be reduced. Banks are required legally to equip their premises with cameras and alarms. Some banks in high-crime areas limit access to the lobby and require customers to show identification before being allowed in the bank. Bulletproof shields placed in front of teller's stations are another safety measure.

During robberies, banks employ various measures to help catch or identify robbers. By using a foot pedal or device in the cash drawer, tellers can activate silent holdup alarms. Also tellers may give the robber decoy or marked money. Some banks prepare special bundles of money that contain an exploding device filled with dye.

Yet, the best security measure is attentive employees who know and follow bank procedures. To help prevent a bank robbery or reduce its impact if one occurs, bank employees

- Strictly abide by the bank's procedures for opening and closing the bank.
- Remain alert for suspicious vehicles, people, and circumstances.

- Jot down the license number of suspicious vehicles in the parking lot or near the building.
- Greet customers by directly looking into their eyes. Take notice of whom they are serving.
- Keep information about bank procedures and operations confidential.

## INSIDER FRAUD

Employee theft, embezzlement, and other forms of insider fraud cause greater losses each year than bank robberies. Banks are particularly vulnerable to insider fraud because so many of their employees work with large sums of money, securities, and other financial assets. Insider fraud can result in significant financial losses and loss of confidential information. If it goes undetected for a prolonged period, insider fraud can threaten a bank's safety and soundness.

The most common type of employee fraud is asset misappropriation, such as embezzling money or stealing blank cashier's or treasurer's checks. Employees also may overcome information security controls to access accounts and move money electronically.

Banks try to minimize insider fraud by carefully screening prospective employees. The Federal Deposit Insurance Act prohibits banks from hiring convicted felons. During the hiring process, most banks perform thorough background checks on prospective employees by calling references, obtaining a credit report, and taking other precautions.

The best defense against insider fraud is a corporate culture in which high standards of ethical behavior are expected and are reinforced by a clearly articulated and well-enforced employee code of conduct.

## CURRENCY COUNTERFEITING

Check counterfeiting is not the only type of counterfeiting. Banks also must be on the alert for counterfeit money. High-resolution scanners and printers are used to forge paper currency as well as counterfeit checks.

To combat using digital imaging technology to counterfeit currency, the U.S. government began introducing new currency in 1996 that incorporates counterfeit-resistant features. These features help tellers authenticate notes and make it difficult for criminals to produce counterfeit notes. The U.S. government took its anti-counterfeiting further in October 2003 when the Federal Reserve unveiled a newly redesigned $20 bill. Redesigned $50 and $100 bills followed in 2004. The new designs co-circulate with old-design notes until the old-design notes gradually become worn and are removed from circulation.

The $20 bills, introduced in 2003, maintained the traditional U.S. currency appearance. They are the same size and have the same, but enhanced, image of Andrew Jackson on the face of the note and the White House on the back. Subtle green, peach, and blue colors featured in the background are the most noticeable difference. The redesign also features a blue eagle in the background and a metallic green eagle and shield to the right of Jackson's portrait.

**Did You Know ...**

In 1995, less than 1 percent of counterfeit notes detected in the United States were digitally produced. By 2002, that number had grown to nearly 40 percent.

*(U.S. Secret Service)*

Hand examination is the most effective method for detecting bad notes. Most tellers can detect counterfeit U.S. currency by hand examination. The new currency contains additional security features that can help bank employees quickly determine whether a note is real or fake. All bank employees should be familiar with these characteristics. The following details security features of the new $20 bill.[2]

| Feature | Description |
|---|---|
| Watermark | A faint image, similar to the large portrait, is part of the paper and can be seen from both sides of the note. |
| Security thread | A plastic strip embedded in the paper runs vertically up one side of the note. On both sides of the note, the words "USA TWENTY" and a small flag are visible along the thread. Under ultraviolet light, the thread glows green. |
| Color-shifting ink | When tilted, the number "20" in the lower right corner on the face of the bill shifts ink color from copper to green. |
| Microprinting | Microprinting is on the face of the note in two new areas. Bordering the first three letters of the "TWENTY USA" ribbon to the right of the portrait, the inscription "USA20" is printed in blue. "THE UNITED STATES OF AMERICA 20 USA 20" appears in black on the border below the Treasurer's signature. |

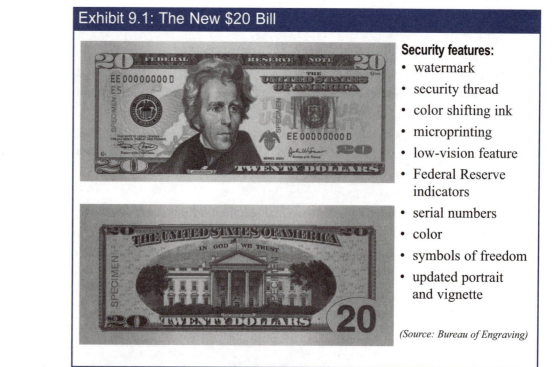

**Exhibit 9.1: The New $20 Bill**

**Security features:**
- watermark
- security thread
- color shifting ink
- microprinting
- low-vision feature
- Federal Reserve indicators
- serial numbers
- color
- symbols of freedom
- updated portrait and vignette

*(Source: Bureau of Engraving)*

| | |
|---|---|
| Low-vision feature | The large numeral "20" in the lower right corner on the back of the bill is easy to read. |
| Federal Reserve indicators | A universal seal to the left of the portrait represents the entire Federal Reserve System. A letter and number beneath the left serial number identifies the issuing Federal Reserve bank. |
| Serial numbers | The unique combination of eleven numbers and letters appears twice on the front of the note. |
| Color | Subtle background colors of green, peach, and blue are on both sides of the note. The words "TWENTY USA" are printed in blue in the background to the right of the portrait and small yellow numeral 20s are printed in the background on the back of the bill. |
| Symbols of freedom | On the front are two American eagle symbols of freedom. The large blue eagle in the background to the left of President Andrew Jackson's image and the smaller green metallic eagle to the lower right of the portrait. |
| Updated portrait and vignette | The oval borders and fine lines surrounding the portrait on the front and the White House vignette on the back of the previous note were removed. The portrait has been moved up and shoulders extended into the border. Additional engraving details were added to the vignette background. |

Another form of counterfeit currency is altered or "raised" currency. One or two ends of the corners of a smaller denomination bill, such as one dollar or a five-dollar bill, are replaced with the ends or corners of a larger bill such as a 10, 20 or 50. The bill is redeemed for the value of the "raised" amount.

## Exhibit 9.2: Know Your Money—Raised Banknote

Compare the denomination numerals on each corner with the denomination written out at the bottom of the note (front and back) and through the Treasury seal.

Compare the suspect note to a genuine note of the same denomination and series year. Pay particular attention to the portrait, vignette, and denomination numerals.

*(Source: United States Secret Service. www.ustreas.gov/usss/money_raised_notes.shtml)*

# SAFEGUARDING THE NATION

Occasionally, an event reminds everyone of the critical importance of banks and other financial institutions to the economic vitality of the United States. On September 11, 2001, terrorists attacked and destroyed the twin trade towers in New York City. Not only is New York City home to the New York Stock Exchange, it is home to many of the largest and most important banks, securities firms, clearing and settlement

organizations, and payment system operators in the country. Despite the terrible loss of life and the enormity of the damage, the nation's financial markets and payment systems continued to function almost without a pause.

The events of September 11 underscored how the fortunes of the banking industry and our nation are inextricably linked. Banks play a vital role in assisting the federal government and law enforcement agencies in fighting crimes that threaten the economic stability and national security of the United States.

## TERRORISM

The events of September 11, 2001, gave terrorism a new meaning for all Americans. Terrorism kills and destroys innocent lives. It has a wider purpose, however, to spread fear and disrupt economic and financial activity. Because they play a central and very visible role in the U.S. economy, banks are targets for domestic or foreign terrorist groups. Banks are active in curbing money laundering and identifying and cutting off sources of funds for terrorist groups, and so are at risk.

Weapons used to cause terror are wide-ranging and unpredictable, as demonstrated by the use of aircraft and anthrax-tainted letters in terrorist attacks just weeks apart in 2001. Bomb threats are among the most common types of terrorism affecting banks. Banks must take them seriously or risk potentially devastating consequences.

Today, most banks are prepared for terrorist acts or other catastrophic emergencies. They have disaster recovery programs and **business contingency plans** for resuming critical functions. Keeping employees apprised of the risks posed by potential terrorist acts and how to respond is an important part of contingency planning. Employees need to know how to protect themselves, co-workers, and customers.

**Business contingency plan**—A plan for maintaining or resuming business operations should unexpected events occur.

**Money laundering**—Moving large amounts of illegally obtained cash through many bank accounts to hide the source of the money.

## MONEY LAUNDERING

**Money laundering** is associated with many crimes, from racketeering and drug dealing to terrorism. Banks are the first line of defense in the battle against the illegal flow of money. They report financial transactions that may be associated with criminal fund raising and fund transfer activities. They are obligated to exercise due diligence in knowing who their customers are and judging whether transactions are legitimate. Banks also assist the federal government by freezing the assets of organizations or individuals suspected of terrorist activities.

## BANK SECRECY ACT

The Bank Secrecy Act (BSA) requires banks to record and report certain financial transactions as a way of curbing illicit activities. Under BSA, banks must file currency transaction reports (CTRs) on all deposits, withdrawals, and exchanges of currency that exceed $10,000.

Since its passage more than 30 years ago, BSA has been amended many times to expand its scope. For example, in 1986, Congress made money laundering a federal crime and allowed laundered funds to be seized and forfeited. Banks were required to have a formal BSA compliance program. In 1990, Congress created the Financial Crimes Enforcement Network (FinCEN) to concentrate on detecting financial crimes. In 1994, FinCEN took over responsibility for BSA.

In the late 1990s, the emphasis of the regulatory agencies shifted from the technicalities of reporting large currency transactions to monitoring and reporting suspicious activities. Banks were required to file a suspicious activity report (SAR) when they detected or suspected that a crime had been committed within or through the bank.

## USA PATRIOT ACT

After the September 11 terrorists attacks, detecting and reporting suspicious activities became a national imperative, especially because of the close link between money laundering and the funding of terrorist activities. On October 31, 2001, Congress enacted the Uniting and Strengthening America by Providing Appropriate Tools Required to Intercept and Obstruct Terrorism Act (USA PATRIOT Act). The act contained several anti-money laundering provisions, including a requirement that, at the request of federal regulators, banks provide records relating to their anti-money-laundering compliance or their customers. Moreover, customer identification program requirements, effective in 2003, imposed significant mandatory identification procedures for both loan and deposit customers of financial institutions.

Effective in 2004, banks must use a new SAR form that includes check boxes for identifying suspicious activity as terrorist financing or identity theft. Some of the warning signs of possible terrorist financing activity include:

- using a business account to collect funds, which are then sent to a smaller number of foreign beneficiaries in a country associated with terrorism
- an unusually high volume of wire transfer activity from a business account
- multiple individuals structuring transactions under the currency transaction reporting threshold
- large currency withdrawals from a business account not normally associated with cash transactions
- same-day transactions at the same bank using different tellers
- shared addresses, which are also business locations, by persons involved in currency transactions
- circumventing identification requirements by purchasing money orders in small amounts

**Did You Know ...**

Financial institutions filed approximately 300,000 SARs during the period from July 1, 2002, to June 30, 2003.

*(Financial Crimes Enforcement Network, U.S. Treasury Department)*

## FREEZING ASSETS

As part of foreign policy, the federal government uses economic sanctions against individuals, terrorist organizations, and countries hostile to the U.S. government. The Office of Foreign Assets Control (OFAC) in the Department of the Treasury maintains a list of individuals and entities subject to sanctions, which may include blocking accounts and freezing assets. Banks are required to regularly check their records to identify assets owned by individuals or organizations that appear on the OFAC list. When a match is found, the bank is required to take action so the funds cannot be withdrawn from the bank and be used for illegal activities. Specific procedures govern the handling of frozen assets and blocked accounts.

# SUMMARY

- Banks are responsible for ensuring the security and confidentiality of customer information. Computer attacks, including unauthorized intrusions and viruses, can threaten the integrity of customer information. Banks also are required to maintain meaningful policies governing the privacy of customer information, disclose their policies, and offer customers an opportunity to opt-out of information sharing with third parties.

- Identity theft is one of the fastest growing financial crimes. Banks are using the latest technologies to thwart identity theft. Comprehensive information security procedures that emphasize employee vigilance are the best way to curb identity theft and other personal privacy invasions.

- Banks and bank customers face ongoing assaults from fraud artists. Federal banking agencies issue fraud alerts and have exposed phishing and advance fee fraud. Bank card fraud, or using a stolen card or number to fraudulently purchase goods or services, is common also.

- A bank must safeguard itself as a corporate entity. Occasionally, banks are victimized from within—unethical or irresponsible behavior can occur any-where in a bank. An inattentive board or audit committee, a senior management that rewards wrong employee practices, or an employee who embezzles poses a threat to a bank's safety and soundness. The best antidotes to these kinds of behavior are high standards of corporate governance and a strong code of ethics. Other threats to banks and their assets are check fraud, bank robbery, and currency counterfeiting.

- Banks play an important role in safeguarding our nation. Banks assist federal and state law enforcement agencies in fighting criminal activity, especially terrorism and money laundering. By filing currency transaction reports and suspicious activity reports, and by freezing the assets of suspected terrorist individuals and organizations and states subject to sanctions, banks help protect the United States against terrorism, money laundering, and other financial crimes.

[1] OCC Advisory AL 2001-4, Identity Theft and Pretext Calling, May 16, 2001.

[2] Bureau of Engraving and Printing. www.moneyfactory.com/newmoney/main.cfm/currency/new20

# SELF CHECK & REVIEW

1. What is the "opt-out" privilege?

2. What identity theft deterrents can banks use to protect customer information?

3. What are some measures taken to keep bank cards from being stolen and misused?

4. What are some scams that have prompted recent alerts from federal banking agencies?

5. What is the bank employee's role in safeguarding bank assets?

6. List at least three signs of fraudulent checks.

7. What can a bank employee do to prevent bank robberies?

8. How are banks helping to protect the United States and its economy?

# ADDITIONAL RESOURCES

**Resources**

*ABA Technology News Digest.* **www.aba.com/Industry+Issues/eAlertNews.htm**

*ABA Toolboxes (Safeguarding Customer Transactions; Bank Robbery Deterrence, Financial Privacy and others),* Washington D.C.: American Bankers Association, **www.aba.com/about+aba/abatoolboxes.htm**

*Advance-Fee Loan Scams Campaign,* Federal Trade Commission. **www.ftc.gov/bcp/menu-credit.htm**

*Avoiding Credit and Charge Card Fraud,* Federal Trade Commission. **www.ftc.gov/bcp/menu-credit.htm**

*Basic Facts About Money Laundering,* Financial Action Task Force on Money Laundering. **www1.oecd.org/fatf/MLaundering_en.htm**

Bureau of Engraving and Printing. **www.moneyfactory.com/newmoney/**

*Common Fraud Scams,* Federal Bureau of Investigation. **www.fbi.gov/majcases/fraud/fraudschemes.htm**

*Consumer Protection (identity theft, phishing scams, privacy and opting out),* ABA Education Foundation. **www.aba.com/Consumer+Connection/default.htm**

*Credit, ATM and Debit Cards: What To Do If They're Lost or Stolen,* Federal Trade Commission. **www.ftc.gov/bcp/menu-credit.htm**

*Credit Card Loss Protection Offers: They're the Real Steal,* Federal Trade Commission. **www.ftc.gov/bcp/menu-credit.htm**

*Financial Institution Fraud,* Federal Bureau of Investigation. **www.fbi.gov/hq/cid/fc/fifu/fifraud/fif.htm**

*Guidance on Preparing a Complete & Sufficient Suspicious Activity Report Narrative*, Financial Crimes Enforcement Network. **www.fincen.gov/pub_fincen_reports.html**

*ID Theft: When Bad Things Happen to Your Good Name*, Federal Trade Commission. **www.ftc.gov/bcp/conline/pubs/credit/idtheft.htm**

Internet Fraud Complaint Center **www.ifccfbi.gov/index.asp**

*Know Your Money,* U.S. Secret Service. **www.ustreas.gov/usss/know_your_money.shtml**

*Public Awareness Advisory Regarding "4-1-9" or "Advance Fee Fraud" Schemes*, U.S. Secret Service. **www.secretservice.gov/alert419.shtml**

*SDN and Blocked Persons*, Office of Foreign Assets Control. **www.ustreas.gov/offices/eotffc/ofac/sdn/index.html**

**Learning Check**

# Answers to Self Check & Review

## Chapter 1  Banking and You

1.  *If all bankers are expected to sell products and services as part of their job, why is sales and business development a separate career path for bankers?*

    While all bankers are salespeople for the bank, banks must focus on the sale of their products and services in order to be competitive. In larger banks, the sales teams specialize according to product. Retail banking, business banking, insurance sales, investment products, and trust services are all examples of sales avenues open to bankers.

2.  *During a period of several years, a bank has experienced losses whereas other banks have been profitable. Who ultimately is accountable for the bank's poor financial performance?*

    Although senior management, led by the bank president, makes the day-to-day operating decisions, the board of directors ultimately is responsible for the bank's financial performance and must answer to the stockholders. The board of directors has the power to appoint the bank's officers.

3.  *What are nontraditional bank services, and why do banks want to provide them?*

    Nontraditional bank services include insurance and securities. Because of the Gramm-Leach-Bliley Act, banks, insurance companies, and brokerage firms now offer each other's products and services. Banks want to offer nontraditional products in order to compete on an equal basis with the other providers and to provide a full range of services to their customers.

4.  *How do banks contribute to their communities?*

    In addition to providing deposit and credit services to individuals and businesses in the community, banks contribute time, effort, and funds to develop, restore, and enrich their communities. Bank employees have a history of service to charitable organizations, and banks sponsor many community-minded events.

5. *What are the benefits of banking partner and affiliate relationships?*

These alliances can provide significant cost savings, greater choice for consumers, and a high level of customer service.

6. *Why might a bank consider acquiring or merging with another bank?*

Through mergers and acquisitions, some banks are eliminating duplicate efforts and becoming more profitable. Banks also combine forces as a way of entering new geographic areas to expand their market share.

## Chapter 2   The Evolution of Banking

1. *What is the role of banks in the U.S. economy?*

Banks fund loans, offer financial services to consumers and businesses, provide access to the payment system, create money, help expand and contract the money supply, and are a force for economic and social change.

2. *What is inflation?*

A continuing increase in the level of prices in an economy caused by too many dollars and too few goods to be purchased.

3. *Why is the National Bank Act of 1863 important?*

The National Bank Act founded the banking system. It contained four major provisions that created national banks, created the Office of the Comptroller of the Currency, introduced the national banknote, and established a system of required reserves.

4. *What is meant by dual banking system? Does the dual banking system exist today?*

Dual banking system refers to the fact that both national banks and state-chartered banks developed over the course of U.S. history. These two structures still exist today.

5. *What was the singular achievement of the Federal Reserve Act?*

The singular achievement of the Federal Reserve Act was the creation of a central bank—the Federal Reserve System, commonly called the Fed.

6. *What Federal Agency was created by the Banking Act of 1933 and why?*

The Federal Deposit Insurance Corporation (FDIC) was created to protect depositors at FDIC-insured banks?

7. *What are the four basic duties of the Federal Reserve?*

The Federal Reserve's duties fall into four general areas:
- Conduct the nation's monetary policy by influencing money and credit conditions in the economy in pursuit of full employment and stable prices
- Supervise and regulate banking institutions to ensure the safety and soundness of the nation's banking and financial system and to protect credit rights of consumers
- Maintain the financial system's stability and contain systematic risk in financial markets
- Provide certain financial services to the U.S. government, the public, financial institutions, and foreign official institutions, including playing a major role in operating the nation's payment system

8. *What events contributed to bank failures in the 1980s and early 1990s?*

Poor loans were a major contributing factor to bank failures during this period. Banks that loaned heavily to less developed countries suffered large losses when many of those countries defaulted on their loans. The United States also went through a prolonged economic slowdown during the late 1980s and early 1990s. Real estate sales in many parts of the country plummeted, and large amounts of office space remained unoccupied in major cities. As a consequence, real estate developers started defaulting on loans. Bankruptcies in other industries, such as the oil and gas industries, also contributed to the poor performance of bank loan portfolios.

9. *What legislation guarantees that a bank customer's financial records will be kept private? What are the basic privacy provisions?*

The privacy provisions in the Gramm-Leach-Bliley Act give customers the right to instruct banks not to share their personal information with nonaffiliated third parties. The law prevents financial institutions from providing certain account information to unaffiliated third-party marketers. It also requires financial institutions to establish a privacy policy and disclose the policy to customers at account opening and annually thereafter. The law also requires financial institutions to implement technical, physical, and administrative safeguards to protect the security and confidentiality of customer information.

10. *What are five regulatory groups with the authority to supervise bank activities?*

Federal Reserve System
Office of the Comptroller of the Currency (OCC)
Federal Deposit Insurance Corporation (FDIC)
Office of Thrift Supervision (OTS)
State banking departments

## Chapter 3   Managing and Reporting Bank Investments and Performance

1. *What is a bank's largest asset? Its largest liability? Its largest income and expense items?*

   A bank's largest asset is loans, which generate the majority of revenues. A bank's largest liability is deposits, which provide funds for making loans. A bank's largest income item is the interest income from loans, whereas the largest expense item is the interest paid on deposits. Another large expense item is salaries and employee benefits.

2. *Why is accurate financial data so important to bank stockholders and investors? To federal and state regulators? To customers?*

   Stockholders and investors require accurate financial data as a predictor of growth potential. Federal and state bank examiners evaluate a bank's financial reports to determine its true financial condition and ascertain whether sufficient capital is available. Customers are interested in the financial stability of a bank so their money is put to productive use and they do not lose their savings.

3. *What would be the consequences if a bank chose to overemphasize liquidity while neglecting other factors in funds management? What would be the consequences of overemphasizing safety at the expense of liquidity and income?*

   If a bank emphasized liquidity only, keeping large supplies of currency in its vaults as a protection against increasing customer demands for funds, the percentage of deposits available for lending would shrink. The drop in loanable funds would impair the credit function and reduce income. If a bank tried to achieve ultimate safety, it would never assume any risk in putting deposits to profitable use, and the potential to maximize loans would not be reached. This situation would result in lost income opportunities and failure to serve the credit needs of the community.

4. *Distinguish between the discount rate and the prime rate.*

   The discount rate applies to short-term credit extended by the Federal Reserve to banks. The prime rate is a base rate that reflects a bank's determination of such factors as its cost of funds, overhead, loan portfolio risk, and profit objectives.

5. *List at least three measures of bank performance, other than net income.*

   Return on assets ratio, return on equity ratio, capital ratio, net interest spread, and earnings per share.

6.  *What is the net worth of a bank with the following assets and liabilities?*

|                                        | (in thousands of dollars) |
| -------------------------------------- | ------------------------- |
| Cash on hand                           | $45,400                   |
| Investments                            | 76,600                    |
| Loans (net of reserve for loan losses) | 224,300                   |
| Fed funds sold                         | 35,800                    |
| Fixed assets                           | 18,900                    |
| Other assets                           | 12,200                    |
| Deposits                               | 312,700                   |
| Fund funds purchased                   | 68,600                    |
| Other liabilities                      | 4,300                     |

Assets = Liabilities + Net Worth

or

Assets - Liabilities = Net Worth

Assets = $413, 200 ($45,400 + 76,600 + 224,300 + 35,800 +18, 900 + 12, 200)

Liabilities = $385,600 (312,700 + 68,600 + 4,300)
Net Worth = $27,600 ($413,200 - $385,600)

7.  *What is the net profit (or loss) of a bank reporting the following revenues and expenses?*

|                                      | (in thousands of dollars) |
| ------------------------------------ | ------------------------- |
| Interest and fees on loans           | $253,700                  |
| Interest and dividends on investments | 22,100                    |
| Interest paid on deposits            | 158,800                   |
| Salaries, wages, and benefits        | 70,300                    |
| Taxes                                | 11,000                    |

Net profit = Revenue - Expenses

Revenue = $275,800 ($253,700 + 22,100)

Expenses =  240,100 ($158,800 + 70,300 + 11,000)

Net profit = $35,700 ($275,800 - 240,100)

8.  *What is the earnings per share for a bank with an average of 5,360,000 shares of stock outstanding and net income of $12,450,000?*

Earnings per share = Net income ÷ average number of shares of its stock outstanding during the period

Earnings per share = 12,450,000 ÷ 5,360,000 shares

Earnings per share = $2.32 per share

9. *In what three ways are banks improving fee income?*

Banks are improving fee income by increasing existing fees, charging fees for previously free services, and entering fee-based lines of business.

10. *Why is it important for a bank to establish a financial plan (a budget)?*

A financial plan or budget allows a bank to plan expenditures carefully and to set earning objectives. A budget is the vehicle planners use to forecast future conditions and achieve overall goals.

## *Chapter 4   Deposit Accounts*

1. *Why are deposits so important to banks?*

Deposits from checking, savings, and money market deposit accounts and certificates of deposit provide a majority of the funds banks use to lend and invest and thus make payments.

2. *What are the basic differences and similarities between a checking account and a savings account?*

Checking accounts are transaction accounts. Deposits made to noninterest earning checking accounts are payable on demand. Usually, the customer intends to withdraw checking account funds in the near future to pay bills and meet expenses. Checking accounts also may pay interest. Such accounts are known as negotiable order of withdrawal or NOW accounts.

Customers generally place funds in savings accounts to set aside money for future needs and to earn interest. Technically speaking, savings account funds are not immediately available to the depositor. Although rarely applied, a bank can require a seven-day notice of withdrawal from a savings account.

Checking accounts and savings accounts do not have maturity dates. Deposits and withdrawals can be made at any time. Thus, unlike a time deposit account, such as a certificate of deposit, no interest penalty is imposed for withdrawal from a checking or savings account.

Also, under Federal Reserve's Regulation D, checking account deposits are subject to reserve requirements. Savings account deposits are not subject to reserve requirements.

3. *How do automatic transfer services benefit a customer?*

With ATS, a customer can write checks that exceed existing checking account balances, and the bank, by prior arrangement (preauthorization), will move funds automatically from the customer's savings account to the checking account to cover the checks.

4. *What deposit account would you recommend to a customer who wants to earn interest and would also like the option of writing a small number of checks (three or less) per month?*

A Money Market Deposit Account offers higher annual percentage yields than savings accounts. This account also allows a limited number of monthly transfers (six per month—three by check and three by preauthorization).

5. *What options do customers have for making deposits into their accounts, other than going to their bank?*

EFT, ATS, ATM, wire transfer, Internet banking, direct deposit, and deposit by mail.

6. *How do account transactions differ for joint accounts held as joint tenancy versus tenants in common?*

With a joint tenancy account, each account holder may make transactions and only one signature is required. When one account holder dies, the funds in the account typically pass to the surviving account holder(s) in accordance with state law and without need to establish an estate. Tenants-in-common accounts require the signatures of all the account holders for transactions. From the bank's perspective, tenants-in-common accounts need greater monitoring. If the bank pays checks with only one signature when it has agreed to require the signatures of all the account holders, it could be liable to the account holders who did not sign the checks or withdrawals.

7. *When opening a deposit account, why is it important for a bank to establish the authority of the customer to use the account? What three steps does the bank take to accomplish this when opening an account?*

When an account is opened, the bank enters into a contractual relationship that gives customers the ability to extend credit to themselves, provides customers with the vehicle to convert checks and other instruments into cash, and creates a number of other situations that could result in a loss to the bank. Three steps the bank takes to open an account include
- establishing the identity of the person opening the account
- determining that the person has the legal capacity to open the account
- ensuring that the person is authorized to open the account

8. *What types of deposit transactions are covered under Regulation E?*

Regulation E covers electronic funds transactions, ATM transactions, point-of-sale debit transactions, online banking transactions through the Internet, and most consumer-initiated telephone transfers.

## Chapter 5   Payments

1. *What five things make a check negotiable?*

   Negotiable checks are (a) payable to bearer or to order, (b) an unconditional order to pay, (c) payable for a specific (fixed) amount of money, (d) payable on demand or at a definite date, (e) in writing and signed by the drawer.

2. *Who are the parties to a check?*

   The parties to checks are the drawer, the payee, and the drawee. The drawer writes the check. The payee is the one to whom the check is written. The drawee is the bank that holds the drawer's account and pays the check.

3. *Explain the difference between a blank endorsement and a special endorsement. Discuss when each is used.*

   A blank endorsement consists simply of the signature of the payee or other holder of the instrument. A blank endorsement can be used for any purpose and allows flexibility and ease of transfer. In a special endorsement, not only does the previous holder sign the instrument, but the holder also names the party to whom rights to the instrument are being transferred.

4. *What are the differences among a cashier's check, teller's check, and certified check?*

   Cashier's checks are issued by the bank and drawn on that bank. The bank is both drawer and drawee.

   Teller's checks are issued by one bank but drawn on another bank. The issuing bank has the same obligation for teller's checks as for cashier's checks.

   Certified check is a customer's check accepted by the bank on which it is drawn. The drawee sets funds aside from the customer's account to a 'certified checks outstanding' account and places an official stamp or signature on the check. The original order to pay is transferred to the bank's promise to pay.

5. *In check preparation, proof, and encoding, the depositary bank performs what functions?*

   Check (item) preparation includes removing staples, paper clips, and rubber bands. All items are arranged to face forward and right side up. Only the items that are to be captured are sent through the proof and encoding function. During proofing, each transaction is reviewed to see that the dollar amount of the debits equals the dollar amount of the credits. This is where errors in addition, extra items not reflected on the deposit ticket, and items listed but not included are found. During encoding, MICR data are imprinted on checks. High-speed reader-sorters can then read the MICR data and capture information, such as the amount, account numbers, and check numbers, which expedites transaction posting and disposition of check clearings.

6. *Give some examples of checks that might be rejected from the normal posting process and require handling as exception items.*

Checks may require special handling as "exception items" for such reasons as the funds in the account may be insufficient to pay the check, an uncollected balance may not leave enough in the account to pay the check, there may be a stop payment on the check, or there may be a hold placed on the account.

7. *Identify some differences and similarities between signature-based and PIN-only debit cards.*

PIN-only cards can be used at ATMs and at POS at some merchant locations. Signature debit cards can be used at these locations and more merchant locations. PIN-only debit card transactions are processed online and require the use of a PIN. Signature debit cards can be used with either a PIN (on-line transaction) or a signature (off-line transaction).

All debit cards have a magnetic strip that allows the customer to perform routine financial transactions, such as withdrawals, deposits, transfers of funds between accounts, and payments.

8. *Define dual custody and provide one example where it is used.*

Dual custody (dual control) is a security technique that uses two or more separate entities or people operating together to protect sensitive functions, information, or assets. Both entities or people are equally responsible for physically protecting materials involved in vulnerable transactions. Currency is prepared for shipment and received using dual control.

9. *In reference to a stolen or lost ATM card, explain the cardholder's and bank's liability for unauthorized transactions.*

Under Regulation E, if a cardholder notifies his or her bank within two days of learning of the loss or theft of the debit card, the liability for the unauthorized transaction is no more than the amount of the transaction, up to a total of $50.

## Chapter 6   Lending

1. *List the reasons why the lending function is so important to the bank.*

   • Of the three cornerstones of banking—the deposit, payment, and lending functions—the lending function represents a significant source of income.

   • Lending is one of the most traditional elements in the relationship between a bank and its customers.

   • Under the Community Reinvestment Act, banks are evaluated and given a public rating on their record of helping to meet the credit needs of their communities, including home mortgage and small business and small farm lending.

- The quality of a bank's loan portfolio often is critical to its survival.

- Loans are essential to the functioning of the U.S. economy, supplying financing for such needs as business operations, home and vehicle purchases, and college tuition.

2. *What is the difference between open-end credit and closed-end credit? Give some examples of open-end and closed-end consumer loans.*

Open-end credit is a revolving line of credit on which a borrower may draw for an agreed-upon period. The balance may fluctuate from zero up to the maximum amount allowed. Two examples of open-end credit are a home equity line of credit and a credit card. Closed-end loans involve an agreement with the borrower specifying the total amount of the loan, the maturity date, the number of payments, and their due dates. An auto loan or home equity loan are examples of closed-end loans.

3. *Why are home equity loans and home equity lines of credit popular with consumers?*

Interest paid on these loans is usually tax deductible. Also, the interest charged is typically lower than other loan products, because the loan is secured by the borrower's residence.

4. *If a business wants to purchase a piece of equipment, what loan type is appropriate— working capital loan or term loan? Why?*

A long-term loan is appropriate, because the funds will be used to purchase equipment. These term loans have maturities of one to five years. Working capital loans are short-term (typically 90 days) and generally are used to purchase raw materials or finance other short-term needs.

5. *Name the five "C's" of credit. Is collateral the most important "C"? Why or why not?*

The five "C's" of credit are character, capacity, collateral, capital, and conditions. A loan request should not be approved solely on the basis of the value of collateral. Collateral should be viewed as a secondary source of repayment only.

6. *What are some electronic advancements in loan services and loan processing?*

Some electronic advancements include: preauthorized automatic debits to make loan payments; providing lending information, calculators and loan applications on the Internet with quick decision replies; and electronic underwriting programs that use credit scoring technology.

7. *What are some activities involved in loan administration?*

Loan administration activities include:
- mailing regular statements
- receiving and posting agreed-upon payments
- maintaining current address information
- ensuring that the bank's security interest is recorded, filed, and returned to the bank
- answering customer inquiries
- reporting the loan to various credit reporting agencies
- maintaining files and documentation for review and examination by internal and external auditors and by regulatory agencies
- taking the loan off the books when the final payment is received

8. *What roles do bank directors play in the overall lending function?*

Bank directors represent the highest authority on policy-making for the lending function. The board of directors' responsibilities include:
- determining the types of loans to be made
- tightening credit standards when warranted
- establishing and monitoring legal lending limits and minimum loan amounts
- determining loan policy
- assigning credit authority
- authorizing all loans above a stipulated amount
- reviewing the loan portfolio for meeting local credit needs and complying with the CRA
- conducting periodic reviews and audits

9. *What laws should a loan officer be aware of when making a mortgage loan?*

The Equal Credit Opportunity Act, Truth in Lending Act, Community Reinvestment Act, Home Mortgage Disclosure Act, and Real Estate Settlement Procedures Act are among the laws that affect home mortgage lending.

## Chapter 7   Specialized Products and Services

1. *What are the basic legal obligations of a trustee?*

***Acting as a "prudent" investor.*** An investor, and in the case of trusts, a trustee, who acts with care, skill, diligence, and sense of responsibility in the management of investments in a customer's portfolio.

*Segregating trust assets*. Keeping trust assets separate from those of all other trusts and from the bank's own assets.

*Preventing conflicts of interest*. Having no personal interest in any investments bought or sold for trust funds and by not purchasing or benefiting in any way from property or assets held in trust.

2. *What personal (individual) trust services do banks typically provide?*

   estate settlement
   trust administration
   guardianships
   personal agency services

3. *What corporate trust services do banks typically provide?*

   corporate agency services
   employee benefit services

4. *What is the primary difference between a testamentary trust and a living trust?*

   Testamentary trusts are created under the terms of a decedent's will. A living trust does not involve a decedent. It is created voluntarily by an individual who executes a trust agreement and transfers property to the trust that is managed professionally by the trustee.

5. *What are nondeposit investment products?*

   Nondeposit investment products include stocks, bonds, mutual funds, and annuities. They are termed "nondeposit" to differentiate them from bank deposit products like checking and savings accounts. Nondeposit investment products are not insured by the Federal Deposit Insurance Corporation, are not guaranteed by the government, and may involve loss of principal. Banks that sell nondeposit investment products must give customers explicit disclosures to avoid customers confusing uninsured products with insured bank products. Nondeposit investment products generally are sold through broker dealer firms, third party or affiliated.

6. *What types of cash management services help a corporate customer optimize the interest earned by deposits or reduce the interest expense of loans?*

   Controlled disbursement accounts, such as zero balance accounts, help businesses optimize day-to-day cash management by establishing an automated link between different deposit accounts or a deposit account and a line of credit. When excess funds are available in a checking account, they can be transferred automatically to a concentration account, usually an investment account, or used to reduce the outstanding balance on a line of credit. Cash concentration services allow a business that has accounts at numerous banks to pool the balances in a concentration account, which can then be invested at a higher rate of return than the business could otherwise earn on separate accounts.

7. *What types of customers need capital market services? What are some examples of capital market services that banks provide?*

Capital market services are useful to corporate customers who need money to finance operations and growth. Banks assist such companies in accessing the public and private equity and debt markets. Capital market services range from specialized lending to underwriting, structuring, and distributing corporate debt.

8. *What types of insurance could be sold to a customer who has just taken out a mortgage loan?*

Opportunities for insurance sales to mortgage borrowers include property insurance, liability insurance, and title insurance.

9. *How does a letter of credit protect the interests of both the buyer and the seller of goods?*

A letter of credit guarantees that the exporter (seller) will be paid if all the terms of the contract are met, and that payment on behalf of the importer (buyer) will not be made unless and until the contract has been fulfilled.

10. *Your company is importing widgets from Europe. Each widget costs €100 euros. The current exchange rate is: €1 euro = $1.15 U.S. dollar How much does each widget cost in U.S. dollars?*

€100 (euros) x 1.15 (U.S. dollar exchange rate) = $115 U.S. dollars

## Chapter 8   Building Relationships: Sales and Customer Service

1. *Do employees who rarely interact with bank customers have a role in building customer relationships? Why or why not?*

Employees who perform jobs where there is little direct face-to-face contact with customers still have an important role in the relationship-building process. Bank employees who are responsive to other bank employees' requests are providing customer service and supporting relationship building. Focusing on delivery standards is providing customer service and building relationships. A bank will have difficulty convincing customers that it cares about their business when back-office personnel regularly make errors when posting customer transactions.

2. *What are some ways a bank employee can demonstrate responsiveness to customer needs?*

Demonstrating responsiveness includes acknowledging customers as they approach, being ready to help them, listening carefully to understand the customers' needs, taking responsibility for the problems they present, working as a team member with other bank employees, solving problems promptly and accurately, resolving special problems in a friendly and caring manner.

3. *What are the benefits of cross-selling and referrals?*

A bank that effectively cross-sells additional products and refers business to other departments or affiliates expands its customer relationships, helps customers meet their financial goals, and sells more products, both immediately and over the long-term. When employees cross-sell and make referrals, customers get the impression that the bank values their business and has their financial interests in mind.

4. *What are some of the things customers do in anticipation of making a purchase?*

In anticipation of purchasing a product, customers often look through newspaper ads, talk to other people, and read information pamphlets and promotional brochures. When contemplating a loan, a customer may request a loan application. Often a prospective customer will call the bank or approach an employee in person to solicit information about financial products.

5. *What is the difference between a product feature and product benefit?*

A product feature is a characteristic of the product, whereas a product benefit describes how the product will meet customer needs.

6. *What steps are involved in bringing a new product to market?*

Bringing a new product to market entails multiple steps under the direction of a product development team. The process begins with market research and the profiling of customers, the market, and the bank's competitors. The product development team solicits and screens new product ideas, tests the concept, performs a business analysis, develops the product, test markets the product, introduces the product to market, and performs ongoing product monitoring.

## *Chapter 9   Safeguarding Customers, Bank Assets, and the Nation*

1. *What is the "opt-out" privilege?*

It provides consumers with some control over how their personal information is used. Banks are required to disclose their privacy policies to customers and to give customers a reasonable opportunity to elect not to have their "nonpublic personal information" shared with third parties for marketing or other purposes. This ability is called the "opt-out" privilege.

2.  *What identity theft deterrents can banks use to protect customer information?*

Banks train employees to be vigilant in safeguarding customer information and in helping customers know how to safeguard their information. By law, banks must have security procedures in place and employees must follow them. For example, bank employees should not divulge customer information without the caller first providing a personal identification number (PIN), password, or some other identifier known only to the person, such as answers to these questions: "What is the name of your first pet?" or "Where were you born?" Secure identifiers normally are established at account opening.

3.  *What are some measures taken to prevent bank cards from being stolen and misused?*

Bank cards usually are sent through the mail. To thwart their theft, the customer must call a toll-free number to activate the card. Banks also send a follow-up notice stating that the card has been sent and needs to be activated. Card holders must sign the backs of their cards so that merchants can match the signature on the card to the signature at the point of sale. Card issuers use sophisticated software to monitor account activity. If unusual activity on an account occurs, some card issuers will freeze or flag the account until the transactions can be verified with the cardholder.

4.  *What are some scams that have prompted recent alerts from federal banking agencies?*

Phishing, advance fee fraud, and credit card protection fraud are some of the schemes that have prompted agency issuances. The agencies explain the frauds and caution banks and bank employees to be on the lookout for them.

5.  *What is the bank employee's role in safeguarding bank assets?*

The bank's expectations for employee conduct, both professionally and personally, are communicated usually in a code of ethics. A code of ethics helps employees decide what is in the best interests of the bank versus their own personal interests. In addition, employees should abide by the policies and procedures established by bank board of directors and management to implement laws, regulations, and other bank-specific safeguards.

6.  *List at least three signs of fraudulent checks.*

- Check lacks perforations, is stained or discolored, or has an odd "feel." Most check paper has the same weight and texture.
- Check number is either missing, does not change, or is low (between 100 and 500). Ninety percent of returned checks have low check numbers. Low check numbers indicate a recently opened account and, therefore, a potentially more risky check.

- Font used to print the customer's name looks visibly different from the font used to print the address.

- Additions to the check are hand written.

- Customer's address or bank's address is missing.

- Evidence of erasures or alterations.

- MICR numbers are missing or are shiny. Fraudulent checks often substitute regular toner or ink for magnetic ink.

- MICR encoding does not match the check number, the bank district, or the routing symbol in the upper right-hand corner of the check.

- Name of the payee appears to have been printed by a typewriter. Most payroll, expense, and dividend checks are printed by computer.

- Word VOID appears across the check.

- Check lacks an authorized signature.

7. *What can a bank employee do to prevent bank robberies?*

- Strictly abide by the bank's procedures for opening and closing the bank.

- Remain alert for suspicious vehicles, people, and circumstances.

- Jot down the license number of suspicious vehicles in the parking lot or near the building.

- Greet customers by directly looking into their eyes.

- Keep bank procedures and operations confidential.

8. *How are banks helping to protect the United States and its economy?*

Banks help combat the illegal flow of money used to finance illegal activities such as racketeering and terrorism. Banks file suspicious activity reports when they detect or suspect that a crime has been committed within or through the bank. Banks also have established stringent customer identification programs to verify the identity of individuals opening bank accounts. Banks also check their records to identify assets owned by individuals or organizations appearing on the federal Office of Foreign Assets Control list of individuals and foreign terrorist organizations and countries that are subject to sanctions. When a match is found, the bank blocks the account or freezes the assets.

# *Glossary*

**401(k) plans**—See defined contribution plans.

**ABA Institution Identifier**—A unique identifying number assigned by the American Bankers Association (ABA) under the national numerical system to facilitate sorting and processing checks. It has two parts separated by a hyphen. The first part identifies the city, state, or territory in which the bank is located, and the second part identifies the bank itself. It appears in the upper right-hand corner of checks as the numerator (upper portion) of a fraction and in the MICR line.

**Account**—A relationship involving a credit established under a particular name, usually by deposit or loan.

**Accounting**—The process of organizing, recording, and reporting all transactions that represent the financial condition and performance of a business, organization, or individual.

**Acquisition**—The process of buying or acquiring some asset, such as a block of stock, or an entire company.

**Adjustable-Rate Mortgage (ARM)**—A mortgage on which the rate is subject to periodic adjustment. The rate usually is tied to a widely published market rate of interest or index.

**Administrator**—A party appointed by a court to settle an estate when the decedent has left no valid will or the named executor cannot or will not serve.

**Adverse action**—Under the Equal Credit Opportunity Act, the action when a creditor denies a consumer's request for credit, reduces an existing credit line, or changes the terms, rate, or amount of a request. The creditor must advise the borrower in writing of the reasons for the denial of the request or change in terms.

**Agency**—The relationship between a party who acts on behalf of another, and the principal on whose behalf the agent acts. The principal retains legal title to property or other assets.

**Altered check**—A check on which a material change, such as the dollar amount, has been made. Banks are expected to detect alterations and are responsible for paying checks only as originally drawn.

**American Bankers Association (ABA)**—Established in 1875 and based in Washington, D.C., the ABA represents banks of all sizes on issues of national importance for financial institutions and their customers.

**Annual Percentage Rate (APR)**—The finance charge expressed as an annual percentage of the funds borrowed. It results from an equation that considers the amount financed, the finance charge, and the term of the loan. APR allows a comparison of credit costs regardless of the dollar amount of the costs or the length of time over which payments are made.

**Annual Percentage Yield (APY)**—A percentage rate reflecting the total amount of interest paid on a deposit account, based on the interest rate and the frequency of compounding for a 365-day period.

**Annual report**—A formal financial report issued annually to stockholders by a corporation. The annual report generally includes a set of financial statements (balance sheet, income statement, cash-flow statement, and footnotes), the auditor's report, and a review of the year's accomplishments.

**Annuity**—An investment that provides a systematic payment for a period of time, such as a specified number of years.

**Asset**—Anything owned by a business or consumer that has commercial, exchange, or book value. May consist of property or claims against others.

**Asset-liability management**—Management of bank assets and liabilities to produce maximum long-term gains for shareholders.

**Asset recovery**—Taking action on problem loans, including collecting late payments and restructuring loans.

**Attorney-in-Fact**—An individual authorized by another to act on his or her behalf.

**Audit**—An examination of accounts (usually by an independent accountant) to evaluate that financial information is accurate and prepared in conformity to generally accepted accounting principles (GAAP).

**Authentication**—Proving or validating a person's identity.

**Automated Clearing House (ACH)**—A clearing facility operated for the convenience of banks in a particular region, generally through the regional Federal Reserve bank. An ACH electronically processes interbank credits and debits.

**Automated Teller Machines (ATMs)**—Electronic facilities, located inside or apart from a financial services institution's premises, for handling many customer transactions automatically.

**Automatic Transfer Service (ATS)**—A service by which a bank moves funds from one type of account to another for its customer on a preauthorized basis.

**Available balance**—The portion of a customer's account balance on which the bank has placed no restrictions, making it available for immediate withdrawal.

**Availability schedule**—A list indicating the number of days, subject to the terms of Regulation CC, that must elapse before deposited checks can be considered converted into usable funds.

**Average daily balance method**—A method for calculating deposit account interest earned by multiplying the daily rate times the number of days in the compounding period times the average daily balance.

**Balance**—The amount of funds in a customer's account. It may refer to the book (ledger) balance, which simply shows the balance after debits and credits have been posited; the collected balance, which is the book balance less float; or the available balance.

**Balance sheet**—See **Statement of Condition**.

**Bank card fraud**—Using a stolen bank card or account number to fraudulently purchase goods and services.

**Bank examination**—Detailed scrutiny of a bank's assets, liabilities, capital accounts, income, and expenses by authorized representatives of a federal or state agency.

**Bank Insurance Fund**—An insurance fund created in 1989 under the Financial Institutions Reform, Recovery and Enforcement Act to hold the deposit insurance premiums paid by commercial and mutual savings banks for potential use in paying depositors of failed banks.

**Banker Acceptances (BA)**—A time draft (bill of exchange) drawn on and accepted by the bank on which it was drawn (stamped 'accepted' and signed by a representative banker). It may be created when payment is by a letter of credit. The bank accepting the draft assumes the obligation of making payment at maturity on behalf of the buyer or buyer's bank.

**Banking Act of 1933**—48 Stat. 162 (1933). Federal legislation that created the FDIC, set the dividing line between commercial and investment banking, and prohibited the payment of interest on deposits. Sections 16, 20, 21 and 32 are known as the Glass-Steagall Act, stipulating the separation of commercial banking and investment banking (see **Glass-Steagall Act**).

**Banknote**—A note issued by a bank promising to pay the amount of money designated on the face of the note when presented to the bank. Currency issued by an individual bank.

**Batch**—A group of deposits, checks, records or documents that have been assembled for processing and proof.

**Bearer**—Any person or company that has physical possession of a check or other negotiable instrument with no name entered on it as payee. Any bearer can present such an instrument for payment.

**Beneficiary**—The party who is to receive the proceeds of a trust, insurance policy, letter of credit, or other transaction.

**Benefit**—The value the product or service features give to customers to meet their needs, such as make money, save money, save time, provide convenience, or provide security.

**Blank endorsement**—The signature of the payee creating a bearer instrument that can be negotiated without other endorsement.

**Board of directors**—The governing body of a corporation ultimately responsible for its financial performance, consisting of individual directors who are elected by the stockholders.

**Board of governors**—The seven-member group, appointed by the President of the United States and confirmed by the Senate for 14-year terms, that directs the overall operations of the Federal Reserve System.

**Bond**—A long-term debt instrument. The issuer (a corporation, unit of government, or other legal entity) promises to repay the stated principal on a specified date at a specific rate of interest.

**Brokerage firm**—A business that arranges contracts for the purchase and sale of stocks and bonds.

**Bulk filing**—A method of filing checks in bundles that are sorted by statement cycle.

**Business contingency plan**—A plan for maintaining or resuming business operations should unexpected events occur.

**Buying on margin**—Using borrowed funds, plus some equity, to purchase assets such as stock.

**Capital**—Funds invested in a company by the owners, such as stockholders, for use in conducting business. The owner's original investment plus any profit reinvested in the business.

**Capital ratio**—A measure of profitability determined by dividing the stockholders' equity by total assets.

**Capitalization**—The total amount of equity and debt securities issued to finance the operations of a corporation.

**Cash concentration**—A service whereby businesses have disbursement accounts at numerous banks and pool balances in one account, the concentration account, to be invested for a higher return than would be possible in separate accounts.

**Cash item**—An item that flows through the collection process without need of special handling, for which a bank is willing to give immediate but provisional credit to a customer's account.

**Cash letter**—An interbank transmittal form, resembling a deposit slip, used to accompany cash items sent from one bank to another.

**Cash management**—Cash collection, payment, concentration, and information services provided to bank customers to expedite collecting receivables, controlling payments, and managing cash efficiently.

**Cashier's check**—A bank's own check drawn on the bank and signed by an authorized official. It is a direct obligation of the bank.

**Cashing**—Delivering money in exchange for a check drawn on another bank.

**Certificate of Deposit (CD)**—A time deposit account that earns interest and is payable at a definite date in the future or after a specified minimum notice of withdrawal. The account may be represented by a formal receipt for the funds deposited.

**Certified check**—A customer's check presented to a bank to be authenticated and guaranteed. By its certification, the bank guarantees that sufficient funds have been set aside from the customer's account to cover the check amount when payment is demanded.

**Charge-off**—A loan, obligation, or cardholder account the bank no longer expects to collect and writes off as a bad debt.

**Charitable trust**—A trust having a charitable organization as the beneficiary.

**Chartered**—Authorized by a federal or state regulatory body to conduct banking business.

**Check**—A draft signed by the maker and payable to a person named or to a bearer upon presentation to the bank on which it is drawn.

**Check truncation**—Electronically capturing the essential information on a conventional paper check and transferring the electronic information, not the paper check, though the clearing system.

**Clearing**—The process by which checks or other point-of-sale transactions are moved, physically or electronically, from the point of origin to a bank or other financial institution that maintains the customer's account.

**Clearing House Association**—A voluntary association of banks that establishes a meeting place for the exchanging and settling of checks drawn on one another.

**Club account**—An account offered by a bank to encourage customers to make periodic small deposits for future expenditures such as holiday purchases.

**Code of ethics**—A formal set of guidelines that represent a company's policies of corporate governance and individual conduct.

**Collateral**—Specific property pledged by a borrower to secure a loan. If the borrower defaults, the lender has the right to sell the collateral to repay the loan.

**Combined statement**—A bank statement that combines information from a number of accounts. Depending on the software capabilities of the bank, the statement may contain checking, savings, time deposits, bank card usage, and loan information on one statement form.

**Commercial loan**—A loan to a business to meet short- or long-term financing needs.

**Commercial paper**—Short-term, unsecured promissory notes issued by major corporations of strong credit standing as a means of borrowing.

**Common stock**—Securities evidencing ownership of a corporation and generally giving the shareholder voting rights. The rights of holders of common stock are inferior to those of holders of the corporation's bonds, preferred stock, and other debts.

**Community Reinvestment Act**—A federal law mandating that federal bank regulators regularly evaluate how financial institutions help meet the credit needs of their communities, including low- and moderate-income sections of the local community, and publicly rate the bank's performance.

**Compliance program**—The policies and procedures that a bank establishes and follows to ensure that it is adhering to all applicable federal and state laws and regulations.

**Comptroller of the Currency**—The head of the Office of the Comptroller of the Currency. The Comptroller, appointed by the President and confirmed by the Senate, is responsible for chartering, examining, and supervising all national banks.

**Computer virus**—A computer program that copies itself in other personal computer programs. These viruses may attack data and crash computer systems.

**Conflict of interest**—A situation in which an action taken by an individual in an official capacity may benefit that individual personally, to the detriment of the employer.

**Conservatorship**—See **guardianship**

**Construction loan**—A short-term loan to finance the cost of constructing a home or other building. The loan is usually repaid when construction is completed, and usually from the proceeds of the permanent mortgage loan.

**Consumer loan**—A loan extended to consumers, either individually or jointly, primarily for buying goods and services for personal use.

**Contingency**—In accounting, a contingency is a possible gain or loss to an enterprise. Depending on whether the contingency is probable, reasonably possible, or remote, and whether the contingency is reasonably estimable, different accounting treatments are prescribed.

**Controlled disbursement account**—An account drawn on an affiliate or branch of the primary bank and processed at another check processing facility. Checks processed throughout the day are totaled, and the customer is informed of the amount at the end of the day. The customer makes payments by transferring money from concentration (investment) accounts or from the company's line of credit.

**Corporate bond**—Long-term debt obligations issued to investors by corporations to finance expansion.

**Corporate governance**—The manner in which directors, management, and auditors handle their responsibilities toward shareholders. It is the way a company is managed and its assets accounted for and reported to the public.

**Corporate resolution**—A document, filed with a bank by a corporation, that defines the authority given to the corporation's officers and specifies who may sign checks, borrow on behalf of the corporation, and otherwise issue instructions to the bank and conduct the corporation's business.

**Corporation**—A business organization treated as a legal entity and owned by a group of stockholders (shareholders). The stockholders elect the directors, who serve as the active, governing body to manage the corporation's affairs.

**Correspondent bank**—A bank that maintains an account relationship or engages in an exchange of services with another bank.

**Counterfeit**—Any fake currency, coin, or bank card made to appear authentic.

**Credit**—(1) An advance of cash, merchandise, or other commodity in exchange for a promise or other agreement to pay at a future date, with interest, if so agreed. (2) An accounting entry to the right-hand (credit) side of an account, decreasing the balance of an asset or expense account or increasing the balance of a liability, income, or equity account.

**Credit card**—A plastic card used by the cardholder to obtain money, goods, or services, possibly under a line of credit established by the card issuer.

**Credit life insurance**—Insurance that pays off the insured loan if the borrower dies while the loan is still outstanding.

**Credit risk**—The risk that the borrower cannot or will not repay a loan with interest as scheduled.

**Credit scoring**—A technique that uses a mathematical formula to determine the likelihood that a borrower will repay a loan, given adverse circumstances.

**Credit union**—A voluntary cooperative association of individuals having some common bond, such as place of employment, organized to accept deposits, extend loans, and provide other financial services.

**Creditor**—Any party to whom money is owed by another.

**Creditworthiness**—The ability and willingness to repay a loan, largely demonstrated by a credit history.

**Cross-selling**—A marketing and sales practice whereby additional products and services are offered to a current customer.

**Currency**—Paper money, as opposed to coin.

**Currency Transaction Report (CTR)**—A report required by the Bank Secrecy Act for transactions involving more than $10,000, unless exempted under one of the provisions of the act.

**Custody**—An agency service, whereby the bank safekeeps the assets and collects the income for the individual. A custodian buys and sells securities when instructed specifically to do so by the customer or the appointed agent. Service is provided for individuals, correspondent banks, and government agencies.

**Daily balance method**—A method for calculating deposit account interest earned by multiplying each day's ending balance by the daily rate and then adding together all the daily accruals during the compounding period.

**Debit**—(1) An accounting entry that increases the balance of an asset or expense account or decreases the balance of a liability, income, or equity account. (2) A charge against a customer's balance or bank card account.

**Debit card**—A plastic card enabling the card-holder to purchase goods or services, the cost of which is immediately debited to his or her bank account.

**Declaration of loss**—A written statement signed by the purchaser or the payee that a check has been lost, stolen, or destroyed, and the check was not transferred by the person making the claim.

**Deferred annuity**—An annuity providing for payment of income beginning at a future date.

**Defined-benefit plan**—A retirement plan whereby the employer typically invests a set amount each pay period on behalf of the employee during the working years. On retirement, the employee receives periodic income for life, with the income amount being defined as a function of years employed and income pattern while working.

**Defined contribution plan**—A retirement plan whereby the employer makes contributions into the plan as a percentage of current pay or profits. Typically each employee makes a contribution of a certain percentage of pay and the employer matches that contribution to a stipulated percentage. Also typically, the employee directs the investment, and the retirement benefit is a function of investment performance and accumulated fund value.

**Depositary bank**—A bank in which a check is first deposited. The bank also may be the paying bank (drawee) if the check is drawn on, payable at, or payable through the bank.

**Direct deposit**—The process by which the issuer of a payment delivers information regarding the payee and the amount of the payment directly to the payee's bank for credit to his or her account.

**Direct send program**—The method of check collection in which deposited checks are presented directly to their drawee banks for settlement. (Also known as direct presentment.)

**Disability insurance**—Insurance that provides a source of income to workers in the event they become disabled or sick for an extended period.

**Discount rate**—The rate of interest charged by the Federal Reserve Banks on loans they make to financial institutions.

**Dishonor**—The refusal of a drawee or drawer to pay a check, draft, note, or other instrument presented.

**Disintermediation**—The withdrawal of money from a financial institution and deposit of the funds in another type of investment product in order to earn higher rates of interest.

**Diversification**—A method of decreasing the total risk of investments by investing funds in assets of different kinds.

**Dividend**—A periodic payment, usually made each quarter, by a corporation to its stockholders as a return on their investment. All dividend payouts must be approved by the corporation's board of directors.

**Draft**—A signed order by one party (the drawer) addressed to another (the drawee) directing the drawee to pay, in the future, a specified sum of money to the order of a third person, a payee.

**Drawee**—The party on whom a draft is drawn and who is directed to pay the sum specified.

**Drawer**—The party who instructs the drawee to pay funds to the payee. (Also known as maker.)

**Dual banking system**—The banking system in the United States today whereby a bank may be chartered under the state or federal government.

**Dual custody (dual control)**—A security technique that uses two or more separate entities or people operating together to protect sensitive functions, information, or assets. Both entities are equally responsible for physically protecting materials involved in vulnerable transactions.

**Due from account**—An account held by a bank (account owner bank) with another bank (account servicing bank) that represents funds 'due from' the other bank on demand.

**Due to account**—An account serviced by a bank (account servicing bank) on behalf of another bank (account owner bank) that represents funds due to the other bank on demand.

**Earnings per share (EPS)**—A determinant of a company's profitability, obtained by dividing the net income by the number of outstanding shares of common stock.

**Edge Act Corporation**—A nationally chartered corporate subsidiary of a bank established under Section 25(a) of the Federal Reserve Act to engage in international banking and investment.

**Electronic funds transfer (EFTS)**—Using automated, electronic, technology to move funds without paper checks.

**Encoding**—Inscribing or imprinting MICR data on checks, deposit slips, debit and credit tickets, or other bank documents.

**Endorsement**—A signature (other than the signature of the maker, drawer, or acceptor) that is made on an instrument, such as a check, for negotiating the instrument, restricting payment, or transferring liability of the instrument to another party.

**Equity**—The stockholders' investment interest in a corporation, equaling the excess of assets over liabilities and including common and preferred stock, retained earnings, and surplus and reserves.

**Estate**—The sum total, as determined by a complete inventory, of all the assets of a decedent.

**Exception item**—An item that cannot be paid by a drawee bank for one reason or another, such as a stop payment or insufficient funds.

**Executor**—A party named in the decedent's valid will to settle an estate and qualified by a court to act in this capacity.

**Feature**—A characteristic of the product or service. For example, the interest rate or maturity period.

**Fed funds**—Excess reserves held by member banks in accounts at the Federal Reserve that are loaned with interest on a daily basis to other member banks.

**Fed funds rate**—The interest rate charged by a Federal Reserve member bank that lends Fed funds to another member bank.

**Federal Deposit Insurance Corporation (FDIC)**—The agency of the federal government established to provide insurance protection, up to statutory limits, for depositors at FDIC member institutions. All national banks and all Fed member banks must belong to the FDIC; other commercial banks and savings banks may join also.

**Federal Open Market Committee (FOMC)**—The Federal Reserve committee that sets monetary policy and issues guidelines for open-market operations. It purchases and redeems U.S. government obligations through the Federal Reserve Bank of New York to implement monetary policy.

**Federal Reserve banks**—The 12 district institutions that deal with member banks and maintain branches and check-processing centers as necessary. Each district bank is owned by its members.

**Federal Reserve notes**—The paper money (currency), constituting the largest part of the nation's money supply, issued by the 12 Federal Reserve banks and officially designated as legal tender by the federal government. Each note is an interest-free promise to pay on demand.

**Federal Reserve System**—The central monetary authority for the United States, created by the Federal Reserve Act of 1913 and consisting of the 12 district banks and their branches, plus the member banks that are the stock-holders and legal owners.

**Fedwire**—The Federal Reserve's electronic funds transfer system.

**Fiduciary**—An individual, bank, or other party to whom specific property is turned over under the terms of a contractual agreement and who acts for the benefit of another party on a basis of trust and confidence.

**Finance charge**—The total cost, including interest, that a borrower pays for obtaining credit.

**Financial Holding Company (FHC)**—A corporation that owns, controls, or otherwise has the power over the voting stock in one or more banks. All finance holding companies come under the jurisdiction of the Federal Reserve.

**Float**—The dollar amount of deposited cash items that have been given immediate, provisional credit but are in the process of collection from drawee banks. (Also called uncollected funds.)

**Floor plan loan**— Loans made to dealers for maintaining inventory.

**Foreclosure**—A legal procedure undertaken to permit a creditor to sell property that is collateral for a defaulted loan.

**Foreign exchange**—Trading in or exchange of foreign currencies for U.S. funds or other foreign currencies.

**Forgery**—The legal term for counterfeiting a check or other document with the intent to defraud.

**Fraud**—Intentional misrepresentation of a material fact by one party so that another party, acting on it, will part with property or surrender a right.

**Funds management**—Management of all items on the balance sheet, including assets, liabilities, and capital to optimize a bank's earnings without taking excessive risk or liquidity exposure in order to achieve liquidity, safety, and income.

**General power of attorney**—The attorney in fact is authorized by the principal to act for his or her benefit in all matters.

**Glass-Steagall Act**— Four sections of the Banking Act of 1933. Section 16 limited bank securities transactions for customer accounts only and securities underwriting for bank investments and government securities only. Section 20 prohibited Fed member banks from affiliating with investment banking companies. Section 21 prohibited investment banking companies from accepting deposits. Section 32 prohibited management ties between banks and investment banking companies.

**Grace period**—A specified extension of time beyond a due date for making a credit payment.

**Gramm-Leach-Bliley Act** (GLBA)— The financial modernization law that permits banking organizations to engage in a broad range of financial activities, including incidental and complementary activities. The law created the financial holding company structure, which owns companies engaged in nonbanking activities. It also includes provisions on financial privacy and security and ATM disclosures.

**Growth assets**—Assets with potential to increase in value. Stock and stock mutual funds are common examples. These products, offered through third-party or affiliated broker-dealers, are not FDIC-insured.

**Guardianship**—A trust relationship, established by a court appointment, in which a trustee holds in safekeeping and manages certain property for the benefit of a minor or incompetent person. (Also known as conservatorship.)

**Hold**—A restriction on paying all or any part of the balance in an account.

**Holder**—A person who is in possession of a negotiable instrument and who is entitled to receive payment of the instrument.

**Holder in due course**—One who holds a negotiable instrument, such as a check, and who takes the instrument for value, in good faith, without notice that it is overdue or dishonored, without knowledge that it has an unauthorized signature or is altered, and without knowledge of claims to the instrument or defenses against payment.

**Home equity loan**—A type of real estate credit in which the homeowner borrows against the value of his or her residence through a second mortgage. A variation, the home equity line of credit, allows the borrower to draw on the credit line at anytime.

**HUD-1 Settlement Statement**—A disclosure required by the Real Estate Settlement Procedures Act that itemizes the settlement services provided by the lender and the fees associated with these services.

**Identity theft**—A crime involving the possession of identifying information not lawfully issued for that person's use or the attempt to access the financial resources of that person through the use of illegally obtained identifying information.

**Immediate annuity**—The payout annuity for disbursing funds to an annuitant, usually periodically and usually for a lifetime or set period.

**In-clearing capture**—The process whereby the Fed presents a cash letter to the paying bank and the paying bank prepares the items for capture (reading), performs the capture run, and settles for the checks.

**Income Assets**—Assets that provide greater income-earning potential but not growth in investment value. These investments are not FDIC-insured, and the income generated can be taxable or tax deferred. Bonds or fixed income mutual funds are examples.

**Income statement**—See **profit and loss statement**.

**Indenture**—A contract underlying a bond issue that is signed by the issuing corporation and by the trustee acting for the bondholders. It sets forth the rights and responsibilities of the corporation, trustee, and bondholders, and the terms of the security issue.

**Indirect loan**—A loan involving three parties: the borrower who obtains financing, a merchant (or dealer), and a bank.

**Individual Retirement Account (IRA)**—Tax-deferred account into which a customer, subject to tax-law restrictions, may make deposits and earn interest for saving for retirement. Penalty-free withdrawals are allowed after the depositor reaches age 59 ½.

**Inflation**—A continuing increase in the level of prices in an economy, caused by too many dollars and too few goods to be purchased.

**Insider**—Under Regulation O, an executive officer, director, principal stockholder, or person with related interests.

**Installment loan**—A loan made to an individual or business, repaid in fixed, periodic payments.

**Institutional Trust**—A trust established by large investing bodies, such as insurance companies, pension plans and profit-sharing funds of corporations.

**Insufficient funds**—See **nonsufficient funds**.

**Insurance**—A contract which, for a fee (premium), one party agrees to pay a sum to another party if the latter suffers a loss. The insurer takes on the risk, and the insured is the protected party.

**Interest rate spread**—The difference between the interest banks pay on deposits and the interest banks earn on loans and investments.

**Investment**—The exchange of money, either for a promise to pay at a later date (as with bonds) or for an ownership share in a business (as with stocks).

**Irrevocable letter of credit**—A letter of credit that stipulates no changes can be made without the full consent of both the buyer and the seller.

**Issuer**—The corporation, person, or government whose note, bond, stock certificate, or other financial instrument is offered for sale.

**Item capture**—Reading and storing electronic information from the magnetic ink character recognition (MICR) line of a check.

**Joint tenancy**—Property held by two or more parties on an equal basis, conveying rights of survivorship.

**Kiting**—Attempting to draw against uncollected or nonexistent funds for fraudulent purposes. A depositor issues a check, overdrawing an account at one bank, and deposits into that account a check drawn on insufficient or uncollected funds at another bank.

**Legal lending limit**—The maximum amount of money a bank can lend on an unsecured basis to a single borrower or combination of financially related borrowers. It is established by law and is expressed as a percentage of the bank's capital and surplus.

**Letter of credit**—An instrument issued by a bank, substituting the credit standing of the bank for the credit standing of the buyer of goods. It guarantees that the bank will pay the seller, if all the terms of the contract are met, and protects the buyer by assuring that no payment will be made until the contract has been fulfilled.

**Leverage**—The use of debt securities or borrowed money to increase the return possible on equity capital.

**Liability**—(1) An amount owed. (2) A source of financing such as a deposit in a bank. (3) A legal obligation to make good some loss or damage that results from an action or transaction.

**Life insurance**—Insurance that provides payment of a sum to survivors on the death of the insured. Many types of life insurance are sold. Two basic categories of insurance products are term life and whole life insurance.

**Line of credit**—Open-end or revolving line of credit on which a borrower may draw for an agreed-upon period. The balance may fluctuate from zero up to the credit line's maximum amount. Two examples of open-end credit are a home equity line of credit and a credit card.

**Liquidity**—The ability of a bank or business to meet its current obligations.

**Living trust**—A trust that becomes operative during the lifetime of the settler. Typically used to provide outstanding management and reduce the cost of probating an estate.

**Loan**—A business contract in which a borrower agrees to pay interest for the use of a lender's funds.

**Loan agreement**—A written agreement between lender and borrower that defines the rights and obligations of both parties.

**Loan loss reserve**—An amount reserved (or set aside) to cover possible loan losses. The loan loss reserve is built up through deductions from net income. As loan losses occur, they are charged to the reserve.

**Loan pool**—A group of loans packaged together to serve as collateral for a security.

**Loan review**—The function of examining loan documents to ensure accuracy, completeness, and conformity with the bank's loan policies and regulatory requirements.

**Local check**—A deposited check drawn on another bank in the same Federal Reserve check processing region.

**Lockbox**—A service in which a bank assumes the responsibility for receiving, examining, processing, and crediting incoming checks for a customer to reduce mail, deposit, and collection time.

**London Interbank Offered Rate (LIBOR)**—An international money market interest rate that represents the average rate offered by banks for the interbank placement of eurodollars. Banks often add percentages above LIBOR to determine the interest rate.

**Magnetic Ink Character Recognition (MICR)**—Magnetic codes on the bottom of a check that allow a machine to read the check. The code can include the check amount, the account number, the bank's routing number, and the check serial number.

**Market risk**—The risk that the market value of a security will decrease because of interest rates and other market conditions.

**Market share**—One seller's portion of the total sales of a product, usually measured as a percentage.

**Marketing concept**—An organizational philosophy that influences and directs all bank operations. It consists of customer satisfaction, total company effort, profit, and social responsibility.

**Marketing customer information file**—A software program that can sort and analyze customer information and that can serve as a customer information database.

**Matched funding**—An asset-liability management technique, whereby the maturity of loans is matched with the maturity of deposits.

**Maturity**—The date on which a time deposit, note, draft, bond, or acceptance become due and payable.

**Merchant banking**—The buying and selling by banks of shares in the unregistered securities in companies.

**Merger**—The combination of two or more enterprises, such as banks. Usually involves exchanging securities or issuing new securities, or both.

**Monetary policy**—General term for the actions taken by the Federal Reserve to control the flow of money and credit.

**Money**—Legal tender, coin, and currency declared by a government to be the accepted medium of exchange.

**Money laundering**—Moving large amounts of illegally obtained cash through many bank accounts to hide the source of the money.

**Money market deposit account (MMDA)**—A type of savings account created in 1982 that pays a market interest rate and allows account holders limited check-writing privileges.

**Money supply**—The sum of all the funds that individuals and businesses have immediately available for spending in the domestic economy. The U.S. money supply consists of M1—the sum of currency, demand deposits, traveler's checks, and other checkable deposits; M2—M1 plus overnight repurchase agreements and eurodollars, money-market mutual fund balances, money-market deposit accounts, savings and small time deposits; M3—M2 plus large time deposits, term repurchase agreements, term eurodollars, and institution-only money market mutual fund balances.

**Mortgage loan**—Real estate credit, usually extended on a long-term basis with the mortgaged property as collateral to secure the loan.

**Municipal securities**—Debt instruments issued by state and local governments and their political subdivisions.

**Mutilated currency**—Currency that is torn, written on, missing a portion, or otherwise damaged.

**Mutual fund**—A mutual fund is an investment company whose primary activity is investing, usually in a diversified portfolio of securities. The stockholder in a mutual fund buys shares from, or sells them back to, the mutual fund in a direct sale, not through a stock exchange.

**National Automated Clearing House (NACHA)**—A trade organization that provides marketing and education services and establishes rules, standards, and procedures that enable firms to exchange automated clearing house (ACH) transactions.

**National bank**—A commercial bank that operates under a federal charter and is supervised and examined by the Office of the Comptroller of the Currency.

**Negotiable Certificate of Deposit**—A transferable receipt issued by a commercial bank on return of a customer's deposit. Bank agrees to pay the amount deposited plus interest to the bearer at maturity. These are issued in large denominations, usually for a minimum of $100,000.

**Negotiable instrument**—An unconditional written order or promise to pay a certain sum of money. The document must be easily transferable from one party to another. Every negotiable instrument must meet all the requirements of Article 3 of the Uniform Commercial Code.

**Negotiable Order of Withdrawal**—See **NOW account**.

**Net interest income**—The difference between interest income and interest expense.

**Net worth**—Assets minus liabilities of a business. This is the owners' equity. (Also called stockholder's equity.)

**Night depository**—A convenience facility provided for merchants who wish to deposit their receipts after business hours. A small vault, located inside a bank but accessible outside the premises, is used.

**Non-cash item**—An item that cannot be processed in bulk and requires special handling. Usually receives deferred credit until final settlement.

**Noninterest income**—Income a bank derives from sources other than interest (for example, fees and service charges, trading income, investment securities gains, and other income).

**Nonlocal check**—A deposited check that is drawn on another bank located in a different Federal Reserve check processing region. (Also known as a transit check.)

**Nonmember bank**—A state-chartered bank that is not a member of the Federal Reserve System.

**Nonsufficient funds**—An expression indicating that a check or item drawn against an account exceeds the amount of collected funds in the account.

**Notary public**—A public officer who takes acknowledgment of or otherwise attests or certifies deeds and other writings or copies of them, usually under his or her official seal, to make them authentic.

**Note**—See **promissory note**.

**NOW account**—An interest-earning transaction account on which check-like instruments (negotiable orders of withdrawal) may be used. This transaction account is not a demand deposit account. The bank must reserve the right to require the depositor to give seven days' advance notice before withdrawing funds, a requirement that is rarely imposed.

**Office of Thrift Supervision (OTS)**—An agency of the Treasury Department that regulates federally chartered savings and loan associations.

**On-us check**—A check deposited or negotiated for cash at the bank on which it is drawn.

**Open market operations**—Sales and purchases of government obligations by the Federal Open Market Committee to influence the size of the money supply and to control the flow of money and credit. Used by the Fed to implement monetary policy.

**Originating depository financial institution (ODFI)**—A financial institution that receives automated clearing house (ACH) payment instructions and forwards the entries to another financial institution to transmit payments.

**Outsourcing**—The practice of turning over part or all of a bank's operations to a third-party provider.

**Outstanding check**—An issued check that has not yet been presented for payment to, or paid by, a drawee.

**Overdraft**—A negative (minus) balance in an account, resulting from the paying (posting) of checks for an amount greater than the depositor's balance.

**Paperhanging**—A type of check fraud, whereby someone intentionally writes checks on closed accounts. They obtain blank checks by improper means or by reordering checks on closed accounts.

**Participation**—A loan whereby an originating bank sells all or some of it to another financial institution. They are used to manage risk and meet borrowing requirements that exceed the bank's legal lending limit.

**Partnership**—A business operated by two or more individuals in non-corporate form. The rights and duties and responsibilities of the partners usually are covered in a partnership agreement.

**Partnership agreement**—A legal agreement stating the contributions each partner has made to the business, the nature of the business, and the proportions in which each partner will share in profits or losses.

**Partnership resolution**—A document containing language certifying that the name of the partnership is exactly the same as provided to the bank and lists who is authorized to write checks and sign for loans on behalf of the partnership.

**Payee**—The beneficiary of the check; the person or entity to whom it is payable.

**Paying**—Delivering cash in exchange for an on-us check.

**Paying agent**—An agency service, whereby the bank makes interest or dividend payments to holders of stock or bonds issued by a corporation or government unit. The agent is responsible for redeeming debt issues as they mature. (Also known as dividend disbursement agent.)

**Payment system**—A communication system that permits the exchange of information necessary to carry out transfers of funds. The payment system extends from point of acceptance through to the paying bank.

**Pension plan**—An arrangement evidenced by a written agreement providing for the accumulation of funds from a corporation or its employees or both to be used for monthly or other periodic payments to employees of the corporation after their retirement.

**Personal agency**—Services provided by trust departments, such as safekeeping, custody, investment advising, and managing. Under an agency arrangement, the bank is given specific authority by the individual who retains the legal title to the assets.

**Personal representative**—A party appointed by a court to carry out the terms of a will. This court appointment occurs if no executor was named in the will or if the named executor cannot serve.

**Phishing**—Imitating legitimate companies in e-mails to lure people to share passwords or credit-card numbers. A consumer scam.

**PIN-only debit card**—A plastic card enabling the cardholder to purchase goods or services or withdraw cash online after entering a personal identification number. The cost of the transaction is debited from the cardholder's bank account (also known as an ATM card).

**Point of sale**—A terminal used to transfer funds from a bank account to pay for purchases.

**Posting**—The process of adding deposits to an account balance and subtracting checks and other withdrawals.

**Power of attorney**—A legal document that authorizes a person named as an agent (attorney-in-fact) to act on behalf of another person (the principal).

**Preauthorized payment**—A convenience service offered by banks, whereby customers request funds be transferred from their accounts to pay a creditor on a regular basis.

**Presentment**—Demand for payment of a negotiable instrument made by the person entitled to payment.

**Primary reserves**—Bank reserves that provide immediate liquidity but do not generate income. Primary reserves consists chiefly of cash assets, cash in vault, reserves at the Federal Reserve bank, balances due from banks, and cash items in the process of collection.

**Prime rate**—A base rate that a bank establishes that reflects its determination of cost of funds, overhead, loan portfolio risk, profit objectives, and other relevant factors.

**Principal**—A party who appoints another to act on his or her behalf, for example, as an agent or attorney-in-fact.

**Private sector**—That part of the economy owned and operated by corporations and individuals, and not government (public sector).

**Probate**—The judicial determination concerning the validity of a will and all questions pertaining to it. The first step in settling an estate. (Also the name of the court that handles this process.)

**Problem loan**—A loan in which the prospect of collecting repayment under the original terms is unlikely.

**Profiling**—Identifying relevant characteristics to gain insight about the need for a product in the marketplace. ·

**Profit-and-loss statement**—A financial statement that shows a summary of a firm's income and expenses for a specific period. (Also called income statement, earnings statement, or operating statement.)

**Promissory note**—A written document with the maker's (borrower's) promise to pay a certain sum of money to the payee (bank), with or without interest, on demand or on a fixed or determinable future date.

**Proof department**—The unit in a bank that sorts and distributes checks and other work and arrives at a control figure for all transactions.

**Proprietorship**—See **sole proprietorship**.

**Prudent investor**—An investor, and in the case of trusts, a trustee, who acts with caution, skill, diligence, and sense of responsibility in managing the investments in a customer's portfolio.

**Public funds accounts**—Accounts established for any government, agency of government, or political subdivision.

**Purchase decision**—In the buying process, the culmination of prepurchase activity, in which information gathered to reduce the risk associated with a decision about a product is assessed and the purchase is then made.

**Raised currency**—One or two ends of the corners of a smaller denomination bill, such as one dollar or a five dollar bill, are replaced with the ends or corners of a larger bill such as a 10, 20 or 50. The bill is redeemed for the value of the "raised" amount.

**Ratio analysis**—A technique for analyzing a financial statement that examines the relationships among certain key values reported in the statement.

**Reader sorter**—Electronic equipment with the ability to read, sort, and process MICR encoded checks and documents.

**Receiving depository financial institution (RDFI)**—A financial institution that receives the automated clearing house (ACH) entries from another financial institution and posts the entries to the payees' accounts.

**Reconcilement**—The process of comparing and balancing one account record against another to provide a proof.

**Redlining**—Excluding potential borrowers because they are from a certain geographic area, regardless of whether they otherwise meet all other criteria of creditworthiness.

**Referral**—Directing a potential customer from one area of the bank, such as consumer lending, to another area, such as insurance, to help the customer obtain information about or purchase another product or service.

**Registrar**—An agency service, whereby the bank maintains records of shares canceled and reissued so that an overissuance does not occur. The corporation establishes the maximum number of shares of stock that may be issued.

**Reserve requirement**—A monetary policy control rule, issued by the Federal Reserve, that requires a bank to set aside a portion of its cash assets against its outstanding checkable deposits.

**Restrictive endorsement**—An endorsement whereby the payee or other holder of a check restricts the purpose for which a check may be used. The most common restrictive endorsement, used for depositing an item to an account, is "For Deposit Only." Endorsed this way, the instrument can be used only for deposit to an account. Any other use is prohibited.

**Return items**—Checks, drafts, or notes that have been dishonored by the drawee bank or maker and have been returned to the presenting party.

**Return on Assets (ROA)**—A financial measurement that indicates how efficiently a bank's assets are being used. Determined by dividing net income (profit) by average total assets.

**Return on Equity (ROE)**—A financial measurement that indicates how efficiently a bank's equity (capital) is being used. Determined by dividing net income (profit) by average total equity.

**Revocable letter of credit**—A letter of credit that may be cancelled at any time by the issuing bank.

**Revolving credit**—See line of credit.

**Right of survivorship**—The right of the surviving tenant(s) to take full possession of specific assets, such as account funds, upon the death of the other tenant(s), without establishing an estate and subject to state laws.

**Risk-based pricing**—Charging a different interest rate on the same loan (terms and amount), depending on a customer's credit scores, credit history, and other indicators of creditworthiness. Customers in higher risk categories are offered higher interest rates.

**Risk rating**—A system measuring the loan's quality on the basis of the borrower's liquidity, the loan's profitability, and other criteria approved by bank's board of directors and recorded in the loan policy.

**Safe assets**—Traditional bank products like checking, savings accounts, money market accounts, and certificates of deposits. They are used to meet everyday life expenses and often provide a small investment return. Many of these products, which are FDIC-insured, are liquid.

**Safekeeping**—An agency service, whereby the bank accepts, holds, and returns upon request the stocks, bonds, or other assets that the individual delivered to it.

**Sarbanes-Oxley Act**—A federal law intended to improve the governance of public corporations by holding boards of directors, management, and auditors to high standards of conduct and accountability.

**Savings account**—An interest bearing account that a depositor may use to accumulate funds gradually from earnings or income.

**Savings and Loan Association (S&L)**—A federally or state-chartered thrift institution, formerly known as a building society, that accepts various types of deposits and uses them primarily for home mortgage loans.

**Savings bank**—A thrift institution specializing in savings accounts but also offering other types of deposit relationships, including checking accounts. Many are federally chartered and are allowed to make commercial loans and offer other services.

**Savings Association Insurance Fund**—An insurance fund created in 1989 under the Financial Institutions Reform, Recovery and Enforcement Act to hold premiums paid by savings and loan associations for potential use in paying depositors of failed S&Ls.

**Secondary mortgage market**—Transactions involving selling and purchasing existing mortgages. Mortgage loans originate in the primary mortgage market. The sale of those loans occurs in the secondary market.

**Secondary reserves**—Funds invested in high-quality, short-term assets that can be quickly converted to cash without major loss.

**Secured loan**—A loan in which the borrower has pledged some form of collateral to protect the lender in case of default.

**Securitization**—Packaging loans as a unit to be sold to outside investors. The loans are no longer assets to the bank, although the bank may still continue to service them for investors.

**Security interest**—The right a lender has to obtain possession of the collateral, sell it, and retain the proceeds (up to the amount of the remaining debt) in the event the borrower is unable to repay the loan.

**Self-check digit**—A suffix numeral used by bank computers, using a programmed formula to test the validity of a bank number or account number. (Also known as check digit.)

**Settlement**—(1)For an estate, the distribution of an estate by an executor or administrator; (2) The conclusion of a transaction, completing all necessary documentation, making all necessary payments, and where appropriate, transferring title.

**Share draft**—A bill payment device offered by some credit unions. Members of a credit union can write these check-like instruments against their savings share accounts.

**Signature**—A sign or mark made by a drawer or maker of a negotiable instrument. A signature may include a thumbprint and may be typed, printed, or stamped.

**Signature-based debit card**—A plastic card enabling the cardholder to purchase goods or services or withdraw cash offline upon signing a receipt. The cost of the transaction is debited from the cardholder's bank account. The card, which may be used for online transactions as well, may carry a VISA or MasterCard logo.

**Smart Card**—A card embedded with a microprocessor that gives it the capacity to compute or to communicate information and store data.

**Sole proprietorship**—A business owned and operated by one person.

**Special endorsement**—An endorsement that names another designated person. The endorsement may state, "Pay to the order of," and then the payee signs under that statement. Only the designated person can negotiate the check. A special endorsement can be used if the payee is sending it to another person through the mail.

**Special Power of Attorney**—The attorney in fact is authorized to act for the principal only for certain specified matters.

**Spoofing**—An attempt to gain access to a system by posing as an authorized user.

**Stale dated check**—A check bearing a date six months or more in the past, prior to its presentment.

**Standby letter of credit**—A letter of credit that is paid when something does not happen. Normally, they are not drawn against, have a period of one year, and may be renewed. They reinforce a customer's credit standing.

**State bank**—A commercial bank chartered by the state in which it is headquartered.

**Statement**—The record prepared by a bank for a customer, listing all debits and credits for the period and the closing balance in the account.

**Statement of Condition**—A detailed list of assets, liabilities, and owners' equity (net worth), showing a company's financial position at a specific time. (Also known as a balance sheet.)

**Statement savings**—A savings account in which a periodic statement, usually computer generated, replaces the traditional passbook.

**Stock**—The generic term for common and preferred shares issued by a corporation, evidencing ownership.

**Stockholders**—The owners of common or preferred stock in a corporation. (Also called shareholders.)

**Stop payment**—A depositor's instructions to his or her bank (the drawee) directing the bank not to pay a previously issued check or item.

**Stored value card**—A prepaid card that stores funds often for a specific purpose. As the card is used, the amount is deducted from the card until the balance is completely used.

**Substitute check**—A paper reproduction of the original check that contains an image of the front and back, bears the full MICR line as allowed by industry standards for such checks, conforms in paper stock and dimensions according to standards, and can be processed through automated check systems.

**Sweep**—A prearranged automatic transfer of funds in an account, above a specified amount, to an investment pool, an interest-earning account, or to pay a line of credit.

**Systematic risk**—Risk that affects security prices in general and cannot be diversified away. It is caused by underlying national and international economic and political conditions.

**Teller's Check**—A check issued by one bank and drawn on another bank or payer. The bank is obligated to pay the check. The drawee bank maintains the check supply and the teller's check account.

**Tenancy-in-common**—The holding of property by two or more persons in such a manner that each has an undivided interest that, upon the death of one, passes to the heirs or devisee(s) and not to the survivor(s).

**Testamentary trust**—A trust established by the terms of a will. It empowers a trustee to manage assets for a beneficiary and becomes active after the maker's death and settlement of the estate.

**Time deposit**—A deposit account carrying a specified maturity date, usually bearing interest and restricting the depositor's ability to make withdrawals before the maturity date.

**Trading account**—Account holding securities that are actively bought and sold to make a profit. Trading-account positions are often tailored to current and anticipated customer needs, underwriting obligations, and trading strategies.

**Transaction account**—A bank account that allows for the transfer of funds to third parties.

**Transfer agent**—An agency service whereby the bank is responsible for changing the title of ownership on the corporation's shares of stock, as required when shares change hands.

**Transit item**—A nonlocal item, such as check drawn on a bank located in another Fed processing region.

**Truncation**—A generic term for the various banking systems designed to reduce the need to send or physically handle checks for customers' accounts.

**Trust**—A relationship in which one party holds property for another party, based on a trust agreement and fiduciary principles of law.

**Trustee**—Person or entity that takes control of the trust property and administers the trust.

**Trustor**—Person creating the trust.

**Underwriting**—The assumption of a risk for a fee such as for insurance or investments. Insurance underwriting guarantees a cash payment in the event of a loss or casualty. Firm commitment investment underwriting, as opposed to a best effort investment underwriting, guarantees the sale of a securities issue.

**Unfit currency**—Currency of such poor quality (limp or dirty) that it cannot be recirculated.

**Uniform Commercial Code**—A set of common laws adopted by all states to govern commercial and financial transactions between parties. Many states adopted their own amendments to the code.

**Universal life insurance**—Life insurance that gives policy owners the ability to set and vary their own premium levels, payment schedules, and death benefits, within certain limits.

**Unsecured loan**—Bank credit extended without collateral.

**U.S. Treasury bills**—Marketable U. S. Treasury securities with maturities of one year or less.

**U.S. Treasury notes**—Interest-bearing security issued by the U.S. Treasury with original maturities greater than one year but less than five years.

**Value**—The worth of a product or service.

**Variable life insurance**—A form of life insurance in which the cash value of the policy may fluctuate according to the investment performance of separate account funds. The policy owner chooses among various funds offered by the insurer.

**Variable rate loan**—A loan that allows the lender to make periodic adjustments in the interest rate according to fluctuating market conditions. (Also referred to as adjustable-rate loan.)

**Vault cash**—That portion of bank's cash on hand that is left in its vault as an immediate reserve.

**Ward**—A person who by reason of minority, mental incompetence, or other incapacity is under a court's protection either directly or through a guardian or another party.

**Will**—A formal, written, witnessed instrument by which a person gives instructions for the disposition of his or her estate.

**Working capital**—The liquid funds available to a business for its current needs. It is current assets less current liabilities.

**Wrongful dishonor**—Dishonor of a properly payable check by the drawee (paying bank).

**Yield**—(1) In investments, the rate of return expressed as a percentage of the amount invested. (2) In loans, the total amount earned by a lender, expressed on an annual percentage basis.

**Zero-balance accounts**—Accounts in a controlled disbursement program; they are a group of bank accounts controlled by a master concentration account.

 *Index*

401(k) plans, 132

## A

ABA Institution Identifier, 91-92
accounting
    accurate, 32
    methods, 44-49
    responsibilities, 7, 32, 171-172
    standards, 32
    *see also* Sarbanes-Oxley Act
accounts
    in trust, 74, 129, 133
    ownership and type, 73-76
    reconcilement, 72
    transaction accounts, 65-68, 78, 102
    transfers, 152, 154
acquisitions, *see* mergers and acquisitions
adjustable-rate mortgage, 112, 157
administrator, 74, 130
advance fee fraud, 169, 170
adverse action, 119
advisory services
    capital markets, 138
    investments, 131, 133
agency services
    corporate, 132
    personal, 131
alterations, 118, 172, 173
altered
    check, 89-90, 172
    signature, 88
American Bankers Association, 91
American Institute of Banking (AIB), 6
Annual Percentage Rate (APR), 24,
    118, 122

Annual Percentage Yield (APY), 79
annual report, 44, 47, 59, 117-118
annuities, 10, 96, 133-134, 139
annuity, 29, 69, 134, 156
APY, 79, 152
Asset and Liability Management
    Committee, 50
assets
    distribution, 101
    growth, 136
    income, 135
    management, 138
    safe,135
    safekeeping, 131
    *see also*, return on assets
asset recovery, 119-120
ATM, *see* automated teller machines
attorney-in-fact, 73
audit, 5-7, 27, 31-32, 44, 121, 171-172
authentication, 169
authority
    corporate account signers, 76
    to open accounts, 75, 77
    to use accounts, 73, 75-76, 78
Automated Clearing House (ACH), 23,
    36, 136
Automated Teller Machines (ATMs), 23,
    65, 154
Automatic Transfer Service (ATS), 70
availability
    funds, 54
    schedule, 71, 103
    *see also* Expedited Funds
    Availability Act
availability schedule, 71, 78, 102

average daily balance method, 79

## B

balance
    inquiries, 4, 70, 119
    *see also* proof department
balance sheet, 44, 46, 47, 58, 59, 66
bank cards, 65, 72, 96, 110,168-169
    fraud, 168, 169
bank funds, 50
bank holding companies, 8, 26, 28, 37, 139
Bank Insurance Fund (BIF), 27
bank investments, 37, 45, 47, 49, 51,
    53, 55-57, 59
bank products and services, 10, 153-154
bank regulators, 11, 36, 49, 133
bank robbery, 174
bank services, 8, 23, 110
banker acceptances, 141
Banking Act of 1933, 21-23, 26
Banking Act of 1935, 21-23
banknote, 17-20, 177
    national, 19
    *see also* Federal Reserve notes
bank-provided endorsement, 89
batch, 90, 92, 99, 100
bearer, 85, 87-88
beneficiary, 74, 102, 129
blank endorsement, 88
board of directors and management
    responsibilities, 171
board of directors
    bank organization, 6-7
    corporate governance, 171
    corporation, 75-76
    loan policy, 120
board of governors, 33-35
bonds
    brokerage firms, 25
    collateral, 118
    community, 53
    corporate, 57, 134
    income asset, 135
    insurance, 139
    investment, 133-134, 139
    municipal issues, 56, 134
    mutual funds, 134
    national bank, 20
    risks, 134

    Treasury, 19
    trust services, 128-129
book balance, 95
brokerage firm, 20, 25-26, 66, 109, 133
brokerage services, 132
broker-dealers, 133,135,136
budget, 58-59
budgeting, 58-59
bulk filing, 95
business analysis, 158
business contingency plan, 178
business owners, 11, 24
buying on margin, 21
buying process, 157

## C

capacity
    account opening, 77-78
    agent, 131
    fiduciary, 131
    five Cs of credit, 116
    legal, 77
capital markets, 128, 138
capital, 58-59
    original, 57-58
    requirements, national banks, 18
capital ratio, 58
card issuers, 168-169
career opportunities, 5
cash concentration, 137
cash item, 19, 71, 92, 102
cash letter, 92, 94
cash management, 68, 128, 136, 155
cash
    check to, 85-89
    concentration, 68
    equivalent, 97
    items, 71
    management services, 68,
    136-137, 155
    on hand, 46
    primary reserves, 51
Cashier's check, 86
cashing checks, 89-90
central bank, 17, 18, 32
Certificate of Deposit (CDs), 17, 23,
    52, 67, 134, 155-156
    collateral, 118
    negotiable, 23, 57

safe asset, 135
savings, 153
certified check, 86
charge-off, 46, 59, 120
Charitable and Institutional Trust, 130
chartered banks, 18, 25, 28, 37-38
check clearing, 96, 97
   services, 36, 54
   system, Federal Reserve Act, 20
check collection system, 19-20, 23
   National Bank Act, 18-20, 31
check fraud, 172, 173
   alteration, 72
   bank programs to combat, 173-174
   counterfeiting, 172, 175
   forgery, 173
   kiting, 172, 174
   paperhanging, 173
checks
   cashing, 90
   counterfeit checks, 172, 175
   kiting, 172, 174
   negotiable instruments, 85
   payment, 84-103
   processing, 91-98
   receipt by the paying bank, 89, 94
   routing symbol, 91
   safekeeping, 35, 131
   sorting, 91-93, 101
   standards, 103
   substitute, 71,96-97,103
   transfers, 97, 102
   truncation, 71
   types, 86
check payment process, 23, 86-87, 89, 103
checking account deposits, 26, 65, 95
   see also demand deposits
Clearing House Association, 99
clearing house, 23, 35-36, 65, 92-94, 99, 132, 136
closed-end credit, 111
code of ethics, 3, 172
coin, 18, 35-36, 46, 65, 70-71
collateral, 21, 54, 56-57, 109-118, 121
collected balance, 94
collection
   processes, 19-20, 23, 35-36
   receipt, 67, 69,71
   services, 92, 100

combined statements, 96
commercial banks
   examinations, 27, 172
commercial loan, 26, 109-123, 155
commercial paper, 57, 109
common stock, 56
community involvement
   banks, 12
   economy, 11
   image, 4
   reinvestment, 24, 57
   role, 10
   support, 11
   see also Community Reinvestment Act
   see also Gramm-Leach-Bliley Act
Community Reinvestment Act, 11, 24, 39, 51, 109, 121-122
competitive profile, 159
compliance, 3-7, 29, 118, 121-122, 168, 172
   compliance program, 179
Comptroller of the Currency, 6, 17-19, 31, 121-123, 166
   see also Office of the Comptroller of the Currency
computer attacks, 165-166
computer virus, 165
conflict of interest, 3
conservatorship, 131
construction loan, 111, 112
consumer loan, 110, 116-119, 123
consumer protection, 21, 23-24, 39, 116, 121
consumer protection laws, 24, 116
consumer scams, 169
contingencies, 47
contingency, 178
controlled disbursement account, 137-138
corporate agency services, 131-132
corporate bond, 57, 134
corporate fiduciary services, 131
corporate governance, 3, 6, 29, 31, 52, 171
corporate structure
   corporations, 76
   partnerships, 76
   unincorporated, 77
corporate resolution, 75

corporation, 6
account, 76
Edge Act and agreement, 37
governance *see* Sarbanes-Oxley Act
legal name, 76
stockholders, 76
*see also* Federal Deposit Insurance
Corporation (FDIC)
correspondent bank, 46, 92-93, 101,
131, 136
correspondent, 92-93, 101, 141
cost of funds, 34-35, 54-55, 109, 112
costs
APR, 23
asset and liability management, 50
check, 20
closing, 123
coin and currency, 71
fee income, 57
funds, 54
interest rates, 151
labor, 97
terms, *see* Truth in Lending Act
counterfeit
banknotes, 17, 19
checks, 72, 172
currency, 175-177
identity, 77
courtesy, 4, 153
Coverdell Savings Accounts (education
IRAs), 67
credit card
introduction, 23-24
liability, *see* Regulation E
merchant, 138
open-end credit, 110
processing, 98
risk, 54, 111
theft, 166-167
credit card protection fraud, 169-170
credit life insurance, 139-140
credit
availability, 34-35
needs, 112
policy, tools, 116, 120,
reporting, 116, 119, 123
risk, 53, 57
credit scoring, 117
credit union, 6, 25-26, 66, 109
creditworthiness, 53, 108, 112, 116,
121, 122

cross-selling, 10, 155
currency counterfeiting, 175
currency
counterfeiting 175-177
global exchanges, 143
transaction report, 179
custody services, 131
customer identification program, 30,
77, 179
customer relationships, 110, 148-149,
151, 155-156
customer service, 148-160
banks, 11-12
importance of, 4
customers
access, 164-166, 175
contracts, 25, 31
expectations, 151-154
financial data, impact of, 34
name usage, 169, 172-174
marketing concept, 149-150
profile, 159
purchasing process, 156-158
support, 158

## D

daily balance method, 79
debit card, 73, 97
electronic payment, 97
PIN-only, 73, 97
processing, 98
signature based, 68, 97
debit
automatic, 111
payment, 111
debts, 57, 84, 130
decentralized reserves, 20
default, 54, 56, 110, 112, 116, 128
deferred annuity, 134
defined contribution plan, 132
defined-benefit plan, 132
demand deposits
interest, 22
savings and time deposits vs., 65-66
deposit function, 51, 64
deposit services, 136
depositary bank, 87, 89-90, 92, 94, 103
depositors
interest expenses, 50, 54
liabilities, 45
liquidity, 51

safety, 52
traditional, 9
Depository Institutions Deregulation
    and Monetary Control Act of
    1980, 26
deposits, 64
    accounts, 65-68
    base, 79
    function, 64
    history, 65, 72
    items, types of, 70
    regulations, 78
    safety, 65
    services, 68
    types, 70
direct deposit, 65, 69, 78, 99, 135-136, 154
direct presentment, 92
disability insurance, 139-140
disbursing agent, 132
disclosures
    customer satisfaction, 150
    *see* Regulation E, Z
    settlement statement, 123
discount brokerages, 133
discount operations, 34-35
discount rate, 34-35, 55
dishonor, 88, 90
    wrongful, 90
disintermediation, 25, 31
districts, 20, 32-33, 94
diversification, 56, 134
dividends, 134, 136
    paying or disbursing agent, 132
documentation
    account ownership, 73
    estate accounts, 75
    government, 77
    guardianship accounts, 75
    lending process, 114-120
documents, 92
    examination, 95
    sorter, 90, 92
drafts, 57, 142
    accepted, 128, 142
    liability of, 45-46
drawee and drawer, 84-90
dual banking system, 18, 37
dual control, 101
dual custody, 101, 136
due from banks, 45-46

duties of the federal reserve system, 32

### E

e-commerce, 5, 7, 23
earnings per share, 58
electronic banking services, 8, 150, 153
electronic bill payment, 23
electronic check, 23, 96, 138
    presentment (ECP), 89
electronic check processing, 96
Electronic Fund Transfer Act, 24, 39,
    70, 78, 97, 99, 102
employees, 2-6, 11-12
    benefit services, 3, 5-6, 9
    role, 2
    training, 6
encoding, 59, 90-92, 94, 173
    function, 90, 94
endorsement, 87-89, 103
endorser, 88, 90
equity, 45
    buying on margin, 21
    capital, 116
    home, 157
    investment, 28
    loans, 122
    markets, 138
    net worth, 45, 47
    return on, 58
    securities, 133
estate, 128
    account, 73
    planning, 135
    settlement, 130
ethics, code of, 3, 72
ethical behavior, 171-172, 175
Eurodollars, 55
exception item, 94
executor, 74, 130
Expedited Funds Availability Act, 78
    *see* also Regulation CC
expenses
    budget, 59
    interest, 22, 50
    profit and loss, 47-48
    *see also* Regulation X

### F

FACT Act, 30-31
Fair Credit Reporting Act, 30, 123,165

FBI, 170, 174

FDIC, *see* Federal Deposit Insurance Corporation

Features
  account types, 68
  currency, 175-176
  insurance, 139
  product, 159-160
  purchasing, 157-158
  *see also* Regulation DD

Fed funds, 34, 46, 48, 55, 109

Fed funds rate, 34, 55

Fed tools and their effects, 35

Federal Deposit Insurance Act of 1935, 23

Federal Deposit Insurance Corporation (FDIC), 22, 36-37, 52, 133

Federal Open Market Operations, 35

Federal Reserve, 16-38

Federal Reserve Act of 1913, 20, 128

Federal Reserve System, 19
  banks, 20, 33-34, 36, 102
  banks withdrew from membership, 25
  board 20, 22, 28,
  chairman, 34
  creation, 17
  districts, 33
  duties, 32
  fee for services, 35
  influences, 34
  loans, 16, 20, 34
  membership, 25
  note, 17, 19-20
  ownership, 17
  regulations, summary, 32, 36
  role and responsibilities, 29-32
  routing symbol, 91
  services, 20
  structure, 32-35

Federal Savings and Loan Insurance Corporation (FSLIC), 27

Fedwire, 35-36, 92, 102

fees
  for services, 123
  income, 57, 151

fiduciary, 74
  accounts, 73-75
  corporate, 131
  fee income, 57
  trust, 129, 139

finance charge, 24, 111, 122

financial data
  impact of, 34, 49

Financial Holding Companies (FHC), 8, 28, 56, 139

financial holding company, 9-10, 139

Financial Institutions Reform, Recovery and Enforcement Act of 1989 (FIRREA), 27

financial performance, 6, 31, 58, 119

financial planning, 128, 135, 156
  bank's, 128-135
  customer's, 135

financial privacy, 24, 28, 29, 151, 154

financial services
  electronic, 136, 138, 141

financial statements, 32, 44, 49, 59, 117, 119, 167

First Bank of the United States, 17-18, 31

fixed assets, 46, 109, 113

float, 19-20, 71, 173-174

floor plan loan, 113

for deposit, 88-89

foreclosure, 112, 119

foreign check, 71

foreign exchange, 8, 141, 143

forgery, 172-173

fraud
  bank card, 168
  schemes, 169

freezing assets, 180

Funds Availability Act, 78, 102

funds management, 8, 50-52

funds transfer, 102, 170

## G

Garn-St Germain Act, 28

Garn-St Germain Depository Institutions Act of 1982, 26

general power of attorney, 73

Glass-Steagall Act, 21-22, 26, 28, 31

global banking
  credit operations, 141-142
  currency exchanges, 143
  deposit services, 136
  services, 141

grace period, 111

Gramm-Leach-Bliley Act, 4, 10, 28, 31, 128, 139, 154, 165

growth assets, 136

guardianship, 74, 129, 131
    accounts, 129, 131

## H

holder
    account, 26, 74, 77
    bond, 128
    *see also* Uniform Commercial Code

holder in due course, 8-,89, 103

home banking, 23

home equity loan, 24, 109-111, 119,
    122, 154

HUD-1, 123

Human Resources, 3, 5, 8

## I

identifiable person, 85, 87-88

identification
    accounts, 75
    customer, 30, 78
    deposit accounts, 73
    establishing, 74, 77
    needs, 156
    PIN, 73, 97
    purchasing, 156
    unincorporated organization, 77
    *see also* USA PATRIOT Act

identifying marks, 86

identity theft, 29, 30, 166-167, 169, 179

image statements, 95-96

immediate annuity, 134

incentives, 149

in-clearing capture, 94

income
    asset, 135
    sources, 47
    tax refund, 36

income statement, 44, 47
    consolidated, 45, 48

indenture, 128

Individual Retirement Account (IRA), 11

inflation, 17, 18, 35

insider, 31, 121-122, 175

insider fraud, 175

institutional trust, 130

insurance
    payment, 139
    products, 10, 139

underwriting, 139

interest checking, 26, 65-66
    *see also* NOW accounts

interest
    calculation of, 122
    checking, 66
    demand deposits, 65
    income, 52, 110
    net spread, 27, 58
    paid, 54-55, 111-112
    received, 50

interest rates
    APY, 79, 152
    base, 54-55
    CDs, 25, 68-69
    consumer protection, 23
    loans, 112
    money market, 69
    Savings and Loans, 27
    spread, 58
    *see also* Federal Deposit Insurance
    Corporation

international banking, 8
    *see* Global Banking

Internet banking, 6, 8, 23, 72, 97, 100,
    150, 154, 155, 157, 169

Internet banking payments, 97, 100

Internet
    account information, 72
    banking services, 6, 8, 67, 72
    electronic media, 8, 70, 97
    lending, 116
    management, 7
    payment methods, 97, 100, 157
    phishing, 169-170
    statements, 68

investment advice, 133, 135

investment products
    brokerage, 26
    in-house, 133
    insurance, 139
    management, 135
    precautions, 133
    regulations, 96
    services, 132-133, 155

investments
    advisor, 131
    management, 135
    manager, 131
    required, 135, 138
    risk, 133-136

irrevocable letter of credit, 142
issuer
    fraud, 168-170
    investments, 53
    municipal issues, 57
    requirements, 56
    risks, 134
issuing bank, 19, 86, 98
item capture, 91-92

## J

joint payees, 87
joint tenancy, 73

## K

kiting, 172, 174

## L

legal lending limit, 113, 121
legal requirements, 56, 85, 103, 121
lending function, 51, 108, 120
lending process, 108, 114-116, 119
letters of credit, 8, 141-142
leverage, 58, 139
liabilities
    management, 114-115, 117
    parties to negotiable instruments, 21
liability
    deposits, 66
    insurance, 139-141
    *see also* Regulation E
LIBOR, 55
life insurance, 28, 109, 139-140
line of credit
    closed-end, 111
    loans, 157
    open-end, 110
    working capital, 112
    zero-balance accounts, 138
liquidity, 8, 22, 46, 50-53, 56, 64,108
living trust, 130
loan agreement, 118-119
loan documentation, 118
loan loss reserve, 46, 52, 58, 120
loan policy, 108, 113, 120
loan pool, 114
loan review, 7, 119-120
loans
    business, 16, 76, 111, 114
    commercial, 112

consumer, 9, 16, 110, 117, 121
government, 113-114
losses, 26
portfolios, deteriorating, 26
risk, 111-114
local check, 92, 94
lockbox, 23, 136
long-term loan, 27, 50, 54, 109, 112

## M

Magnetic Ink Character Recognition
    (MICR), 23, 86, 90
    line, 91
    line, in-clearing capture, 91
    placement of data on checks, 91
mailbox theft, 168
market crash, 21, 22
market risk, 53, 56-57
market share, 12, 149, 159-160
marketing concept, 149-150
matched funding, 50-51
merchant banking, 10, 28, 56, 139
mergers and acquisitions, 2, 12
Monetary Control Act of 1980, 26
monetary policy, 19, 32, 35
    administration, 35
    tools, 34-35
money center, 19-20, 141
money laundering, 29-30, 77, 102,
    178-180
Money Market Deposit Account
    (MMDA), 26, 67,68, 78, 153
money market mutual funds, 96
money supply, 16, 17, 20, 34-35
    growth rate, 18, 34-35
    increasing and decreasing, 35
mortgage loan, 99, 111-112, 114, 123
mortgages, 54, 69, 110, 112, 114
municipal issues, 56-57
mutilated currency, 101
mutual fund, 10, 25, 28, 69, 96, 133-136

## N

National Automated Clearing House
    (NACHA), 99
national bank
    created, 18-26
    examinations, 27
    FDIC, 27
    limits, 123
    notes, 19

OCC, p. 19
required membership, 25
reserves, 19
*see also* National Bank Act
National Bank Act of 1863, 18, 20
National Currency Act, 18
negotiable instrument, 23, 84-86, 88,
96, 103
Negotiable Order of Withdrawal
(NOW) accounts, 66
net interest income, 27, 48
net interest spread, 27, 50, 58
net profit, 58
net worth, 45,47
night deposit, 68-69, 89
night depository, 69, 89
noncash items, 71, 102
noninterest income, 57
nonlocal checks, 94
nonsufficient funds, 57, 94
notary public, 86
NOW accounts, 26, 65-67

## O

Office of the Comptroller of the
Currency (OCC), 18-19, 36-37, 123
*see also* Comptroller of the Currency
Office of Thrift Supervision (OTS),
27, 36-37, 123
on-us check, 89, 92, 95
open market operations, 35
open-end credit, 110
Originating Depository Financial
Institution (ODFI), 99
outsourcing, 11-12
outstanding check, 19
overdraft, 74, 90, 117

## P

paperhanging, 172, 173
participation, 113, 139
parties to, 84
partnership agreement, 75
partnership, 11, 73-77, 170
partnership resolution, 75
payable on demand, 71, 85
payee,
check alteration, 172-173
check inspection, 174

internet banking, 100-101
negotiable instrument, 84-89
Regulation CC, 78-79
paying agent, 132
paying checks, 57, 89-90, 172
payment services, 7, 23
payment system, 11, 16, 32, 69, 84,
97, 101-102, 174, 178
payments
cashing checks, 89
cash management, 136-138
debits, 99
direct deposit, 70
deposit, 64, 99
electronic, 65, 79, 96-97, 99
fee income, 57
loans, 112
net interest spread, 50
paying checks, 89
problem, 120
Statement rendering, 95
tax, 69
*see also* Regulation EE
pension, 56, 69, 99, 132, 135, 136
pension plan, 135
performance
measurements, 46, 59
ratios, 49
standards,
personal agency, 129,131
Personal Identification Number (PIN),
72, 97, 99, 168
personal
banking, 3, 7, 12
customer service, 3
fraud, 169-170-171-173
identification, 168
identity theft, 30, 166
information, 165-166
privacy, 29, 154-155
professional appearance, 154
safety, 167, 174
trust, 128-129
*see also* Code of Ethics
*see also* Regulation B
personal representative,130
phishing,169-170
PIN-only debit card, 67, 97
point-of-sale (POS), 65, 72, 97-98
terminal, 65
transactions, 65

power of attorney, 73
preauthorized payment, 100, 102
prepurchase activity, 157
presentment, 23, 89, 92
    through correspondents, 92
    through the Federal Reserve, 92
pricing, 112, 123, 150, 160
primary reserve, 51
prime rate, 55, 112
principal, 73, 88, 112, 114, 115
privacy
    financial privacy, 29, 39, 151,
    154, 165
    identity theft, 30
    responsibility, 29
    *see also* Fair Credit Reporting Act
    *see also* Gramm-Leach-Bliley Act
private sector, 18
probate, 74, 130
problem loan, 119-120, 172
processing
    check clearing, 20, 84, 92
    combined statements, 96
    correspondent banks, 93
    deposit related, 69, 71
    electronic, 24, 96
    Federal Reserve, 36, 94
    fee income, 57
    offline transactions, 73, 98
    operations, 5
    services, 136
product development, 158, 159, 160
profiling, 158, 159
profitability, 150
    budget, 59
    lending, 115
    measures, 58
    marketing concept, 149-150
    risks, 53
profit-and-loss statement, 44, 47, 48
promise
    certified check, 86
    fraud, 170
    negotiable instrument, 84-85
promissory note, 71, 109, 111-112, 118
proof department, 59
proofing, 90
property insurance, 139-141
proprietorship, 73-75
prudent investor, 129

prudent investor principle, 129
public funds, 56, 73-74, 76
purchase decision, 148, 156-158
purchasing, 4, 110, 114, 134-135, 156, 158
    postpurchase assessment, 156, 158
    prepurchase activity, 156
    purchase decision, 156-157
pyramiding of reserves, 19-20

## R

raised currency or raised bill, 177
ratio analysis, 49
ratios, 49, 58
reader-sorter, 90, 92, 94
Receiving Depository Financial
    Institution (RDFI), 99
Redlining, 122
Referral, 155
Registrar, 132
Regulation B, 59, 119, 121,
Regulation CC, 59, 78, 95-96, 102-103
    endorsement, 103
Regulation D, 59, 78
Regulation DD, 78-79
Regulation E, 78, 102, 168
    Electronic Fund Transfer Act, 102
Regulation EE, 59
Regulation J, 102
Regulation X, 59, 122
Regulation Z, 59, 121-122, 168
regulations, 32, 36, 37, 38,
    by category, 59
    corporate governance, 171
    deposit, 78
    payments, 102-103
    lending, 121-123
regulators, 11, 36, 49, 133, 169, 179
    authorities, 58, 102
required reserves, 17-19
reserve requirement, 16
    deposits, 64, 66
    Federal Reserve, 19-20, 34-35
    Funds management, 54-55
    *see also* Regulation D
reserves, 22, 25-26, 34
    decentralized, 20
    early banking system, 17-20
    equity, 45
    liquidity, 51-52
    loan loss, 45, 58

primary, 51

pyramiding, 19-20

requirements, 19-20

secondary, 51

restrictive endorsement, 88

return items, 20, 36

return on assets (ROA), 46

return on equity (ROE), 46

returned checks, 95, 173

revocable letter of credit, 142

revolving credit, 110

risk, 6, 50

cashing checks, 90

controlling, 50

credit cards, 111

credit , 53

deposit account, 77

diversification, 56

factors, 54

Federal Reserve, 32

income, 52

investments, 56-57

loans, 53, 115

market risk, 53

paying checks, 89

portfolio, 112

rating, 120

safety, 52

term, 54

risk-based pricing, 123

robbery, 174

routing symbol, 91, 173

## S

safe assets, 135

safeguarding information, 167

safekeeping, 9, 35, 108, 118, 131, 164

Sarbanes-Oxley Act, 3, 31-32, 171

savings account

cross-sell, 155

customer, 152

direct deposit, 136

need, 153, 156

product, 153

safety, 135

statement settling, 95

see also Money Market Deposit
Account

Savings and Loan Association, 25

savings and time deposits, 65-66

Savings Association Insurance Fund

(SAIF), 27

savings bank, 6, 25, 27, 37, 109

schemes, 30, 169, 172

Second Bank of the United States, 17-
18, 31

secondary mortgage market, 114

secondary reserves, 51

secured loan, 54, 110, 120

Securities Exchange Act of 1934, 22

Securitization, 28, 138

security interest, 118-119

settlement

direct presentment, 92

electronic, 174

estate, 129-130

Federal Reserve services, 36

merchant, 138

processing, 98

see also Regulation X

settling, 102, 130

share draft, 66

short-term loan, 20, 50, 54, 109, 112-113

signature-based debit card, 67, 72, 97

smart card, 97, 99

sole proprietorship, 73-75, 78

sorter, 90, 92, 94, 96

sources of credit, 109, 116

special endorsement, 88

special power of attorney, 73

spread, 20, 27, 50, 58, 165

standby letter of credit, 142

state bank, 18-19, 21, 26, 36-38, 128

state banking departments, 36-38, 121

state-chartered banks, 18, 25, 28, 37-38

statement of condition, 44-47, 59

statement rendering, 95

statement savings, 67, 157

stop payment,73, 75, 89, 90, 94, 102

stored value card, 97-99

structure

Federal Reserve bank, 34

Federal Reserve system, 33

organizational, 4, 10, 132

Savings and Loans, 25

substitute check, 23, 71, 96-97, 103

suspicious activity report (SAP), 179-180

sweep, 135

systematic risk, 32

**T**

telephone banking, 67, 154-155

teller
- accounts, 68
- automated (ATM), 6, 70, 154
- check fraud, 173
- cross-sell, 155
- forgery, 173
- identity theft, 167
- opportunities, 5
- safety, 174

Teller's check, 86

tenants-in-common, 73

testamentary trust, 130

time deposit accounts, 64-66, 79

time deposit, 24, 45-46, 64-67, 78-79, 96, 157

title insurance, 141

tools
- customer, 116
- Federal Reserve, 34-35
- USA PATRIOT Act, 30

trade name, 74-75

trading account, 45, 48, 135

traditional financial services, 9

training, 5, 6, 12, 160

transaction account, 65-68, 78, 102

transaction report, 179-180

transfer agent, 132

transfer funds, 65, 73, 173

transit item, 92

truncate, 71, 97

truncation, 97, 152

trust
- accounts, 75
- committees, 172
- fiduciary, 74
- opportunities, 5, 8
- services, 128-129, 131-132

trustee, 128-131, 150, 153

Truth in Lending Act, 24, 31, 116, 121

Truth in Savings Act, 24, 78-79

types of bank checks, 86

types of bank investments, 56-57

types of credit information, 116

types of endorsements, 88

**U**

U.S. banking system, 16-18, 21

U.S. government agency obligations, 56-57

U.S. government obligations, 35, 53, 56-57

U.S. Treasury bills, 56

U.S. Treasury notes, 56

unauthorized signature, 88

unconditional order, 85

underwriting,
- insurance, 28
- loan, 117
- securities, 10, 22, 26, 28, 133, 138-139

unfit currency, 101

Uniform Commercial Code (UCC), 85, 89, 90, 103

unincorporated organizations, 76

universal life insurance, 139

unsecured loan, 54

USA PATRIOT Act, 30-31, 77, 102, 179

**V**

variable life insurance, 139

verification, 77, 95

viruses, 165

**W**

ward, 74, 131

will, 170

wire transfers, 16, 65, 102, 154

working capital, 112-113

wrongful dishonor, 90, 103

**Y**

yield, 53, 56, 67, 79, 157

**Z**

zero balance accounts, 138